Your Towns and Cities

Brighton

in the Great War

DOUGLAS d'ENNO is a historian, linguist and journalist who has made an exhaustive study of the impact of the First World War not only on Brighton but also on Britain's fishermen and their vessels (the first volume of his *Fishermen Against the Kaiser* was published by Pen & Sword in 2010, with research continuing for the second). After a career which included several years spent applying his linguistic and editorial skills in a publishing environment and – primarily – as a translator/reviser in public service, he has devoted himself to writing and research. Through contributions in the past to *The Argus* and local/community publications, he has established a reputation as a leading authority on Brighton and the surrounding area. Published works include *The Saltdean Story* (1985), *The Church in a Garden* (2001), *Foul Deeds and Suspicious Deaths around Brighton* (published by Wharncliffe/Pen & Sword in 2004), *Brighton Crime and Vice 1800-2000* (published in 2007, also by Wharncliffe/Pen & Sword), and a number of 'then and now' pictorial books on the Brighton area and on Sussex. A book on the county's railway stations through time is in

Your Towns and Cities in the Great War

Brighton
in the Great War

Douglas d'Enno

Pen & Sword
MILITARY

First published in Great Britain in 2016 by
PEN & SWORD MILITARY
an imprint of
Pen and Sword Books Ltd
47 Church Street
Barnsley
South Yorkshire S70 2AS

ISBN 978 1 78303 2 990

Printed and bound in England
by CPI Group (UK) Ltd, Croydon, CR0 4YY

Pen & Sword Books Ltd incorporates the imprints of
Pen & Sword Archaeology, Atlas, Aviation, Battleground, Discovery,
Family History, History, Maritime, Military, Naval, Politics, Railways,
Select, Social History, Transport, True Crime, and Claymore Press,
Frontline Books, Leo Cooper, Praetorian Press, Remember When,
Seaforth Publishing and Wharncliffe.

For a complete list of Pen and Sword titles please contact
Pen and Sword Books Limited
47 Church Street, Barnsley, South Yorkshire, S70 2AS, England
E-mail: enquiries@pen-and-sword.co.uk
Website: www.pen-and-sword.co.uk

Contents

Introduction   7

Acknowledgements   9

1. 1914 – The Shadow of War   11

2. 1915 – Doctor Brighton   55

3. 1916 – Tribunals, Hospitals and Holiday Crowds   117

4. 1917 – Prosperity against the Odds   159

5. 1918 – Holding Fast   201

Appendices   243

    1.   Timeline of Selected Events
(from the Armistice to the end of December 1918)   245

    2.   GALLERY – Post-War Remembrance
and Recognition, 1919-22   249

    3.   Theodore Wright VC and Edward 'Mick' Mannock VC   255

    4.   Poem *9 November* by Irene Snatt   257

    5.   The Plaque in Holy Trinity Church   259

Sources and Further Reading   261

Index   265

Introduction

This is the only volume, at the time of writing, to portray in narrative form the history of Brighton during the tumultuous years 1914 to 1918 in all its aspects. Compiled largely from information gathered from the contemporary press and publications, it is intended to serve as a comprehensive chronological record of events, aspirations and achievements during that unforgettable period of upheaval and change. Many of the arresting images it contains, both photographic and line-drawn, have now been published for the first time, being previously inaccessible, save to a few, in private collections.

The volume focuses on day-to-day life in the town rather than on the lives of its servicemen and women, although due attention has been paid to those who died, to those who were wounded and to prisoners of war.

For those interested in details of Brighton's war dead, the town's Roll of Honour is to be found both on the Internet (see Sources and Further Reading, Part C, on page 261) and in printed form in the book *Brighton and the Great War* by Trevor Harkin, published in 2014, which contains a limited amount of additional material on developments in the war locally and the impact of the conflict on the town.

Douglas d'Enno
Saltdean, August 2015

Acknowledgements

A great many people readily assisted me in the compilation of this volume; through their help and support, my task was made decidedly easier.

On the textual side, the now closed History Centre in Brighton, and subsequently the new centre for local archives, The Keep, located north of the city, provided much of the core information needed – and many images. I am grateful to staff members at both locations, especially Shona Milton and Kate Elms, for their guidance. Useful material was also obtained from Brighton's Jubilee Library and Hove Library, whose staff I thank. Help with specific school records was willingly forthcoming from Sue Carnochan (archivist, St Mary's Hall, now part of Roedean School), Jackie Sullivan (archivist, Roedean School) and Mark Gillingham (Archivist, Past & Present Association, BHASVIC (formerly Brighton, Hove & Sussex Grammar School)). Robert Fleming (National Army Museum, London) assisted me in connection with the awards made to Havildar Gagna Singh.

In connection with images (the sources of which are also acknowledged individually in the book), I was very fortunate to have unfettered access to the extensive collections of the following collectors/local historians: Peter Booth, Trevor Cox, Chris Horlock, Robert Jeeves and Tony and Liz McKendrick. Additional pictorial assistance was willingly provided by Liz Finlayson and Flora Thompson of *The Argus,* and by Penny Adamson, regarding the French Convalescent Home, Kemp Town; by Kevin Bacon (Digital

Development Officer, The Royal Pavilion and Museums, Brighton &
Hove), David Carter (war historian), Andy Grant (local historian), Alan
Keys (image restorer), Andy Maxted (Curator Collections Projects, The
Royal Pavilion and Museums, Brighton & Hove), local historians Peter
Mercer, Judy Middleton and Jacqueline Pollard; Matthew Richardson
(war historian), Robin Sharp (holder of family archive) and Rendel
Williams (Sussex postcard expert and private collector).

   For their interest, encouragement and support, I thank my friend and
ex-work colleague David Weiss, local historian Sarah Tobias, Paula
Wrightson (Creative Programme Officer, The Royal Pavilion and
Museums, Brighton & Hove), Jennifer Drury of the My Brighton &
Hove website, and especially author Kate Clarke, who closely followed
my progress from the outset and provided valuable background
material from the press at regular intervals during 2014 in particular.
Sam Tyler kindly allowed me access to St Mark's Church, Kemp Town,
to take a picture. I am indebted also to Roni Wilkinson (Commissioning
Editor), Jonathan Wright (History and Transport Publisher) and Matt
Jones (Production Manager), all at Pen & Sword, and to Carol Trow,
the company's editor for this title, for their valued advice and guidance;
and last, but by no means least, to my wife, Caroline, for patiently
enduring my unreasonable schedule and its effects over a long period.

CHAPTER ONE

1914 – The Shadow of War

Proudly, majestically, the ships of Britain's First Battle Squadron approached Brighton from the west. The flagship of this splendid array of vessels, part of Britain's 'sure shield', was the newly-commissioned HMS *Marlborough* under Vice Admiral Sir Lewis Bayly, KCIV, CVO. She was accompanied by the three other ships of the First Line and the four of the Second, plus the Squadron's light cruiser, HMS *Bellona*.

The date of this impressive visit was Tuesday 30 June 1914, and it was sweltering. The townsfolk of Brighton and Hove were out in force to witness the arrival, their numbers augmented by the large numbers of visitors from far and wide who had come by special trains and motor cars. The vessels anchored well off the town in two lines, just before two o'clock, while crowds of onlookers thronged the Palace Pier, West Pier and the gaily decorated Esplanade.

The *Brighton Herald and Hove Chronicle* (henceforth *Herald*) reported:

> *'The entire front between the piers was fluttering with colour from the lines of streamers stretched from standard to standard, with the brave display of bunting put out liberally by the hotels and boarding houses and with the countless pennons on the masts and the piers.'*

The fleet had set out from Portland under a general scheme by which visitors at seaside towns were given the opportunity during the summer months to see and go on board warships of the British Navy.

In the course of the afternoon, the Mayors of Brighton and Hove

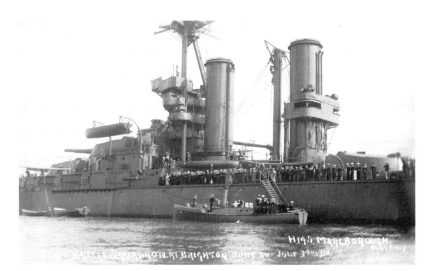

HMS Marlborough *on her visit to Brighton, 30 June–3 July 1914. (Robert Jeeves/Step Back in Time)*

were entertained aboard the *Marlborough* by Sir Lewis, in whose honour, and that of 150 officers, a ball was given at the Royal Pavilion on the evening of the following day. The grounds were illuminated, as was (from 9.30 to 10.30) the fleet – a spectacle enjoyed at close quarters by passengers on board the packed pleasure steamer, *Brighton Queen*, whose owners also ferried the sailors between the town and the vessels at no charge during the Squadron's visit.

On Wednesday 1 July half of the total crew of 2,500 came ashore. The other half visited on the following day. To a rousing welcome and headed by military bands, they split into two contingents, one marching to Brighton's Corn Exchange and the other to Hove Town Hall.

Visit of First Battle Squadron – Officers and Men leaving Hove Town Hall (Trevor Cox collection)

Following a meal at both locations, the men proceeded to the Hippodrome for a show; one was also put on for the remaining crew the next day on the Palace Pier. On Friday, the fleet continued on its tour to Eastbourne, its next scheduled destination. The men had spent a lot in the town. Public houses had done such a roaring trade that some landlords declared they had never seen so much liquid refreshment disposed of in two days.

Nobody, it seems, gave much thought to the prospect of war, even in the month before the calamity descended on the town. The local papers were instead replete with large advertisements for the summer sales from stores like Hanningtons, Athelstan Woods, Soper's at the top of North Street, describing itself as 'Brighton's Drapery Emporium', Hetherington's, with extensive premises in Western Road, offering bargains in china, glass, ironmongery and fancy goods, and the clothing store Needham & Sons on the Castle Square/Old Steine corner site.

Needham and Son's drapers/outfitters on the corner of the Old Steine and Castle Square was established in 1848 on the site of the Castle Inn and some four-storey houses. Today a branch of the Royal Bank of Scotland occupies the site. (Author)

Down at the West Pier and Palace Pier, the paddle steamers *Brighton Queen* and *Albion* were sailing daily from and to a variety of destinations, including Eastbourne, Hastings, Boulogne, Shanklin,

Folkestone, Deal, Bournemouth and Cowes. On the entertainment front, the Hippodrome was offering, *inter alia*, a revue titled *And Very Nice Too*, depicting scenes from the past, present and future (set in 1924), while from the West Pier there was acrobatic diving by Professor Tong and Miss May Victoria and, at its Pavilion, a production of Arnold Bennett's comedy *The Honeymoon* – 'Miss Marie Tempest's Success.'

Within the town, progress was being made on the restoration of the jewels in Brighton's crown: the Pavilion and the Dome. Work on these unique and beautiful buildings had been going on for some months, skilfully and sympathetically remedying the neglect – and worse – of the barely appreciative Victorian age. We can only imagine the amazement, bordering on incredulity, of the *Herald* member of staff who penned a feature on the refurbishment of these splendid edifices upon learning, before long, of the use to which they were to be put.

On 1 August 1914, the paper did, however, remind its readers of the imminence of the threatened war, which had, it stated, 'made its influence felt even in Brighton', for on Wednesday 29 July the Brighton Coastguard had been ordered away and the whole contingent of thirty-two men had left for Chatham depot *en route* for their various ships. At their station on the Lower Esplanade the doors were locked and one solitary man remained on duty.

On 5 August, *The Argus* reported the shattering news of Britain's declaration of war on Germany:

The PSS Brighton Queen *of 1897 was requisitioned in 1914 for minesweeping duties and based on the Thames. She would be mined and sunk off the Belgian coast on 6 October 1915 with the loss of eight lives. (Author)*

'The seriousness of the position is thoroughly realised throughout the county of Sussex, and the goings and comings of Territorials made street scenes animated in all parts of the county to-day. ... Business was, of course, very much unhinged, and there were few firms whose staffs were not depleted by the mobilization orders.

'At the Drill Hall, Church-street, Brighton, the work of mobilization was carried out quickly and efficiently. ... The "call to arms" has awakened the old spirit in many who had left the ranks, but Sir T. Berry Cusack-Smith, KCMG, JP, the commanding officer, is not signing on any new recruits until tomorrow. The Batteries paraded at headquarters at six o'clock this evening to receive further instructions.

'The 4th Battalion Royal Sussex Regiment returned from camp at twelve o'clock last night, the various Companies going to their headquarters at Chichester, Worthing, Haywards Heath, &c. The men were under orders again before mid-day, however, and assembled at convenient points for dispatch to appointed places.

'The railway is being kept busy by the Reservist traffic, and trains loaded with men going to join their colours have passed through the county. Cheering along the railway route was frequent.

'There was an interested knot of spectators around the entrance to the County Ground to witness the mobilization of the 6th (Cyclist) Battalion Royal Sussex Regiment. ... The response to the mobilization order was very gratifying, and several recruits were admitted, including motor cyclists. This branch of the service can be especially useful, and Colonel Somers Clarke [commanding] hopes that suitable men able to ride cycles will respond in large numbers to join the ranks of the Cyclist Battalion.

The 6th (Cyclists) Battalion, Royal Sussex Regiment, leaving the front entrance of the Sussex County Cricket Ground in Hove and heading off down Selborne Road (probably on their way through the town to Hove Station). The Sussex Cricketer public house can be seen in the background. (Trevor Cox collection)

Within days, that Battalion was up to full strength – twenty officers and 489 non-commissioned officers and men, nearly double the number in the run-up to the war. Extra men had been taken on and there were sixty-six names down for any vacancies that might occur. Numerous motorcyclists were also waiting to be enlisted.

Reservists re-joined the colours briskly; among them, fifteen men of the town's police force (three of whom were naval reservists and twelve military) were called up for duty. The town's citizens made due response to the King's appeal for recruits at the recruiting office in Lewes Road. After enrolling, these men – mostly from mechanical departments – were taken over to Preston Barracks for a medical examination. The barracks themselves were a hive of activity, with men hurrying to and fro with accoutrements and fodder. On the big grass space in front of the main building stood rows of field guns. With the batteries of the Royal Field Artillery quartered at the Barracks armed with howitzers, Brighton and Hove had, with various other forces, adequate naval and military equipment.

Mayor John Otter issued an appeal to Brighton men of military age urging them to share with Army Commander Sir John French, 'our fellow-townsman', the 'labours, the dangers, and the glory of enterprise which will be famous through the ages.' Ex-regular soldiers between the ages of 19 and 42 years and other men between 19 and 30, could also enlist at the Town Hall.

New recruits march southward down the Old Steine, watched by onlookers who include many potential servicemen. (Trevor Cox collection)

The energetic Recruiting Officer for the Borough of Brighton was Sir John Blaker, the town's chief magistrate, who told a *Herald* reporter that if every town did as well as Brighton, Lord Kitchener wouldn't have long to wait for his second army. On his first day he raided Brighton Workhouse and came away with seven inmates and seven officials. He also brought in men from Shoreham Workhouse, paid daily visits to the Labour Exchange (enlisting as many as seven on the spot) and visited Beeding Cement Works, which yielded a haul of eight brawny recruits, conveyed into Brighton in triumph in motor cars. Blaker wrote an appeal letter to the *Herald* calling for volunteers. Time, he wrote, was short and the need was urgent.

A valuable record of the enrolment process has been left to us by George Parker, author of the book *The Tale of a Boy Soldier* (QueenSpark 2001). Born in 1898 at 49 Southampton Street, Brighton, he was working when war broke out at the Co-op in Blatchington Road and living at 74 Hanover Terrace. When walking home from work as usual, he called into a recruitment office that had been opened at 20 Church Road, Hove. Within an hour, he was a soldier – at the age of 15¾.

George Parker (1898-1973) joined up when aged nearly 16 and fought in the trenches at both Ypres and the Somme. Although wounded, he survived the war. His memoir, written in 1969, was published posthumously. (Author)

There was a desperate need for men and the town responded. About thirty-five staff from Brighton Corporation's Tramways Department were Reservists and all were called up on the 5th to rejoin the colours. This caused extreme difficulty in the running of the cars, as the August Races were the busiest time for trams in the whole year. The Brighton and Hove Gas Company gave up over a hundred men to the colours while in one solicitor's office a clerk turned up for work as usual one day and was in his uniform by lunchtime! The Cannon Brewery offered staff joining up a weekly sum of not less than five shillings, plus their jobs would be kept open. Another brewery, the long-established Smithers and Sons Ltd, gave every encouragement to no fewer than twenty-seven men of their staff joining the Navy, Army or Territorials. Practically the whole of the First Home Counties Brigade Royal Field Artillery (T), whose headquarters were in Church Street, volunteered for active service abroad.

Territorials, some mounted, others on motorcycles, made their way through the town *en route* for their various headquarters. A line of seventeen motor coaches, commandeered by the government, drew up outside the Library and Corn Exchange on one occasion, to take navvies armed with picks and shovels to Newhaven to dig trenches. Later in the day, the Sussex Yeomanry installed themselves in the Secondary School in York Place, while Pelham Street School was occupied by 100 members of the Army Service Corps (Territorials). On the following evening, the staff of the chemist's Glaisyer and Kemp in North Street worked until midnight to supply drugs and antiseptic dressing to the local troop depot.

THE RIGHT SPIRIT.

Drawn by resident cartoonist C. H. Phelp for Brighton and Hove Society *and published on 10 September 1914 (Royal Pavilion & Museums, Brighton and Hove)*

Many call-ups and troop movements took place that August, witnessed by patriotic crowds, by saddened loved ones and by the curious. On Monday the 24th, Brighton Station was the location of just such a scene when a large party of men, horses and guns left for active service. Two platforms were specially set aside for the departure. The first train left at 11.40 pm and the last at 2.15 on Tuesday morning. All the arrangements went smoothly and, despite the late hour, the men were given a hearty send-off, with warm handshakes and rousing cheers which resounded in the still night air to speed them on their way to who knows where – even the officers were ignorant of their destination.

By the end of the month, the number of men who had enrolled since the 7th, when the recruiting office opened in Lewes Road, totalled nearly 550. This included a number of men from Lewes and Haywards Heath, which fell within Brighton District. It also included over fifty National Reservists and a considerable body of ex-soldiers – men anywhere between thirty and forty-two years of age. Between Monday the 24th and Friday the 28th, 200 men registered.

Yet despite such scenes, Brighton as a town and resort soon returned to something approaching normal. As early as 16 August, the *Sunday Times* commented:

'The foolish war panic which drove many people from our seaside resorts and prevented others from leaving town has fortunately subsided and intending holiday-makers may rest assured that our seaboard is practically as safe now it was in peace time. Already there are signs that the public is banishing its fears and resolving to enjoy as heretofore its well-earned summer vacation. The railways are getting back to their normal working. The Brighton Railway, always to the fore in catering for the needs of holiday-makers, has resumed its cheap ticket arrangements between London and the many delightful resorts on the South Coast. Here one may gaze on the peaceful waters of the Channel and forget for the nonce the horrors of war.'

The *Brighton Gazette* (henceforth *Gazette*) reported that by the 19th 'things were looking a lot brighter all round' and in its issue of the 22nd stated 'Brighton is itself again.' The next day, the *Sunday Times* reiterated the point that there was 'no foundation whatever for ridiculous and idle rumours of danger' and that the resorts on the Kent and Sussex seaboard were perfectly safe.

In September, two major patriotic meetings were held. The first, on the evening of the 7th at the Dome, was a historic occasion, attended by so many men that they filled not only the Dome but the Corn Exchange as well. Among their number were men of recruiting age and over, a Cabinet Minister of the Liberal Government supported by the two Unionist Members of Parliament for Brighton and no less a literary figure than Rudyard Kipling. All came together to confirm the gravest resolution that England had made for a century – the resolution to fight Germany to the death.

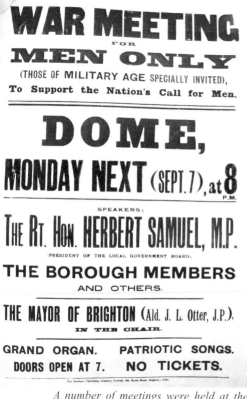

The second meeting, a great War Demonstration held at the Level on the 26th, was preceded by a procession representing the military forces, public bodies, trade unions, friendly societies and other organisations. Starting from Madeira Road (today's Madeira Drive) at 3 pm, it made its way along King's Road, Preston Street, Western Road, North Street, New Road and northwards to the Level. Addresses were delivered from four platforms. John Otter was one of the speakers campaigning for further recruits for Kitchener's Army. Will Crooks MP, the Labour leader who had led off the National Anthem at the memorable prorogation of Parliament, incited his hearers to rally to the assistance of the Empire in the hour of its urgent need.

A number of meetings were held at the Dome to encourage enlistment (Royal Pavilion & Museums, Brighton and Hove)

Noted trade unionist and politician William 'Will' Crooks MP (1852–1921) delivering a rousing speech at the Level in this view captured by the Press Photo Co. of Brighton (Trevor Cox collection)

The Hotel Metropole was the destination and starting-point of Alfred Vanderbilt's horse-drawn *Venture* coach, a service between Brighton and London. It became an early casualty of the war – thirty of its forty splendid horses were commandeered by the government. The American

Members of the Boys' Brigade march past the Queen's Hotel in the great procession on 26 September 1914. (Robert Jeeves/Step Back in Time)

A splendid photo of Alfred Vanderbilt's Venture coach leaving the Hotel Metropole, Brighton, for London. (Epsom & Ewell Local and Family History Centre)

millionaire took the whole business very good-naturedly. Unfortunately, on 1 May 1915, he would be among the many who drowned when the *Lusitania* was torpedoed *en route* for Liverpool from New York.

A pressing issue nationally and locally was the supply of food. Hoarding became a social problem; the rush to lay in stores had been so frantic that many of the shops in, for example, London were unable to cope with it and closed their doors. Panic buying led to rising wholesale prices and to wholesalers being unfairly criticised but it subsided by the end of August.

The price of bread went up by a halfpenny a loaf in Brighton from Monday 3 August and the prices of both home-killed and foreign meat rose considerably. For the moment, the national supply position was not problematic as stocks of the chilled and frozen product were sufficient to meet ordinary needs at the normal rate of consumption, although only for about six weeks. Naturally, uncertainty prevailed. Home supplies represented sixty per cent of total consumption, so imports were vital. Numerous meat-carrying ships had had to be withdrawn from service, causing a great shortage in the supply of the foreign article. Ships from Denmark, which supplied forty per cent of our bacon, had dared not put to sea in the early days of the war, although they began doing so later in the month. Walter Port, Honorary Secretary of the Brighton and Hove Butchers' and Pork Butchers' Association, sent a letter to the *Herald* on the instructions of his members, urging the general public to exercise the strictest economy in their consumption and strenuously guard against waste. Fruit and vegetables were inevitably hard hit. One William Rushton, some years ahead of his time, wrote to the paper suggesting the use of many idle building plots, rent free, for the culture of vegetables during the war and its aftermath.

The impact of the war on groceries and provisions was as yet limited, but sugar – the bulk of which had normally come from Germany, Austria and Russia – was in short supply. Butter, of which large quantities were normally obtained from Siberia, could not get through. Cheese from Canada and to some extent New Zealand was, however, plentiful. Deliveries of provisions at home were delayed due to many suppliers' horses having been impressed for military purposes.

The early days of the war in the town were marked by uneasiness, fear and wild rumour, despite the outbreak of hostilities having been greeted in rousing fashion. The *Brighton and Hove Society* magazine, looking back four years later, recalled:

> *'That Tuesday midnight found the streets of our town being promenaded with cheering crowds waving flags and singing Rule Britannia, God Save the King and The Marseillaise. It was a night of disturbed slumber at the best. For many it was a sleepless night.'*

One concern was the possibility of bombs being discovered in the houses of Germans or other aliens in Brighton. The police, deluged with communications about supposed spies, explosive devices, illicit wireless telegraph apparatus and so on, investigated every complaint however, and were able to assert positively that all these notions were quite groundless. The Chief Constable (William B. Gentle) himself declared categorically that no bombs or explosive material of any kind had been found in any house in Brighton.

The caption to this Punch *cartoon by Percy T. Reynolds dated 9 December 1914 reads: 'Run avay, you leedle poys: don't come here shpying about'.*

PERCY T REYNOLDS –

"RUN AVAY, YOU LEEDLE POYS; DON'T COME HERE SHPYING ABOUT!"

A German named Henry Frederick Eickhoff, 37, living in Mount Street with his 'wife' and six children (he had another six in Germany by his real wife), was charged on 8 September before the Magistrates with failing to register his correct name in accordance with the Aliens Registration Act. He admitted the offence. When at the Town Hall to register in accordance with the Act, he had declared his name to be Henry Frederick Arnold, a name he had used for fifteen years. Despite his assertion that he was a faithful and loyal subject to the government, the Magistrates decided he should be fined £20 plus costs or, in default, perform three months' hard labour.

Aliens were indeed a problem. By 28 August, a total of 1,350 were registered at Brighton Town Hall, with possibly a few more to be added. Interestingly, no fewer than 500 or so were married to English women. Practically every European nation was represented (Germany and Austria to the tune of well over 400) as was every continent. Some 230 'alien enemies' were having expulsion orders enforced against them, full discretion being in the hands of the Chief Constable. All householders had to give notice to the police of the presence of aliens in their houses.

An anonymous correspondent to the *Herald* from St James's Street, whose letter was published on 29 August, confirmed the prevalent feeling that British people did not like anything German and suggested that German Place (which had been originally so named after the proprietor) be renamed Belgian Place, which would also be a little compliment to a brave people. Below the anonymous letter appeared one from 'A.W.H.' of Charlotte Street, who suggested the very same thing. In the event, the street was in that year renamed Madeira Place.

Brighton was invaded by hundreds of French and there was a fair number of them there already studying at language schools. Little groups of French people were often to be seen eagerly studying the war telegrams in the windows of the *Daily Telegraph* office in King's Road, while a number of French and Belgian families who had the means to do so sought sanctuary in various hotels in Brighton.

The *Gazette*, in its issue of 22 August, reported that Brussels had fallen. The Honourable Press Secretary wrote to the *Herald* begging its Editor's cooperation in helping the Belgian Relief Fund by publishing an appeal, which he duly did.

To show solidarity with our Allies, a Grand Belgian, French and Russian Night was held at the Dome. The spacious building was packed to overflowing. The programme opened with Elgar's *Land of Hope and Glory*, resoundingly played by the Municipal Orchestra. The highlight of the evening was Tchaikovsky's *1812* Overture. Naturally, the national anthems of Belgium, France, Japan, Russia and England were played, with the audience respectfully standing in each case.

Preparations for providing hospitality in England for large numbers of Belgian refugees were made and committees were formed in many places. The Brighton Committee, with the Mayors of Brighton and Hove as Chairman and Vice-Chairman respectively,

Poster depicting the plight of the destitute in Belgium (Royal Pavilion & Museums, Brighton and Hove)

was formed towards the end of August. A request came from the Catholic Women's League in London for the towns to receive 150 Belgian children, fifty at a time. Accordingly, through the kindness of Father James Kerwin, the newly-built (1913) St Mary's School in Church Road, Portslade, was placed at their disposal as a hostel. Here the children spent the night before being drafted off into various convents which had agreed to receive them. Miss McNalty undertook the duties of housekeeper and matron, and 150 sets of children's clothes were provided by the Mayoress of Brighton's Working Party.

But when, on 3 September, the first party of refugees arrived, it consisted only of two men, three women, and one child – none of whom were Belgian. All were Russian Jews from Antwerp and Liège; one could speak nothing but Yiddish. The following day, the expected children did begin to arrive, but they came in large and extended families, so the accommodation at the hostel had to be re-arranged and more furniture provided. Between 3 September and 17 October, sixty-nine families from all classes passed through the hostel, the total number, counting all the children, being 230.

Belgian refugees of all ages housed at 13, Chesham Place, Kemp Town. (Royal Pavilion & Museums, Brighton and Hove)

As soon as it became known in Brighton that there were refugees in Portslade, offers of hospitality began to come in. One was from the Crescent House Convalescent Home offering the use of an entire wing of the building, with board and lodging free, for three months, for eighteen women and children. In two instances, in the neighbourhood of Brighton, a large family was provided with a comfortable home and suitable employment through the generosity of private individuals. Miss Gardiner, with the help of friends, took entire charge of a family of twelve and Miss Ormsby took in four families. Architect, writer, musician and property owner, Harry S. Goodhart-Rendel, offered the free use of some of his empty houses in Kemp Town. Number 13, Chesham Place was swiftly opened as a residential home for refugees. Four Flemish nuns, themselves refugees, were placed in charge and twenty-five Belgian peasants were comfortably installed there. A social centre, also courtesy of Mr Goodhart-Rendel, was opened for ladies at 7, Chesham Place, provided with books, newspapers, writing materials and a piano. The Club was open every afternoon either for English lessons or for working parties making garments for Belgian soldiers. Further help came from across the county.

Many well-to-do Belgian families lived in Brighton at their own expense. Their applications for assistance were soon met, however. Houses were therefore taken for them and weekly maintenance grants were made for their support. By February 1915, thirty-four families, making a total of 233 refugees, were being either partially or wholly supported.

The four nuns, themselves refugees, who took charge at 13, Chesham Place. (Royal Pavilion & Museums, Brighton and Hove)

Instead of decorating their church for the Harvest Festival, the congregation of St Anne's Church, Kemp Town, brought gifts of food for the refugees, and an enormous quantity of groceries, flour, bacon, vegetables, tea, coffee, sugar, etc. was given, which entirely filled the west end of the church and was afterwards distributed among all the different Belgian families. From Canada came 200lb of flour, a sack of potatoes, and a fine cheese; similar gifts were sent from Queensland.

On the employment front, offers included work for eight or nine people in a laundry and on a fruit farm in Lancing. Hugh Charles Fairfax-Cholmeley took a party of eighteen to his estate in Yorkshire and gave them employment on the land for six months.

One of the striking drawings from the Brighton Graphic *(issue of 19 December 1914) vividly transferring an image of the destructive impact of the war from Louvain to Brighton. (Royal Pavilion & Museums, Brighton and Hove)*

During August came the first reports of sons of Brighton being killed in action. One such casualty was Second Lieutenant Vincent Waterfall, 23, of 1, Belvedere Terrace on the 22nd. Flying an Avro 504 on a reconnaissance mission from Maubeuge, northern France, near the Belgian border, to monitor the advance of the Germans, he and his observer, Lt Charles George Gordon Bayly, were brought down by enemy ground fire. The loss of their machine was the RFC's first combat loss in the Great War and its wreckage was the first indication to the Germans that the BEF had arrived at the Front. Well known

Second Lieutenant Vincent Waterfall of the 5th Squadron RFC, formerly in the East Yorkshire Regiment, shot down on 22 August 1914. (Waterfall family)

socially in Brighton, the handsome aviator had possessed considerable athletic and sporting prowess and had been an equestrian of note, having won a number of prizes in military point to point steeplechases.

It was on the very day young Waterfall was killed that the first British shot of the war in Europe was fired – by Brighton man Ernest Edward Thomas. Born in Colchester, where his father's regiment was stationed, he attested with the Royal Horse Artillery in May 1899 and transferred on 1 April 1902 to the 4th (Royal Irish) Dragoon Guards. After postings spanning some years in India and South Africa, he arrived in the UK in November 1908. By June the following year he had met and married Ellen Pont in Brighton. She continued to live in Brighton with her in-laws whilst her husband was posted to barracks elsewhere. Their first child was born in Brighton in 1911, followed by a second in 1912. According to his service record, Thomas was re-engaged in Brighton on 23 November 1911. In view of his links, he could be fairly described as a 'Brighton man' when dispatched with the British Expeditionary Force to assist Belgium. Promoted to Lance Corporal on 3 September 1914, he attained the rank of Corporal in 1916 (in which year he received the Military Medal) and Sergeant in 1917.

On 22 August 1914, as mentioned, Thomas's unit encountered a German cavalry patrol on the Mons-Charleroi road at around 6.30am and laid an ambush. The enemy, having become wary, were about to flee when a sabre charge on them was ordered by his Captain, Charles Beck Hornby. Drawing his rifle, Thomas hit a German officer on horseback with that celebrated shot; Hornby, using his sword in this action, was reputedly the first British soldier to kill a German soldier. For the part he played, Thomas was awarded the Military Cross. Later in the war, he received the Military Medal. He was discharged from Brighton's Preston Barracks in 1923, by which time he had settled with his family above a greengrocer's shop at 19, Southdown Avenue. In around 1937 they moved to 68, Stanley Road. Following his discharge, 'Long Tom', as he was known due to his 6ft 3in frame, worked as commissionaire at the nearby Duke of York's Picture House, Preston Circus, where he remained, a familiar figure, until his death in February 1939.

A plaque commemorating the BEF's first shot was unveiled in 1939 at Casteau, six miles north of Mons – at a spot just some 400 metres away from a similar plaque commemorating the last shot in the conflict. In 1964, the 4th/7th Royal Dragoon Guards (as they had become) marked the 50th anniversary with a memorial event in the village, while on 22 August 2014, the centenary of that first shot was commemorated there. Thomas's great-grandson, Ben Thomas, attended, as did two grandsons of Captain Charles Hornby.

Seconds after Thomas's historic shot, another 'first' involving a Brighton man took place in the same action. In an interview given to the *Sussex Daily News* on 14 November 1938, former Sergeant Frederick Chapman, of 29, Upper Lewes Road, recalled:

> *'We went helter-skelter at them [the Uhlans] with our swords drawn, and were face to face with them almost before they were aware of it. All the time we were receiving covering fire on either side as we charged. The Uhlans – there were about eight of them – were captured. I will not arouse any controversy by saying that I took the first prisoner, but I was one of the patrol which scored this first success. The Uhlans were marched back to Brigadier-General de Lisle, who was in charge of the 2nd Cavalry Brigade, for interrogation.'*

Thomas and Chapman were old friends. Both received their Lance-Corporal stripes on the same day and they were promoted to the rank of sergeant together.

The influx of wounded in large numbers – where they would be accommodated, how many would be allocated to the town and what could be done for their medical care and general well-being – was now to become a pressing issue. In Kemp Town, an appeal from the Mayoress of Brighton on behalf of wounded soldiers and sailors led to the generous offer from Mrs Maude Dickinson of Eastern House, Marine Parade, for her house to be used as a hospital should the need arise. Further east, and a little way inland, stood the brand-new John Howard Convalescent Home (today the Brighton Steiner School) for ladies of limited means. This was unhesitatingly offered by Mr Howard to Lord Kitchener in a letter written to him in August. It contained twenty-three single and four double bedrooms, a large dining room, a spacious sitting room, a library and four bathrooms. He had been about to open this home on 14 August but in view of the war and with his age preventing him from joining up, he had decided to offer the building, rent-free, for convalescent military or naval men.

Benefactor John Howard, too old to fight, generously made his new convalescent home available for the accommodation of wounded officers. (Author)

Convalescing officers and two of their nurses near the south-facing front entrance to the building. (Author)

Brighton's Workhouse in Elm Grove had, in early 1914, been renamed the Brighton Poor Law Institution and would be offered to the military as a hospital before the year was out. The 'Kitchener Hospital' opened in January 1915, its 1,050 inmates being evacuated to large houses in Brighton and Hove and to other institutions in the county.

The earliest large-scale provision for the wounded, however, was made in August with the taking over of the new Grammar School in Dyke Road as the 2nd Eastern General Hospital. So suitable was the building that the governors were given only one hour's notice to surrender it. By 29 August, the *Herald* was reporting that fitting-out was pretty well complete, with as many as 520 beds provided.

The *Brighton and Hove Society* magazine enthused:

'If the English Government had searched Brighton or Sussex all over, they could not have found a more beautiful and suitable building for a military hospital than the new and sumptuous buildings of the Brighton Grammar School. They have been transformed in a wonderful short space of time into an up-to-date hospital, with accommodation for over 500 patients. Anyone having the privilege of inspecting it must be struck with its capable and ready condition. ... The great hall makes a magnificent ward, and its airy ventilation is of the very latest and most approved order. There are many other smaller wards presided over by an army of silent-footed nurses in their neat uniforms. Thus, in an atmosphere

The Second Eastern General Hospital on the corner of Dyke Road and Old Shoreham Road, converted from the new Brighton, Hove and Sussex Grammar School. (Trevor Cox collection)

*of peace and rest that seems to bring healing in its wings, our
wounded soldiers may be very sure of the comfort and attention they
have so richly earned.'*

The medical staff were mostly drawn from the staffs of the various
local hospitals and all had specialist knowledge and experience in
medicine and surgery. There were also a further thirteen doctors whose
services would be available should they be required. The school
laundry was converted into an excellent operating theatre, fitted with
an x-ray department and with all the equipment necessary for any
operation. The doctors were supported by a matron, twenty-two sisters
and sixty-eight nurses, recruited from various parts of Sussex and all
belonging to the Territorial Force Nursing Service. They were billeted
at the Convent of the Sacred Heart in Upper Drive, Hove. The
Commanding Officer was Major J. A. Rooth RAMC, a well-known
Brighton doctor. The school was now invested with quite a military
aspect, with a Red Cross flag on its roof, an ambulance wagon within
the grounds and uniformed men closely guarding the gates.

   The pupils displaced from the school were sent back, disappointed,
to their former premises (made available since not yet needed by the
new owners, the Women's Hospital in West Street) at 79 and 80
Buckingham Road. Term would start on the appointed day, namely 17
September. Boarders were housed at 78 Buckingham Road.

   Stanford Road Council School was fitted up as an Auxiliary Hospital

*The pupils pictured here in mid-September 1913 would not be so happy a year later
when they were displaced. (Trevor Cox collection)*

with 60 beds, much to the delight of the children who had an extra week's holiday before being placed in other local schools.

Stanford Road Council School, whose classes were scattered between seven different buildings. These did not return to the main school until December 1919. (Trevor Cox collection)

Then the wounded came. *The Times* of 2 September reported the arrival in England on the previous day of 'further batches' totalling 500. They were taken to various hospitals – 300 to Brighton, 120 to Portsmouth and the rest to Birmingham. A list containing the names, ranks, numbers and regiments of 139 of the casualties appeared in the newspaper on 19 September. Although English regiments predominated, just over a quarter of the men were from Scottish regiments, mainly the Coldstream Guards and the Argyll and Sutherland Highlanders, while Irish regiments accounted for ten per cent of the total.

In Brighton, where thousands of people lined the route, over fifty private motor cars, supplemented by the Police Fire Brigade's motor ambulance and by a number of railway vans for the stretcher cases, conveyed the men from the station to the hospital. Soon a fine fleet of motor ambulances was forthcoming, admirably driven by young ladies, the daughters of well-known townsmen.

One of a number of postcards published by George A. Wiles of Hove showing wounded arrivals at Brighton Station. (Trevor Cox collection)

The men had come, reported the *Herald*,

> *'from one of the most awful sights that the eye of man can look upon, to find – what? Brighton, happy holiday-keeping Brighton, rejoicing in the brilliant sunshine of one of the most glorious summers of recent years, and with almost all its summer holiday attractions in abundant, if not in full, activity.'*

To those who had been lying in trenches night after night, with the shrapnel bursting around them, who had been fighting hard retreats and who had been lying helpless on the ground, their present quarters were an earthly paradise. For nearly two hours the procession – among which there were as many tartan glengarries as khaki caps – continued, the crowds ever changing and increasing, and ever cheering. This was 'the most moving scene that this generation of Brighton has known, [one] that – God grant – no other generation of Brightonians shall ever know.' It was not only the women who had tears in their eyes.

Once the men had settled in, more could be learned about the real war. Most of the casualties were wounded in the legs; some had lost an arm or a hand, but all were cheerful and all told the same story of the fighting:

The *Brighton and Hove Society* magazine of 17 September featured 'A Chat With Our Wounded Tommies':

> *'The sympathies of all Brighton has been directed to the 2nd Eastern Hospital in the Dyke Road, where our wounded soldiers are being so tenderly cared for. To see their bronzed faces above the blue hospital suits and red ties which lend much picturesqueness to their appearance, it strikes one that though the strain they have gone through has been exceedingly great, they are rapidly recovering with the rest and quiet they so richly deserve. ... To learn from their own lips stories of the fierce fighting they have undergone, always against an enemy that outnumbered them ten, twenty, thirty and forty to one and always fighting these difficult and hazardous rearguard actions, brings home to all of us dwelling in ease and comfort in England what our brave little Army is undergoing and suffering for one and all of us.'*

An unusual picture from a contemporary publication of the heroic patients in the hospital grounds. (Author)

Private William Harland of the 2nd Royal Sussex Regiment kept a war diary. He had a foot badly mangled by shrapnel and was recovering in Nicholson Ward. He told the *Herald* about the part played by the Royal Sussex Regiment in that terrible retreat from Mons almost to the walls of Paris. On the dreadful day of 10 September, the Regiment lost forty men killed and eighty-five wounded. Graphically describing his experiences, he recalled lying on the ground when the enemy were only to be seen by a flash of guns on a distant height and by the shells that went screaming overhead. Fortunately, many of the shells were bad; he had one hit the ground right in front of him. To his mind, the Germans were but sheep forced unwillingly to the slaughter – if it wasn't for their officers they wouldn't have fought at all. They did, however, sometimes abuse the white flag, killing their approaching captors. Harland, who had been born in Portslade and had enlisted in Hove, would be killed in action on 17 October 1916 and buried at Thiepval.

In a letter reproduced in part in *The Times* on 7 September, a lance-corporal of the Argyll and Sutherland Highlanders who was shot clean through the thigh at Mons and was in hospital at Brighton wrote:

> *'The Belgian hospital to which I and my wounded comrades were taken was pitilessly shelled by the Germans, men being killed in their beds. The Germans fired on the wounded at every opportunity. Their conduct was brutal in the extreme. The one satisfaction which is ours, however, is that the German loss was terrible.'*

This was probably the convent hospital in Belgium referred to in another account which was full of wounded when the Germans opened fire, the shells bursting in the wards. Many were killed, while others managed to crawl out and were finally picked up by search parties and brought to a safe position. Yet another narrative was told by a sergeant of the Foot Guards of how the wounded were hurried out of a hospital flying the Red Cross Flag at Rouen as the Germans were shelling it.

A trooper from the 4th Hussars graphically described wearisome marching by day and night in a strange country. Thinking they had reached their goal and would get a brief rest away from the enemy, they were suddenly attacked by a horde of Germans, cleverly ambushed in a thick and leafy wood. 'Though we were tired and worn,

*Wounded heroes from the Marne and Aisne battles at Dyke Road. In the foreground is
'Prince', which collected for the Prince of Wales Fund. Third from right on the bottom
row, a Private Richards of Hove is wearing a captured German helmet. (Author)*

we gave them a hot time of it, if only we had been in stronger force,
not one would have escaped.' A soldier of the famous Black Watch,
which was severely mauled and lost many men at Mons and Cambrai,
declared 'One and all our men agree that if we had the same numbers
in the field as the Germans they would not stand a dog's chance.'

The first soldier of the war to be laid to rest in a Brighton cemetery,
according to the *Herald*, was a patient from the hospital. Private Anton
Robert Heren, 25, of the Duke of Cornwall's Light Infantry, died on 6
September 1914. He had arrived at Dyke Road early the previous week
in the batch of 300 wounded and had been one of the few serious cases,
having contracted rheumatic fever on the battlefield at Mons. His
funeral was accorded all the solemn honours that a military funeral
could bestow. A large crowd assembled in Old Shoreham Road to
witness the departure, under armed escort, of the cortege for the
cemetery. A body of soldiers acted as bearers of the coffin, over which
the Union flag was draped. At the graveside, a firing party fired three
volleys as a last farewell.

There was a further intake of wounded on 21 September. Whereas
the first batch had come from the battlefields of Belgium, the new

Soldiers and civilians have made way for an imminent funeral procession for victims of the Aisne from the SEGH. (Trevor Cox collection)

arrivals (a hundred-plus) were fresh from the killing grounds in France. They were survivors of the carnage of the long retreat through that country, the fierce battle of the Marne and the latest protracted fighting around the Aisne. They were, unfortunately, much more seriously injured than those in the first contingent, as many as fifty of them being stretcher cases. Although fatigued and suffering, the men smiled bravely back at the cheering crowds who had waited for them, patiently and subdued, for hours.

The big King's Ward – the lecture room of the Grammar School – was full of cases likely to require protracted care. Many of those less seriously hurt were in other wards, in some of which they were allowed to smoke and see friends. The forethought of the authorities and the organisation of the hospital were, the *Herald* remarked, everywhere excellent.

Concerning the interaction in the early days between the wounded and the public, the *Gazette* recalled, in a feature published in November 1918:

'*During the first autumn of the war the scenes outside the Dyke-road hospital were like a fair. All sorts of things, wanted and unwanted*

by the wounded men, were sold from barrows, pony-carts, baskets,
etc. and handed over the railings to them. They accepted them all
with thanks and smiles, especially the fruit and picture cards, and
when they were given goody-goody or "pacifist" tracts they still
smiled (with a twinkle in their soldierly eye).'

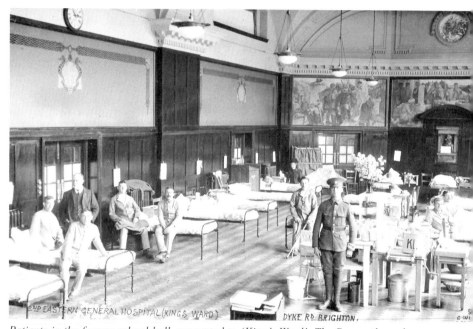

Patients in the former school hall, converted to 'King's Ward'. The Sussex-themed
panels were painted by artist Louis Ginnett (1875-1946), a past pupil. (Peter Booth
collection)

On the morning of Saturday 21 November, Major P.S. Lelean, an
eminent War Office official, and Sir Walter Lawrence, Commissioner
in charge of the Welfare of Indian Troops, visited Brighton Town Hall
to explain that urgent accommodation was required for 600 wounded
Indian troops and to suggest that the Pavilion, Dome and Corn
Exchange would make a suitable hospital. The need had arisen because
there had been a fire on one of the ships moored in Southampton Water
to serve as temporary hospitals, hence the Indian casualties had been
crowded into an adapted hospital in the port. When the King went to
inspect the building on the following day, he saw for himself the need

for proper accommodation to be made available. He assigned responsibility to Sir Walter Lawrence to take action in the matter.

Brighton's Mayor responded by telegraphing to Lord Kitchener, Secretary of State for War, that the Corporation begged to place the buildings at His Majesty's disposal. During the afternoon, an appreciative reply came from the Secretary of the War Office on Lord Kitchener's behalf.

Brighton's Mayor, John Otter, welcomes Indian soldiers to the town in this C.H. Phelp cartoon which appeared in the Brighton & Hove Society *magazine on 3 December 1914. (Royal Pavilion & Museums, Brighton and Hove)*

A transformation of the buildings rapidly took place. The *Brighton and Hove Society* magazine of 26 November commented:

> *'Both the Pavilion and Dome in the course of one day changed from the magnificent concert hall, the ball-room, the suites of banqueting and other chambers, and the ornate corridors, into a vast, but entirely empty building, shorn of everything that could be removed, and prepared for its new use as a large hospital ... It is greatly to the credit of Brighton's town that such a gigantic work could be performed within the hours of Saturday night and Sunday, and ... that such a work was immediately set in successful operation.'*

The Royal Pavilion in peacetime. The banner on the right advertises a concert by the Municipal Orchestra at the Aquarium that evening. (Author)

It was, the magazine remarked, certainly a very happy thought that the casualties should be brought to lie during their treatment within the Orient-inspired decor of George IV's Eastern Palace, where their congenial surroundings would undoubtedly strongly appeal to their Asiatic tastes.

By Wednesday, about 780 bedsteads with bedding, side tables and other hospital furniture had been delivered to the buildings. To meet the tastes and habits of the Indian troops and for their cooking – as they would take no food from the hand of a European – very special arrangements had to be made. Nine kitchens were set up serving the Pavilion/Dome complex, most of them in huts erected on the lawns. These would cater specifically for Muslims (or Mohammedans as they were then generally called) or for either meat-eating or vegetarian Hindus. Since one caste would not mix with another, a plan of the hospital was drawn up in which the operating theatres, anaesthetic rooms, kitchens, bathrooms, lavatories, etc. were all separate. For religious worship, a Sikh temple or *gurdwara* was erected on the Pavilion lawns and, in front of the Dome, space was set aside on a grass plot where the Muslims could pray facing Mecca.

In December, a letter was received by Brighton Town Council from Lord Robert Crewe, the Secretary of State for India, expressing his cordial thanks to the Mayor and Corporation and citizens of Brighton for having placed the Royal Pavilion and Dome, and other public buildings in Brighton, at the disposal of the government for the accommodation of sick and wounded Indian soldiers.

Temporary huts in the Pavilion grounds. The larger one on the left may well have been the Sikh temple mentioned in the text. The other two probably housed kitchens. (Royal Pavilion & Museums, Brighton and Hove)

The first contingent – a small one – arrived at the Pavilion just a fortnight after the request had been received from the War Office. They were put straight into the Music Room and the North Drawing Room.

A party of three reporters from the *Brighton and Hove Society*

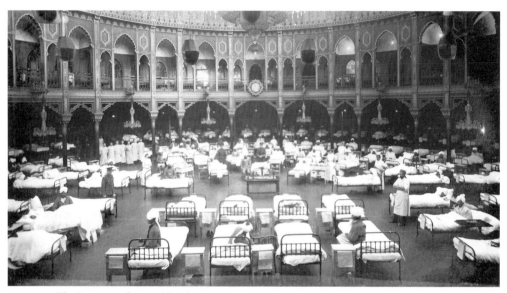

The Dome as a hospital for the wounded. One of a series of official postcards produced by Brighton photographer A.H. Fry for Brighton Corporation. (Trevor Cox collection)

magazine described the transformed buildings and the earliest occupants in a feature (issue of 10 December). In contrast to the blustery and cheerless Sunday weather outside, all was 'warmth, brightness, calm and quietude' when they entered the Pavilion, whose new occupants were:

> *'mostly tall men and graceful, quite dignified in their demeanour, and picturesque in their turbans and flowing robes, as they wander about in knots talking in their native Hindustani, or sitting and conversing upon the various seats. These are the Punjabs. There are also Gurkhas of Mongolian cast of features – short and sturdy. These are the convalescent wounded ... The more serious cases are still at Southampton, expected to arrive on the morrow.'*

Nurses pose with their Indian charges outside the Royal Pavilion. (Author)

A number of patients were delighted to sample from the group a scented mix of antiseptic, award-winning Oriental oils known as 'Dongor' – actually produced locally by Mrs Maude Dickinson of Kemp Town, whose patriotism was noted earlier.

Everything was now prepared at the Royal Pavilion, Dome and Corn Exchange. With around a thousand beds put up and all arrangements completed, a perfect working hospital was in readiness. In the Dome, a great array of beds was arranged symmetrically, with aisles for the doctors, nurses and orderlies. Beside the Dome, the finely-lit Corn Exchange presented another wonderful hospital array, and there was a fully-equipped dispensary under the direction of the Voluntary Aid Corps.

Another Fry photo, here showing the Corn Exchange in use as a hospital for the wounded Indian troops. (Author)

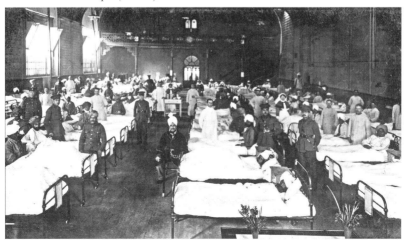

The first large contingent of patients, 345 in number (two full trainloads), arrived on Monday 14 December and of these 145 went to York Place, where visitors remarked on the brightness of the former classrooms, now turned into wards, and the airy gym, now occupied by 60 beds, while the rest went to the Pavilion.

The trains were met by the Chief Constable and there were representatives of the RAMC, the Sussex VAD, the Red Cross and St John Ambulance to handle the 112 patients from the first train (100 of them stretcher cases) and 233 in the second, which had only a few stretcher cases. The casualties were cheered by the crowds which had gathered in the rain – some ladies among them had arrived with 5,000 cigarettes as gifts to show their appreciation, prominent among them being, no doubt, Mrs Frances Pollak from Hove, who would become known as 'the soldiers' friend'. The *Gazette* editorial of 16 December recorded 'scenes of such amazing variety, of colour and animation' and enthused that they found themselves in magnificent hospitals, with the pleasant ease of spring beds, after the hardship of the trenches. Their first impression of the town, however, with its mud-laden streets and

Wounded at the SEGH, Dyke Road, being taken for a ride, September 1914. (IWM Q53312)

dripping umbrellas and mackintoshes, must have been a little dispiriting.

It was doubtless a source of great pride to the townsfolk to learn that one patient at the Pavilion was Havildar (a native soldier who was a non-commissioned officer in British Indian armies) Gagna Singh. He would be decorated by King George V himself with the Indian Order of Merit, the near-equivalent in the Indian Army of our Victoria Cross, for having commanded twenty-five Indians defending a trench who killed sixty Germans before they were overpowered. Singh, the only survivor, snatched a German officer's sword and killed ten men before he fell. He was left for dead, having sustained five wounds.

The non-medical care of the more able wounded took various forms, such as outings, attendance at events and, both away from the premises and on site, the enjoyment of entertainment. Here was a chance for players, artistes and speakers – and of course various townspeople, whether individually or in groups – to do their bit for the men.

In early October, over a hundred of the wounded from Dyke Road attended the performance at the Grand Theatre, North Road, of an exciting military drama, *Second to None* by Walter Howard, which dealt with episodes connected with the Scots Greys. Invited by Ernest Gates, the theatre manager, the men arrived in a series of loaned motor cars and also in a motor charabanc provided by Messrs Tillings. During the interval there was a showing of patriotic pictures connected with the war. When a beautiful coloured portrait of King George was shown, the men all rose to their feet (although many did so with difficulty, being wounded in the legs), and, standing to attention, lustily sang, *God Save the King*. After this moving episode, the band played *It's a Long Way to Tipperary*, which the heroes spiritedly sang from start to finish. The continuation of the play rounded off an enjoyable entertainment, one of a series offered to the wounded by Gates with his compliments.

For several weeks before Christmas, through the kindness of W. H. Boardman, the genial manager of the Hippodrome, various members of that theatre's companies paid visits, between performances, to the Dyke Road hospital to entertain the men. On 22 December, Seymour Hicks, ably supported by Gladys Cooper, greatly amused the patients with *The Bridal Suite*, a story based on the first half hour of married life.

Images of the Grand Theatre, North Road, are rare but this photograph, taken many years after the war, is a valuable record of its appearance. Sadly, the building was destroyed by fire in June 1961. (Chris Horlock collection)

Gifts for the sick and wounded were always appreciated and here working parties of ladies, or individuals, were major contributors (in August, Mrs Magnus Volk began independently organising a series of such parties at 38, Dyke Road for making clothing, bandages and other necessaries for the sick, wounded and destitute). St. Peter's Working Party met twice weekly in the Parish Room and forwarded all the articles to the King's Apartments at the Royal Pavilion, the Central Depot superintended by the Mayoress, Mrs Audrey Otter. Here they would be registered and dispensed as required to various hospitals. One independent worker was Mrs Duncan Furner, whose offerings, made via the Catholic Women's League, took the form of strong canvas kitbags filled with various basic items of clothing, toiletries and stationery.

Women were playing their part in many other ways, of course, taking over the work previously done by their men now serving in the forces. On 22 September, Emmeline Pankhurst gave a stirring address at the Dome to a largely female audience. In her long and earnest speech, she gave her unhesitating support to England's attitude to the war, boldly declaring that 'in taking part in this war we are fighting for our existence as a nation and all the ideals for which our forefathers have fought and sacrificed in the past.' She asked that every man who could should take his part in this war and that women should play their part and secure the welfare of those at home. Plenty of work for women could be found as booking clerks at railway stations, as shopwalkers, and as shop assistants of various kinds. A collection was taken on behalf of Queen Mary's Fund to provide work for unemployed women. This was an issue tackled by Miss Decima Moore of Brighton, who set up the Women's Emergency Corps. This aided the war effort by finding employment for the thousands of women and girls thrown out of work by the conflict; in London alone they numbered between 50-60,000. A large meeting of the Corps, based at Old Bedford College, Baker Street, London, was held on 15 October at the Grand Hotel; it had been arranged by Mrs Otter, who personally presided. It was reported that much had been accomplished in a very short time; workrooms had been opened for needy women, who included typists, shop girls, tearoom attendants, secretaries, lady gardeners, actresses and many others whose work had been taken from them and whose means of livelihood had gone. The Corps later evolved into the Women's Volunteer Reserve.

Munition workers at the Machine Shop, Brighton (Railway) Works, in 1915. At this stage, there is only one woman among the workers but she occupies a central position in the group. (Trevor Cox collection)

Meetings aside, it was resort business which filled the Grand, and indeed all of Brighton's hotels. Visitors flocked to the town during the autumn and winter, especially once the issue of alien workers had been resolved. A White List had been produced by early November of hotels and boarding establishments in which 'Visitors will be SAFE from the possibility of being waited upon by ALIEN ENEMIES as in each case the Proprietors have given a signed document to the effect that no Germans or Austrians are employed at these Establishments.'

=BRIGHTON HOTELS.=

THE WHITE LIST.

Following on our investigation of Hotels in Brighton and Hove ; and the employment therein of Germans and Austrians, we present below the

WHITE LIST

of Hotels and Boarding Establishments at which Visitors will be

SAFE

from the possibility of being waited upon by

ALIEN ENEMIES

as in each case the Proprietors have given a signed document to the effect that no Germans or Austrians are employed at these Establishments.

Fears of being served by German or Austrian staff in a Brighton hotel were allayed by the publication of a White List of 'safe' establishments. (Royal Pavilion & Museums, Brighton and Hove)

The *Brighton and Hove Society* magazine described the scene at one of Brighton's leading hotels:

'Khaki is everywhere; the Hotel Metropole was full of officers on Sunday [1 November]. There were all sorts of uniforms to be seen. The cavalryman, the Highlander, and the ordinary infantry kit, the staff, and many more, to the blue and gold of the naval commander. An officer that commanded much attention was wearing the Black Watch uniform, ... while another was from the Welsh Fusiliers. The Canadian Highlanders were there, too, the dark blue ribbons on their stockings showing up well against the khaki uniforms. All were with friends, and there were numerous parties to be noted. The hall and lounge were full for tea and dinner, while a vast crowd filled every seat for lunch. Many distinguished people made this

rendezvous a most interesting one, especially to the onlooker. Charming music added its enjoyment to the proceedings'.

At the Hippodrome on the previous evening, nearly every other man had worn khaki. Officers, as well as men of all ranks, had imparted the atmosphere of a garrison town to the audience. With numbers of smartly-dressed people present as well, it had been as cheery a place as was to be found in Brighton.

The town's other theatres and both piers provided ample entertainment for all tastes that autumn. On 22 October, the *Brighton and Hove Society* magazine noted that:

'the promise of a crowded winter season is everywhere being fully substantiated, with visitors to the town coming in a steady stream. One of the most popular resorts, both morning and afternoon, is the Palace Pier, and on Sunday there were large and smart crowds both in the Winter Garden [where the Band of the Royal Garrison Artillery performed daily] and on the long promenade stretches the pier possesses.'

With the approach of Christmas and the close of the year, society functions and general entertainments were patronised even more eagerly. At the Theatre Royal, past pantomimes had long been famous for lavish sets, gorgeous dresses and an abundance of rollicking humour. War or no war, this year was to be no different. The show put on was *Jack Horner*, an extravagant production comprising fourteen beautiful scenes and no less than 400 elaborate costumes. Miss Dorma Morgan, well known to variety audiences, was the principal boy. At the Grand Theatre, Ernest Gates' Boxing Day production was *Robinson Crusoe*, in which an expensive and novel effect was introduced by way

A rare view of the inside of Brighton's Hippodrome. (Royal Pavilion & Museums, Brighton and Hove)

of a 2-ton, electrically illuminated, crystal Dreadnought battleship, complete with turrets and barbette guns, which made its appearance as a finale to the first part. There was also a grand submarine ballet and special patriotic and other dances. Miss Maisie Ayling played the lead role.

On Boxing night (a Saturday), the Hippodrome, where 'row upon row of stalls held their fashionable complement' (*Brighton and Hove Society* magazine, 31 December), was packed to the rafters. The Royal York Hotel displayed its famous Christmas Tree and featured the Royal York Orchestra and a Cinderella Dance. In the distribution of presents, dolls dressed and donated by lady visitors to the hotel were sold by auction for charity, the causes this year being the Royal Alexandra Hospital for Sick Children in Dyke Road, the Royal Sussex County Hospital and Chief Constable W.B. Gentle's Police-Aided Scheme for Clothing Destitute Children. On the following Monday, there were again crowds at the Metropole, described by the *Brighton and Hove Society* as 'a most interesting place to pass an hour or so, just to watch the ever-varying assemblages of smart people.' This year, it reported, aristocratic visitors who generally went to the South of France for

A postcard which captures the atmosphere and busyness of Brighton's promenade. On the right is one of the pavilions at the entrance to the West Pier and on the left, in the middle distance, stands the Hotel Metropole. (Author)

Christmastide had flocked to the South Coast as being the nearest imitation in point of climate (although this had admittedly been sadly disappointing). Dress was, it commented, pre-eminently a display voicing fashion's latest moods. War had not destroyed women's love of modish attire yet 'though some looked charming, numbers bordered on the grotesque.'

A brilliant ball, which outshone the three dances given during Christmas week in the Clarence Rooms, ushered in the New Year of 1915 at the Metropole. Again, khaki was very much in evidence against the backdrop of splendid flowers and tall palms. As 1914 died, *Auld Lang Syne* was sung by the vast assembly and all thoughts turned to the national crisis which had overtaken the town since the previous year's gathering. As midnight approached, the lights were switched off and when the clock was heard to strike twelve, wild cheers greeted the New Year amid a burst of light and greetings were heard on every side. Three cheers for the army were followed by three for the soldiers of the king who were present, and three more rang out for the men in the trenches. Then supper was served in the dining-rooms, handsomely decorated in white and gold, to celebrate the opening hours of 1915, with much drinking to the health of present and absent friends. Sidney Hemmings and his well-known band provided music in excellent style and the whole of the fine winter garden was thrown open for use between the dances.

At the Grand, the decorations were also exquisite, both in the beautifully appointed King's Room and the adjoining lounge. The

Cheerful officers and staff at the SEGH, Dyke Road, looking forward to their Christmas dinner. (Author)

handsome overmantels were completely covered with flowers and large palms made quite cosy corners in the corridor and vestibule, where an enormous fire gave a cheery welcome. Miss Clara Waggett's Bijou Orchestra played an excellent and much enjoyed programme of dance music. Here too, of course, *Auld Lang Syne* was sung lustily and, as everywhere, with perhaps a tinge of sadness.

In the *Brighton and Hove Society* magazine, 'Scalpel' bade farewell to the old year in one of his 'Ballads With A Point'. Although devoid of any poetic merit, this extract does mirror the feelings of the day:

GOOD-BYE NINETEEN-FOURTEEN
WE LITTLE THOUGHT A YEAR AGO,
WE'D SEE SUCH THINGS AS NOW,
WE PEACEFULLY WENT TO AND FRO,
NO THOUGHT OF HARM I VOW;
BUT WAR CAME ON US, TRUTH TO TELL,
IN THE YEAR NINETEEN-FOURTEEN,
SO NOW WE'RE GLAD TO SAY FAREWELL
TO THE WORST YEAR EVER SEEN.

[REFRAIN:]
GOOD-BYE NINETEEN-FOURTEEN,
WE'VE HAD ENOUGH OF YOU,
GOOD-BYE NINETEEN-FOURTEEN,
MAKE ROOM FOR THE NEW YEAR, DO;
YOU'VE BROUGHT US LOTS OF TROUBLE
FROM THE KAISER AND HIS SET,
SO CLEAR OUT AND SLOPE,
BETTER LUCK LET US HOPE
IN NINETEEN-FIFTEEN WE SHALL GET.

CHAPTER TWO

1915 – Doctor Brighton

The new year was only into its second day when 130 more British wounded arrived from Dover at Brighton Station, where a large and sympathetic crowd awaited them. They were carefully conveyed by the RAMC men to St Mark's School, Kemp Town, and Stanford Road School. In mid-March there were, unusually, mixed arrivals of Indian and British wounded – three trainloads of the former (582 casualties) and one of the latter (187). All had received their wounds in the British offensive around Neuve Chapelle (10-13 March) in the Artois region of France. The fighting in that area also resulted in ninety-three men (fifty-two seriously wounded) being brought to Brighton on the

St Mark's Church of England School stood on this Arundel Road/Roedean Road corner site from 1895 until demolition in 1983. The bell tower (right) has been preserved at this location. (Chris Horlock collection)

evening of 14 April. Shrapnel wounds seemed to be the most prevalent. The crowd of well-wishers at the station gates was larger than usual and as each car swung out conveying the injured heroes to the Second Eastern General Hospital (SEGH) in Dyke Road, St Mark's School or the Red Cross hospital in Hove, rousing cheers were given.

The tragedy of the heroic fight for the historic 'Hill 60' in Flanders, south of Ypres was brought poignantly to Brighton's notice on 14 May, when a train from Dover arrived with 129 casualties. Eighty of the arrivals were seriously wounded stretcher cases. The scene was repeated in the following month, when ninety-two sufferers arrived straight from the battlefields via Boulogne and the great Kentish port, with casualties again taken off at Hastings and Eastbourne.

The cheering crowd which assembled at the platform barriers on 18 June was larger than had been seen at the station for months. Of the arrivals, twelve were officers; forty of the men had to be borne out on stretchers to the motor ambulances while another forty could walk, or limp, unaided.

In the following month, a Red Cross train brought in 181 Englishmen, Irishmen and Scotsmen from Dover. One man spoke with enthusiasm of the kindness of the poor people of Flanders. 'They will do anything for you; they can't do enough.' Ironically, one of the 158 wounded arriving late in the evening of 14 August, many of them

A very rare view of the interior of the Eye Hospital in Queen's Road (1846–1932) when used for the wounded. (Trevor Cox collection)

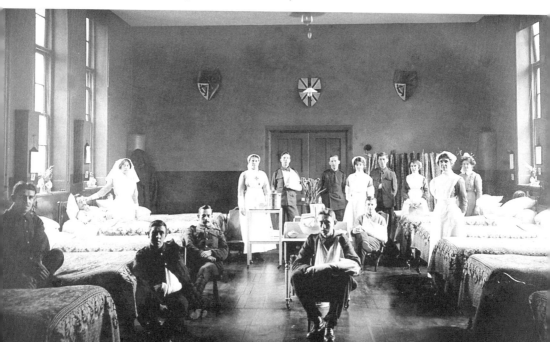

survivors of the terrible fight for the recapture of the trenches at Hooge a few days earlier, had been a stretcher bearer in the trenches. Sixty of the men were too seriously wounded to walk. Due to the blackout there were no lights in the ambulances. From the open cars in which the 'sitting' cases were conveyed, they could see only the mighty canopy of stars over Brighton. Not until around midnight did the last motor ambulance glide away, cheered by the comparatively few people remaining outside the station.

Thirty-two of the casualties from the train which came in on 27 August were taken to the RSCH and accommodated in Bristol, Chichester and Deans wards, while two men placed in York block enjoyed having their beds on the balcony facing the sea.

In September – as always – excellent preparations to receive the trains were in the capable hands of Mr John Roffe, the station superintendent, and Major Brailey, the Transport Officer for Sussex. It was the busiest month so far, with 164 cases arriving on the 2nd, 119 on the 17th, 207 on the 24th, 447 on the 27th and nearly 500 (including Indians) on the 28th. The Indians came in two batches, numbering 130 and 135 respectively, and were assisted by a number of Indian orderlies from Kitchener's Hospital, to which the first batch was conveyed. The second was distributed between the Pavilion and York Place Hospitals. One soldier, who had had a leg amputated, proudly exhibited the cause of his injury – a piece of shrapnel weighing about a pound.

While the British wounded continued to arrive until the end of the year, and indeed throughout the war, incoming convoys of Indians ceased at the end of 1915 due to changes which will be described later. In the meantime, ambulance trains conveyed them to the town on days or evenings which were, by and large, different from those bringing in British wounded; furthermore, they generally came from the west, via Southampton. Among the 200 who arrived on 19 February, most of the men suffered from frostbitten feet and illness rather than wounds (although there were fifty-one stretcher cases). The 582 arrivals in March have already been mentioned. Nearly 400 brave soldiers were brought in on 3 May by two trains. In the first, the Gurkhas were very prominent; their injuries, mainly to their hands, showed that they had fought deadly combat with the knife among the enemy. All were sent to the Kitchener hospital, while those from the second train, containing many bad cases of fractures and gunshot wounds, were distributed among the Pavilion, Dome and York Place hospitals, the latter receiving ninety-one of the 195 heroes. Two trains jointly brought in nearly 300 wounded, mainly Sikhs and Gurkhas, just three days later. One poor fellow had gone out of his mind. He was taken charge of by two of the RAMC men and driven off in a taxi. The occupants of one train were taken to Elm Grove and those from the other were divided between York Place, the Dome and the Pavilion.

The Municipal Secondary School opened at York Place in 1884 and taught technical and commercial subjects. Annexes were added in 1906. Several of the original buildings are still in use. (Tony McKendrick collection)

Mayor Otter stated in an interview given to the *Brighton Graphic and South Coast Illustrated News* (henceforth *Brighton Graphic*) in January 1915, in reference to the wounded, that much had been done in the town for them and it was a sacrifice – worthy of much appreciation – on the part of the townspeople to give up the Dome and Pavilion for a military hospital. The splendid conversions were visited on Saturday the 9th (the first day that year on which rain had not fallen in the town) by King George V and Queen Mary. *The Times* reported:

'The Dome was a wonderful sight with its circular lines of beds and

the picturesque uniforms of the patients who were able to move about, all of whom stood rigidly at attention. Others were able to get up, but a good number lay still in their cots. ... Another young Gurkha, of whom the King took special notice, was a man who had been shot in the jaw and has lost his tongue. His Majesty, through an interpreter, addressed a kindly remark to this man. ... On leaving the Dome the King, turning to the Mayor and the hospital administrators, expressed his entire satisfaction and gratification with all the arrangements. "Nothing," he said, "could be better."'

From the Pavilion the King and Queen went to inspect York Place Hospital, later visiting the Dyke Road Hospital where there were also Belgian wounded. They additionally visited establishments in Kemp Town, where John Howard had the honour of being presented to Their Majesties. They revisited Brighton on 21 August, accompanied by Princess Mary, on which occasion they visited the sick and wounded of the Indian Expeditionary Force at the Kitchener Hospital. Later, in brilliant sunshine, His Majesty conferred distinctions upon a number of heroic Indian soldiers at the Royal Pavilion Hospital, in particular the VC on Jemadar (a rank corresponding to that of Lieutenant in the English army) Mir Dast IOM (Indian Order of Merit) of the 55th Coke's Rifles, Frontier Force. This had been won for most conspicuous bravery and special ability at Ypres on 26 April, when he had led his platoon with great gallantry during the attack and had displayed remarkable courage in helping to carry eight British and Indian officers into safety while exposed to very heavy fire. At the time of this exploit, he was attached to the 57th Wilde's Rifles.

Gallant hero Mir Dast having just been awarded his VC. (Author)

In January 1916, *The Times of India* published an interview with this hero, then in the Lady Hardinge War Hospital, Bombay, in which he described the part he took in the fighting in Belgium and France and also his experiences at Brighton's Pavilion:

'Here I received the kindest of treatment. People of rank and the greatest soldiers and statesmen came to see a humble person like me. Among these were Lord Kitchener and Mr. Chamberlain, and they talked so nicely to me. They expressed their admiration for the work done by the Indian soldiers in the field. Lastly, my happiness was crowned by the visit of his Majesty the King-Emperor. My heart was filled with joy and gratitude when his Gracious Majesty with his own hands pinned the Victoria Cross on me, shook hands with me, and congratulated me on winning the distinguished order. ... Another visit gave me equal pleasure. It was from the Queen Mother, Queen Alexandra, who condescended to come and see me. "How did you like the treatment from your British comrades?" the Subadar was asked. "Splendid," he exclaimed. "They treated us like brothers, even more than brothers. ... Our British officers, too, were very kind. They made no distinction between the British, the Mahometan, or the Hindu soldiers – all were treated alike."'

Mir Dast was retired from active service on health grounds in 1917 with the rank of Subedar (the second highest rank of enlisted Indian soldiers, also spelled 'Subadar' as above).

The Indian hospitals in the town attracted other Royal visitors: Princess Louise (Duchess of Argyll) and Princess Henry of Battenberg visited on 14 January, followed a couple of weeks later by Ex-King Manuel II of Portugal, while Queen Alexandra visited the Royal Pavilion on 24 June. Manuel (also known as Dom Manoel and, in the Brighton press, King Manoel), deposed in 1910, was a friend of George V and was living in exile in Twickenham. He held a post in the Red Cross and cared greatly for the casualties of the war, both in British hospitals and at the Front. The *Sussex Daily News*, reporting his visit, noted:

'In the grand corridor and other parts of the Pavilion and Dome, and even in the grounds, wounded Indians propelled themselves cheerfully in invalid chairs and saluted as the King passed or as he

stopped to say a few sympathetic words to them, but apparently they did not in every instance realize the honour that was being paid them.'

At the Dome, the royal visitor smilingly said some words of encouragement to one young Ghurka to whom Queen Mary had given a flower. In the Corn Exchange, King Manuel was impressed by the excellent arrangements of the long rows of beds and walked slowly up and down among them, warmly expressing his sympathy. Despite some of the cases being very serious, he was informed that neither in the Dome nor in the Corn Exchange had a death yet occurred. After spending some time inspecting the well-appointed operating theatre, he quietly left the grounds via the North Gate.

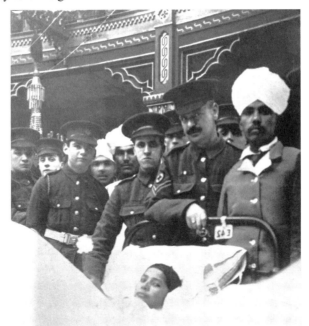

16-year-old Gurkha Pim holds a flower given to him by Queen Mary. (Trevor Cox collection)

The following week, the *Sussex Daily News* reminded readers of the ex-monarch's deep concern for the wounded, as evidenced by his many visits among them in London. He now planned to open 9, Eastern Terrace, through the British Red Cross Society, for as many convalescent officers as it would accommodate. This spacious property with a splendid sea view, formerly owned by Alfred Vanderbilt, was loaned to him by its owner, Admiral the Hon. Sir Hedworth Meux, GCB, Naval ADC to King George, and Commander-in Chief at Portsmouth.

Kemp Town elegance: Eastern Terrace. On the far right is No 9. (Author)

Kemp Town also hosted all the medical cases among wounded British soldiers arriving in mid-January. They were accommodated at 13, Lewes Crescent (once the home of Thomas Cubitt, the builder of thirty-seven houses in Kemp Town), to which had recently been added the adjoining house belonging to Mr Goodhart-Rendel. The block of premises communicated internally via a newly-constructed passage. In the annex there were five well-equipped wards, providing thirty-two extra beds, named Rodney, Hawke, Ceylon, Madras and Australia. Being a branch of the SEGH, the Lewes Crescent hospital was under the administration of Lieutenant-Colonel Rooth CO and Captain Walker while the Matron controlled the nursing staff of four buildings in Kemp Town.

Officers outside 9, Eastern Terrace. On the left, with crutches, is Captain Russell Roberts MC. Second from left is Lt Maurice Sharp of 10th Royal Fusiliers, his very close friend. (Sharp Collection IWM via David Carter/courtesy Robin Sharp)

We know from a letter from Walter Broadbent of Brunswick Square, Hove, to the *Sussex Daily News* on 23 January that 16, Lewes Crescent, on the opposite (eastern) side of the square, was also used for convalescents. He wrote on behalf of the men of the SEGH branch hospital at that address to convey their warmest thanks for a number of gifts donated by various local individuals and he referred to a concert party being brought to the hospital that afternoon.

The Lewes Crescent Hospital at No 16 (left portico). Sussex Square begins on the extreme left. (Author)

A splendid record of convalescence at the Lewes Crescent hospital (note the telescope pointing seaward) by local postcard publisher Arthur Scrace of 7, Herbert Road, Preston. (Robert Jeeves/Step Back in Time)

Presented to King George in January was wealthy Mrs Fanny Barnato, who had fitted out Hove Military Hospital at 38, Adelaide Crescent for European officers of the Indian army, staffing and maintaining it entirely at her own cost. She would go on to place 14, Royal Crescent, Kemp Town, at the disposal of Georgiana, Countess of Dudley, for War Office relief. Here a number of convalescent officers were installed.

During his visit, the King had asked Mr G. Cooper, Chairman of the Brighton Board of Guardians, where the inmates of the Poor Law Institution had been transferred to and was informed they had been accommodated in various houses in Brighton. The King thanked the Guardians, whose patriotic spirit, he said, had been of the most valuable assistance in providing for the wounded Indians.

It was Sir Walter Lawrence (who had secured the Pavilion) who had sought the Guardians' cooperation, sending a telegram to Lord Kitchener as follows:

'The Guardians of Brighton Parish, being of the opinion that the Poor Law Institution and Infirmaries are admirably suited for hospital treatment of Indian troops, beg to place such institution at the disposal of His Majesty for that purpose.'

The offer was accepted. The *Herald* reported on the major problem of removing a thousand people, 'nearly all of them feeble, and four hundred of them really sick', and doing so without exposing them to suffering. Action was taken by a special committee. The placements turned out very well for some inmates, as when ninety-seven ladies were transferred to a luxury block of four houses along the seafront at Aldrington called The Lawns. Others were placed out in the country, for example in Hassocks and Wivelsfield Green. Here, they occupied Wivelsfield Hall, a splendid country house built in 1910. Locally, in Norfolk Terrace, a building which in 1913 had closed as a school (Windlesham House) was used. In Kemp Town, the neighbours of 4 and 6 Sussex Square objected to the arrival of fifty-five sick females and fifty-five sick males respectively, while the transfer of seventy-six sick inmates to 5, Eastern Terrace did not sit well with those living nearby either. Ultimately it took just three weeks to complete the huge operation.

The Kitchener Hospital, formerly the Poor Law Institution, at the top of Elm Grove provided ample accommodation for the wounded. (Author)

On taking over the institution, the military authorities immediately changed its name to the Kitchener Indian Hospital. Much work was needed on it:

'Their original inspection of the building and its contents revealed some unacceptable equipment. They refused to take over the 177

bedsteads which were of sacking and, according to their Medical Officer, full of bugs. The Institution had only one obsolete steam steriliser and the Operating Theatre they described as "not a very modern one". The huge ashpit still in use in the grounds was immediately filled in. Despite these deficiencies it was soon to become a vast, fully operational military hospital. ... The hospital originally accommodated 1,500 Indian patients but orders were received to have as large a number of beds as possible. By the middle of June the number was raised to 1,763 and 2,000 by 1 July. Thirty infectious cases were arranged in groups of five in six wooden huts pallisaded off from the rest of the estate to form an Isolation Hospital. ... Sixty Indian officers were nursed in a separate block and remaining cases were spread among the other buildings.'

Janet Gooch, *A History of Brighton General Hospital* (Phillimore, 1980)

At the third Indian hospital in York Place and Pelham Street, 550 patients could be accommodated.

On 2 February, the *Sussex Daily News* reported that on the previous day, a Monday, three trainloads of wounded Indians, 445 in all, had arrived at the station, representing all the Indian regiments at the Front. There were now, it stated, about 2,000 wounded and invalided men in the three great buildings known as the Indian General Hospital. All the stretcher cases were taken either to the Pavilion or to York Place and the rest to the Kitchener Hospital, this being the first contingent to be sent to it. Three days later, the paper ran a feature on the 'immense preparations still going on at the series of great buildings on the south-western slopes of the Race-hill'. Over the previously uninteresting gates:

'appears boldly the arched inscription: "The Kitchener Indian Hospital"! Turbaned men are standing within; British sentries are on duty outside. About 350 wounded and invalided soldiers of the King-Emperor are already there, and more will soon be coming. There is room for some 3,000 of them and the work in progress suggests that this number of beds are being prepared. All the wounded Indians at Netley and in the special hospital which has been extemporised for them at Brockenhurst, are in due course to

be sent to Brighton, where they are all to be concentrated under
Colonel Neil Campbell's administrative supervision. This is the
King's wish.'

On 20 July, Lord Kitchener himself came to visit the hospital bearing
his name and also the Royal Pavilion.

Local photographer Arthur K. Pink of 29, Dover Road produced a number of internal
and external views of the hospital. Seen here are Blocks C-G. (Trevor Cox collection)

Colonel Sir Bruce Seton, a medical man who had served in India,
was in charge, assisted by a highly efficient staff of Anglo-Indian and
Indian officers, Indian doctors and Red Cross personnel. The various
blocks of buildings had been marked in large black letters on a white
ground, 'A', 'B', 'C' and so on and many Brighton workmen were still
busy making all sorts of improvements indoors and outdoors. Some
outhouses with corrugated iron roofs had already been set up, while
others were being built. The great main block, marked 'A', contained
no wounded as yet but was being beautifully equipped with all the most
modern improvements.

The irregular-sized wards had to be adapted to meet the caste and
religious observances of the Indians. The public were not to be allowed
to stare in from Elm Grove or the hill beyond. To prevent it, hoardings
were put up wherever necessary and high fences erected on the lower
edge of the grounds.

The entertainment of the wounded, in which Brighton excelled, greatly helped the casualties on the road to recovery. The hospitals themselves, large and small, were important and convenient venues. A favourite at the Dyke Road establishment was the Thursday evening Hippodrome Night held in the gymnasium (on 12 August, Marie Lloyd sang sentimental ballads and Will Evans made some of the men 'quite ill with laughing'). At the RSCH, pleasant concerts were arranged in the summer by various ladies. At St Mark's Hospital, Kemp Town, Mrs H. J. Walker laid on a hugely appreciated concert on 12 June and nearly three weeks later Miss Ogilvy did the same at that establishment. On 6 October, the recreation room of the Stanford Road Hospital was crowded with soldiers, mostly from Highland regiments, with the 'Gay Gordons' predominating. It was the latter who laughed the loudest at the funny stories told to them by concert giver Miss Muriel Gray. In December, Mrs Lethbridge gave an entertainment at the Queen's Road Eye Hospital.

Church halls were often used for shows. In April, fifty wounded were entertained in St Bartholomew's Hall, Providence Place, made available by the Vicar, the Rev H. Ross. Most of the guests were being treated at the SEGH, Dyke Road, while others (among them two Belgians) came from the Stanford Road establishment. In that road, at the United Methodist Church, fifty injured Tommies from three local hospitals declared their event on 3 February was 'the treat of treats'. Entertainments were occasionally put on at the Congregational Church Rooms, Lewes Road, hosted by the PSA (Pleasant Sunday Afternoon) Sisterhood. Here there was a recreation room, where billiards, draughts, chess and other games could be enjoyed. In the town centre, a concert was held in March, also on church premises, at the Union Church Hall, Queen Square, the large room of which had been converted into a comfortable recreation room for soldiers. Just over a week later, nearly seventy wounded soldiers were feted in style at St Anne's Hall by the young members of the Girls' Realm Guild, founded 15 years earlier. Mrs Pollak conveyed the soldiers from the three Kemp Town hospitals in her own and other private cars and was responsible for their safe return. The varied programme was followed by a sumptuous tea. The Guild entertained the wounded (over fifty of them, including two Australians blinded in the landing at Anzac Cove) again in mid-December.

A wonderful gathering of helpers and convalescent servicemen at an entertainment hosted by Emily Vokins at her spacious villa, Beechwood, in Withdean. (Robert Jeeves/Step Back in Time)

Theatres also welcomed the heroes. In September, for example, the directors of the Theatre Royal treated them – as they often did – to Saturday matinees. At the end of the play, Mrs Pollak distributed chocolates and cigarettes among the 'boys' and took all her party to Clark's Tea Rooms at the corner of the North Street Colonnade, where they enjoyed a substantial ham tea. The Grand Theatre, under Cecil Gates, welcomed nearly eighty men in March, all of whom greatly enjoyed the adventures of *The Beggar Princess*. Plentiful refreshments were provided.

Outdoor entertainments were also enjoyed. In September, one venue was the Brighton and Hove Ladies' Golf Club. After a delightful drive to Devil's Dyke, some thirty-five wounded soldiers had tea and amused themselves, some playing golf and clock-putting while others rambled over the Downs. Several members of the Club helped to entertain the visitors. Private homes and gardens were liberally opened up to cheer the wounded. On 14 August, a delightful party, with orchestral accompaniment, was held at spacious Fairlie Place in Surrenden Road, the home of Mr and Mrs Emile Moreau. Nearly a month later, Mr and Mrs Clarkson Wallis entertained a large number of patients from the Dyke Road and Stanford Road hospitals at their attractive residence, Springfield. A quiet game of bowls was enjoyed in its garden.

On 1 August 1916, Mrs McSweeney entertained the wounded to luncheon at an unidentified location. (Peter Booth collection)

One unusual venue, courtesy of Mr and Mrs Gosnay of Channel View, Preston Park, was the enclosure in front of the bathing huts opposite the covered Madeira Walk. There, in early July, a splendid tea was given to twenty wounded soldiers from the Stanford Road Hospital. Some of the men were even recovered enough to take a dip. On the nearby Palace Pier back in early February, a matinee had been held at the Theatre in aid of wounded Indians. As the Gurkhas entered, the audience gave them a hearty cheer.

Brighton's taxi drivers 'did their bit' to look after the wounded. On 9 July no fewer than thirty-three cars paraded at the Aquarium after picking up some 150 men at the various hospitals and, in the presence of a large (mainly female) and cheering crowd, started on a forty-mile circular tour, taking in Steyning and Partridge Green. From there they were taken for tea to the Chinese Gardens – also provided by the generous donors – at the Orchard Pleasure Gardens in Hassocks. It meant a real sacrifice for all the cab men to give up a whole afternoon in the busiest month of the holiday season. As for Brighton itself, the *Sussex Daily News* remarked:

'If one town could be said to represent the nation today, Brighton can surely claim to be very representative and this procession from the Aquarium to the Hove boundary and back along the King's-road brought out once more the intense sincerity of our gratitude to these heroic warriors in our great cause.'

At all the places visited, crowds cheered the invalids on their way. To their enormous credit, the cabmen repeated the exercise, this time direct to Hassocks, the following month.

The Indians were sometimes taken even further afield, for example to London. One wrote to a friend about an excursion in August:

'I had the day of my life yesterday for I was one of the chosen for a trip to London and I'm pleased to say enjoyed myself immensely. What a wonderful city it is. Unlike anything I have yet seen and it will always conjure up happy memories long after I am back in India. The kindness and thought about hospital authorities is indeed great, taking so much time for our welfare and gratification - a day that will live to the end of life.'

About the capital, he wrote in a second letter:

'The vastness of it is so very great. I cannot remember one-half that I saw. One thing stood out alone to my mind, and that was the Tower Bridge. A wonderful sight to see the road stand up on its edge!'

That August was a remarkable month in Brighton. The memorable weekend and Bank Holiday Monday were swiftly followed by the first anniversary of the war, while the 15th was National Registration Day, an exercise which kept volunteer enumerators busy for some time. The holiday brought huge crowds, not only to Brighton and Hove but to other resorts in the county. From Friday 30 July to Sunday 1 August, bookings on the London, Brighton and South Coast Railway (LBSCR) were very heavy to all resorts in Sussex and Hampshire. However, 'despite an unavoidable shortage, the staff grappled nobly with the invasion of Brighton' (*Sussex Daily News*, 2 August). These thousands were swelled on the Monday holiday by many more from London and the country. The weather was for the most part splendid throughout, encouraging excursions to outlying places such as Devil's Dyke, Hassocks (for the popular Orchard Pleasure Gardens, mentioned

An attractive poster promoting both Brighton and, oddly, the small, independent SMJR (Stratford Upon Avon & Midland Junction Railway) company which ran a railway network across part of central England, promoting itself as 'The Shakespeare Route'. (Author)

above) and Lewes. The throng of visitors to the Palace Pier on the Monday was one of the largest seen that summer. Lunches and dinners were served at the pier head restaurant and teas in the Winter Garden. The influx of visitors was astonishing. The *Sussex Daily News* acknowledged, on 2 August, that:

> *'Brighton has beaten the record for the August Bank holiday week-end. Another very remarkable feature of this success is that all classes contributed to it. Society was well represented at numerous house parties, the best hotels were absolutely crowded – a somewhat rare experience at this holiday – boarding-house proprietors were so overwhelmed that they had to find apartments outside their own premises. The commercial element was to be seen in apartments in private houses. The influx of vacation visitors on Thursday, Friday and Saturday was unprecedented, and hundreds of residents who let a few rooms at the season had to turn away applicants. ... In fact, a perfect avalanche of holiday folk descended upon the town.'*

The newspaper's pen picture of Brighton's Front under the most glorious conditions of summer expanded on the scene:

> *'On the long line of promenades, the crowd was great as on an ordinary Bank Holiday with the tripper element in full strength. There were all sorts of people – military officers, soldiers in khaki, representatives of the naval service, ladies in smart gowns, young women in characteristic holiday garb and young fellows in straw hats and flannels; but there was one common rule of quiet, decorous enjoyment of the delightfully inspiring scene. It was a moderately dressed crowd ... There was no evidence of extravagance. Groups of many children added to the picturesqueness of the scene. The beach was particularly animated ... Dainty tents formed interesting objects on the shore, and sailing and rowing boats bobbed serenely on the surface of the water. The Madeira-road proved as attractive as usual to holiday visitors, and thousands boarded the cars of Volk's electric railway for trips to Black Rock and the eastern cliffs. One of the most interesting sites on the Front was the march past of a large contingent of the London Volunteer Training Corps. ... A profuse display of bunting from the flagstaff on the West Pier gave the structure an animated appearance. The largest audience of the*

season assembled for the morning and afternoon concerts. ... A
feature of the day was the popularity of tea parties on the veranda
at the Hotel Metropole and Grand Hotel, and in the seaside winter
garden at the Royal Albion hotel. There was also considerable
entertaining in the tents on the beach. The widespread desire of the
people to enjoy the splendid weather imposed a severe strain on the
tramway service to and from the Aquarium terminus and the motor
tourist cars were besieged at every point. The buses had a busy day,
the new service from the Seven Dials to the Sea Front being
extensively utilised.'

Brighton beach was the place to relax and make friends, as this picture from a
contemporary magazine shows. (Chris Horlock collection)

The fourth itself – anniversary day – was respected and reflected on,
both privately and publicly. Several columns in the *Sussex Daily News*
were taken up by a moving review of the previous twelve months.
Titling his feature *4 AUGUST, 1914-15 – SUSSEX AND THE WAR*
YEAR (REFLECTIONS BY A MAN OF SUSSEX), the writer summed
up the mood of the times and of the people:

'At the end of this year of blood and tears we reverently salute our immortal dead and lift up our hearts with renewed hope and confidence towards the future. We pay homage also to our brave sons who are "marching away" across the fair land of Sussex, and we know that our faith in them can never die, because it is based on the diviner faith in the justice of our cause.'

The main public event was the service of prayer and intercession at St Peter's Church. Here the national anthem was fervently sung and at noon, simultaneously with the service in St Paul's Cathedral which the King and Queen attended, a long procession of choristers, clergy, and members of the Town Council and other public bodies in Brighton entered the undecorated parish church singing a hymn *Lord, In This Thy Mercy's Day*. The building was packed, with barely even standing room inside.

St Peter's Church, York Place, where major commemorative services were held. (Author)

The roving enumerators for the new registration scheme enjoyed pleasant weather that month for their duties. The purpose of the 1915 National Registration Act was to compile a register of all persons between the ages of 15 and 65 who were not members of the armed forces. The names were taken, in the week beginning 9 August, of everyone who would be in residence on the night of Sunday the fifteenth. Anyone refusing or neglecting to complete the forms was liable to a £5 fine. By and large, the enumerators found people very willing to fill them out.

The information supplied under the Act provided manpower statistics and also enabled the military authorities to discriminate between persons who should be called up for military service and those who should, in the national interest, be retained in civil employment. The measure was a way of dealing with the labour crisis, since essential industries had been left without key workers after the rush of volunteers to the Front. The government was also keen to identify the shirkers and slackers who were not doing their duty for the war effort. Men in essential industries were 'starred' for exemption from military service. Recruiting officers would pay up to three visits to men who had not enlisted and inquire why. The Register was inevitably also used when conscription was introduced in 1916.

Punch *(3 February 1915) pillories those who have not enlisted. The caption reads: 'Patriotic Old Person (to individual bespattered by passing motor-bus). "THERE, YOUNG FELLER! IT'D NEVER HAVE BIN NOTICED IF YOU'D BIN IN KHAKI!"'*

The *Brighton Graphic* noted on the 26th that on Registration Day, 'it seems there were 30,000 visitors in Brighton and 15,000 in Hove. They came from all parts of the United Kingdom and even from beyond the seas.' Some interesting discoveries were made; for example, one enumerator found in a house which ordinarily accommodated five persons no fewer than twenty-nine residents.

During that summer, and particularly in the autumn, the townspeople of Brighton and, no doubt, visitors to the resort, dug deep into their pockets and purses to support our Allies and other causes. Fundraising usually took the form of flag days, occasionally with associated events and entertainments. It was almost entirely the women of Brighton who, often jointly with those of Hove, organised and participated in the collections.

In May, flags sold to support Poland and the Russian Red Cross raised over £173 and over £462 (which included a £48 contribution from Worthing) respectively. Such responses were very gratifying but nothing could compare with seeing a tangible result from a local appeal. In July 1915 this was secured in the form of a motor ambulance – bearing the name *Brighton*. On 29 April, Audrey Otter, Mayoress of Brighton, had relayed to the local press an appeal to the town from the Duchess of Norfolk, President of the Sussex Branch of the British Red Cross Society and the Order of St John of Jerusalem, to supply an ambulance for use at the Front. These vehicles, costing £600 (including £200 for maintenance and running expenses), were urgently needed. Brighton's would be exhibited in London, together with others similarly supplied by other towns, before being dispatched to the field of battle. By June, the target had not only been reached but exceeded, inspiring the idea of raising money for a second vehicle. On 5 July, at Buckingham Palace, the Queen received the Mayoresses of the various large towns and inspected the ambulances provided by the respective boroughs. Brighton, Hove and Tunbridge Wells had each provided a vehicle which bore a brass plate showing the name of the town which provided it (the Queen stopped at the Brighton ambulance and examined it in detail). After a short ceremonial, the mayors and mayoresses were driven to the Mansion House, where they were received by the Lord Mayor of London and the Lady Mayoress. In September, Mayor Otter received a letter affirming that the ambulance was doing good work in Egypt and in November Mrs Otter reported

Sadly, the flag day for our ally, France, was marred by heavy rain, particularly in the morning. (Robert Jeeves/Step Back in Time)

that a special Christmas parcel had been sent to the driver of the Brighton ambulance in Alexandria.

French Flag Day, held on 14 July (Bastille Day), was a combined effort by the twin towns. The collection and associated events, which raised the magnificent total of just over £1,080, were in support of the *Secours National*, corresponding to the Prince of Wales's National Relief Fund (towards which Brighton had contributed more than £7,000 by November 1915). The *Sussex Daily News* recorded that it was 'almost as difficult to get through the entanglement of pleading maidens as barbed wire'. At the French Convalescent Home at Black Rock, the flags of the Allies were arranged in line on the lawn in front of the building. All of Sussex took its hat off to France. In Rottingdean village, decorated with flowers, more than £11 was raised from the sale of over 1,000 flags, twelve schoolchildren having made admirable collectors.

The former French Convalescent Home (now a residential development called The French Apartments) in de Courcel Road, Kemp Town, was opened in 1896 as a sanatorium and rest home. It offered thirty beds for wounded servicemen. (Author)

Patients at the French Convalescent Home in a view from the lawn facing east (Arundel Street). In the white coat (centre) is George ('Louis') Vintras (1864-1934), whose father founded the Home. George's wife, Grace, a nurse, stands beside him. Their son, Roland, is seated in the middle of the front row. (Penelope Adamson)

Unfortunately, pitiless rain later that day affected the pageant of local volunteer forces (the VTC and Cadets) which started out on Madeira Road. The paraders marched to Hove, where the volunteers from that town were dismissed but the Brighton VTC Battalion and the College, Grammar School and cadet contingents returned eastwards along the front to Brighton, with the VTC band playing *Sussex By The Sea*. At the Court Theatre in the evening, a very successful collection was made from the crowded audience when the lights were put on for ten minutes for the purpose.

Flag days held in the autumn by the

From Punch, *23 July 1915. Caption: 'Officer (who has not lunched). "Now, Sir, You've got to stand here and keep a sharp look-out all over the country. But you're on no account to see the enemy till half-past two."'*

twin towns raised over £572 for Serbia on 7 September and over £843 for Belgium on 2 October.

There were two drives for local funds in September, one the Tobacco Fund and the other a collection for the VTC. The Tobacco Fund was the brainchild of the *Brighton Graphic*, which gave its services entirely free. Through it, our troops could be supplied with cigarettes and tobacco sent duty-free, carriage free, and with free distribution, courtesy of the government, the War Office and the Admiralty.

The flag day in aid of the equipment fund for the 1st (Brighton) Battalion Sussex Volunteer Training Corps, which paraded proudly through the town, was held on the 25th and raised over £478. Although recognized by the government, the VTC had to find its own equipment. Many of the members of the Battalion had already, wholly or in part, purchased their uniforms. Were it not for the donations of their friends and supporters, the men would also have had to pay for their own rifles and other equipment. The proprietor of the Palladium showed a film of an earlier inspection and march past of the Corps in Preston Park and a mass meeting and grand concert were held in the evening in the Market Hall.

Over £185 was raised in a flag day the following month on behalf of the Mayoress of Brighton's Working Party, which by now had moved from the Royal Pavilion to spacious rooms above Lyons at 14, North Street.

The proceeds of just over £1,641 from another flag day held in October, this time on behalf of the British Red Cross Society and the St John Ambulance Association, substantially exceeded even the funds raised in July for France. The total, remarked the *Sussex Daily News*, coming after many flag days for other deserving causes, was regarded as highly creditable to Brighton and Hove. Dubbed 'Our Day', the event was an appeal from the mayors of both towns. A large crowd watched the procession of

The twin towns could show their support for the Belgians by buying flags and attending a concert in Hove. (Royal Pavilion & Museums, Brighton and Hove).

Appeal poster for 'Our' [sic] Day, the annual fundraising event of the British Red Cross Society and Order of St John. (Royal Pavilion & Museums, Brighton and Hove)

mounted police, ambulances, nurses and many wounded heroes proceed along the front at midday. Boosting the collection was money raised at the Grand Hotel in the evening from a delightful concert of vocals and instrumentals (these courtesy of the Grand Hotel Orchestra) given in the lounge.

Unlike the East Coast, the South Coast was not a target from the air or from the sea. 'There is', stated Brighton's Mayor John Otter when interviewed in early January 1915 by the *Brighton Graphic*, 'scarcely any chance of the Germans coming to Brighton. The danger of an invasion down here is extremely remote', although, he conceded, 'possibly the danger of a flying bombardment is a little nearer'. Nevertheless, it was important that Brighton was not illuminated for the enemy. 'We are darkening the streets at night time as much as possible. All bright lights outside shops are subdued, and in some instances the bright lights displayed in the interiors have been reduced.'

Although the first Order on lighting was not issued by the Home Office until 8 April 1915, restrictions had been introduced in London as early as 11 September 1914. In essence, street lights could be left unlit while others could be dimmed or shaded. An editorial in *The Motor* in December 1914 referred to the new regulation issued by the Home Secretary which imposed further restrictions on shopkeepers and contained a new provision requiring all vehicles to carry red rear lights in addition to any headlights as prescribed by law. Bicycles were included, although cyclists were showing 'determined obstinacy' in not adopting rear red lights. The red reflectors fitted voluntarily by a large number of them had, however, admittedly been successful as an interim measure.

On 22 February, Brighton's Chief Constable published a notice in the local press headed DEFENCE OF THE REALM ACT, 1914 which stated that 'inside lights will be permitted undimmed in shop and other windows WHICH

'O is the Order re "lighting at night" (My own little house is the fifth on the right).' From 'An Alphabet of the War' in Punch's Almanack *for 1915.*

CANNOT BE SEEN FROM THE SEA, from this date until further notice. ALL OTHER WINDOWS MUST REMAIN SCREENED.'

Inevitably there were transgressors. On 5 March, Frank Goodchild, 68, of Hartington Road, manager of the Princess Laundry in Whippingham Street, was summoned for having failed, on 15 February, to reduce the intensity of the inside lighting from 6 pm so that no bright light was shed outside. Goodchild pleaded not guilty. He said that as soon as the Order came out, a man had been specially appointed to see to the lights but had omitted to do so on the night in question. At about 8 pm, PC French had called his attention to several windows being brightly lit and the blinds not drawn. The accused's defence lawyer contended that a laundry did not come under the word 'shop' but the Chief Constable, in reply, argued that the laundry was a workshop and that the word 'shop' did not necessarily mean a drapery, grocery or boot shop. After consultation, the Bench held that a laundry was indeed a shop within the meaning of the Order, whereupon the defendant pleaded guilty. William Gentle said the owners of this property had been warned four or five times. The Bench imposed a fine of 50 shillings and costs.

'He won't have the lights down' claimed Bessie Boswell, the owner of an apartment house at 53, Marine Parade, who was summoned in May for not having secured indoor lights on 22, 23 and 25 April so as to be invisible from outside. She was referring to one of her boarders, a baronet and a Justice of the Peace in Yorkshire – someone who should have known better. The police were sorry too, for they did not have sufficient evidence to bring him before the Court. This unreasonable lodger incurred for his landlady a fine of 40 shillings, a deterrent welcomed by the Chief Constable, who thought boarding house keepers in Brighton seemed to be treating the Order very lightly indeed.

On 23 April, the case came up of Sydney Edgar, a butcher, of 136 Albion Hill, for having failed to reduce a bright light at that address on 16 March. Edgar pleaded not guilty. Special Constable Dubbin had gone to the defendant's premises on the night in question, where he saw a big light in the centre of the shop. The doors were open and no blinds or shutters were at the windows, and this caused the light to shine over the road and onto the houses on the opposite side. Dubbin told defendant the light was too strong, and Edgar replied 'Am I to take note of special constables, or what?' Dubbin reminded him of the Lighting Order, and the defendant replied 'Get out of my shop; I don't want to talk to you.' About a quarter of an hour later, Edgar did put some brown and coloured paper round the globe but it had little effect on the light. Giving evidence, he said that the only lighting he had on the premises was a 28-candlepower electric light and an incandescent burner in the centre of the shop. Two witnesses did not think the light complained of had been excessive. The Bench evidently agreed. Advising Edgar to be more careful, it ruled that the case would be dismissed on payment of costs.

Charles Arnold Bleckly of 5, Arundel Terrace received a severe sentence for an offence committed on 2 May. Special Constable Albert Noakes claimed the lights would have been visible several miles out at sea. The night had been particularly dark and the outline of each window had been clearly visible. Since the property was on the seafront, the Bench felt the non-observance had been particularly dangerous. A fine of 60 shillings, or 10 days' imprisonment, was imposed. Another offender, whose light could be seen from the sea a few days earlier, was Thomas Edwardes, 37, of Duke Street. His shop faced down Middle Street and he had done his best to keep the light as low as possible by putting brown paper over the top of the windows.

Special (to Citizen retired for the night, whom he has called up). "Your ground-floor window's open; and now I must report you for showing too much light." From Punch, *issue of 27 October 1915.*

Although liable to a fine of £100, Edwardes, despite having had several previous warnings, was in the event fined 20 shillings or seven days.

On 14 May, George Stone, another butcher, of 14, Elm Grove was summoned for having failed to secure his windows and skylights on the 8th. He pleaded not guilty. Notable about this case was the fact that the Deputy Town Clerk, Mr C.N.T. Jeffreys, said the Special Constables who had visited the premises had been treated in a very offensive manner. They had been carrying out duties which were to a certain extent onerous. It was very much to be regretted that when they were doing their duty in this way they should be subjected to abuse and their authority questioned. Stone was convicted and fined 40 shillings.

Cases came up in abundance that spring, summer and beyond (particularly among boarding house proprietors), the most serious one in terms of the penalty imposed being that of John Hardy, who had a shop in King's Road Arches. On 12 June the door was open and light was streaming out to sea. The defendant, who pleaded guilty, explained

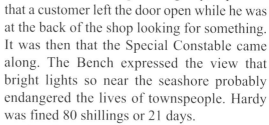

that a customer left the door open while he was at the back of the shop looking for something. It was then that the Special Constable came along. The Bench expressed the view that bright lights so near the seashore probably endangered the lives of townspeople. Hardy was fined 80 shillings or 21 days.

The duties of Special Constables were evidently thankless – and sometimes worse – on the streets. Under the Special Constables Order dated 9 September 1914, they were appointed 'for the preservation of the public peace, and for the protection of the inhabitants, and the security of property in the police area for which, or for any part of which, the justices making the appointment act'. These duties they performed to the best of their ability, despite the difficulties.

Women also wanted to help. There were now two female forces on patrol, which led to some confusion in the town. The situation was set out in a feature published in the *Brighton*

A Special Constable, identity unknown. The Specials did valuable work but could occasionally be over-zealous. (Author).

Graphic on 3 April entitled 'BOBBY – THE WOMAN POLICEMAN':

'Since the publication a few days ago of the fact that in Brighton there had been established a body of women known as Women Police Patrols, a slight misunderstanding has apparently arisen regarding another body of women, also established in the town, known as Women Police Volunteers. Seemingly, whilst the one body has been recognised by the authorities, the other has not sought for recognition, and this not being generally known in newspaper circles, a "general mix-up" was apparently made relating to one or two pictures of the Police Volunteers which appeared in London contemporaries recently.'

HOW SHE MAY HELP.

*In the caption (not reproduced), the fashionable lady's offer to hold bridge evenings and dances for the troops is rejected by the OC, who urges her to join the Women's Police instead. (*Brighton and Hove Society *Cartoon No 509).*

Chief Constable Gentle contacted the *Daily Mail* to state that he disapproved entirely of a body of women at Brighton who were apparently being called the 'Women Police Volunteers' and that he had warned them that they ran a risk if they persisted in using a uniform which more or less resembled the ordinary police uniform. Mrs E.M. Field, Hon. Secretary of the Brighton and Hove branch of the National Union of Women Workers, stated that by contrast Brighton's officially recognised Women Police Patrol Force (already sixty strong and still recruiting) did not wear a uniform but only an armlet. Mayoress Otter pointed out in an interview in the *Brighton Graphic* that the Chief Constable so valued their work that he had placed a room at the Town Hall at their disposal. Their duties were to give proper advice to young girls in the town and to establish clubs, if possible, for their social benefit. They were in no way connected with the 'Women Police Volunteers' who had been at work in Brighton since January 1915 and whose duties were to help the public at large, attempt to uplift the morals of the town, endeavour to protect children compelled to frequent lonely places, guide women and children visiting the town and bring about general improvements which they felt would prove beneficial to all concerned. They particularly required large club rooms, where girls (many of whom met young soldiers at the corners of the streets and were often driven into public houses) could take their men friends and enjoy themselves in a harmless way.

The Volunteers' 'lady-chief', Miss Mary Hare, looking particularly

smart in her uniform and bowler hat, admitted when interviewed by the *Brighton Graphic* that the force had been warned by the Chief Constable. They had sought an interview with him and been told by him to cease their work. 'But', she added,

A group of Women Police Volunteers in Brighton. The picture featured in an article on the WPV in the Brighton and Hove Society *of 3 April 1915.*

'we are out to do good work in Brighton, and we have had unsolicited testimonials to the effect that we have done good. We have had no complaints made against us ... We cannot see any satisfactory reason why we ought to stop and we have decided to continue our duties.'

They wanted to be of service to the general public and aimed to establish a training ground for those women who may later on have opportunities for taking up police duties on a professional footing. They were connected with the suffrage movement but recruits did not need to be suffragettes and would not be asked to become one. There was a similar volunteer body in London which worked in a very friendly way with the Women Patrols of the city. Sometimes they remained on duty until midnight or even later.

Female (un)employment was an ongoing issue. There was initially distress among some women on account of the decreased trade in various business houses supplying luxuries. A great deal was achieved towards alleviating any hardship by the local Relief Committee. Initiatives to help young women thrown out of work through the war included a scheme at 34, West Street partly supported by grants from the Committee. Here, twenty girls made toys, the sale of which yielded the balance of the funding. The thriving enterprise replaced cheap German toys with superior English machine and hand-made ones. Training was directed by Mrs Toyne, the wife of Frederic H. Toyne, Secretary of the Education Committee. Girls up to 14 years of age learning toy-making were paid 4s 6d a week and those from 15 to 17 years over, 6 shillings. Girls showing special talent in making more complicated toys received 10 shillings and more.

Regarding general employment in the town, Mayor Otter said in his January interview that there was currently more employment than there had been of late years due to so many men being taken on for government work, for instance at Shoreham in the building of huts. These works would come to an end and then a substantial fall in employment might be expected but the Corporation would then, through the Distress Committee, provide such work as it could find.

When asked about the call to arms in his January interview, Mayor Otter responded 'We have done very well indeed. I think we have nearly reached the end of men eligible, and with a decided impulse to military service. If matters, however, become more serious than they are now, I think a great many more men will volunteer. I mean men who have fixed occupations now.'

That the recruitment drive was effective was confirmed by Sir John Blaker, who in January declared that recruiting improved with the fine weather and every time the sun shone he saw more recruits dropping in at the Town Hall. He found the New Year was opening very well for Lord Kitchener's Army. Figures to date since the war started were as follows: August, 702; September, 1,405; October, 310; November, 430 and December, 260 – a grand total for 1914 of 3,107.

On 13 March, men of the 9th Battalion of the Royal Sussex Regiment, which was 1,057 strong and billeted at Portslade, marched from there to Brighton in a recruitment drive. As part of the exercise, two little boys in khaki, sons of men serving in the army (Jack Woolgar and Fred Brooker), marched up to any fine upstanding young men they came across and put the enlistment question to them. From the Aquarium, the battalion proceeded to the eastern end of Madeira Road and returned along Marine Parade, watched by a large crowd; it then marched back to Portslade. Sir John Blaker, who organised the event, sported a sign on his car announcing that 500,000 men were still required. At around this time, Brighton Palladium showed a well-

The West Pier with the Hotel Metropole in the background. 'What the Germans would like to see'. From a feature 'BRIGHTON AS THE KAISER WOULD LIKE IT' in the Brighton and Hove Society *of 19 December 1915.*

known patriotic film, *Wake Up, or a Dream of Tomorrow*, based on a story by Laurence Cowen. Its mission was to awaken the fighting spirit in the young blood of the nation and to this end it featured a massive parade of military and naval forces and, dramatically, scenes of destruction showing what would happen if the invader established himself on these shores.

Unexpected support for recruiting came on the evening of 5 April at the Hippodrome, where Harry Lauder, after two encores, made an impassioned recruiting speech which, the *Sussex Daily News* reported, 'roused the audience to the heights'. On 15 May, the newspaper reported that recruiting in Sussex was being well maintained and that out of 800 who had joined the colours from the county during April, nearly half were from Brighton. Horsham and Worthing came next, with 107 and 103 recruits respectively.

To examine how labour conditions could be adjusted in order to release men of military age for service in the army, a conference of employers was held at the Town Hall on the afternoon of the 21st. Mayor Otter, who had convened it at the request of the Home Secretary, presided over a large and representative gathering. He was supported by, among other civic officials, the Mayor of Hove, Councillor A.R. Sargeant JP. There were representatives of the Brighton and Hove Trade Protection Society (BHTPS), the Brighton and Hove Grocers' Association (BHGA), the Butchers' Association and many other major figures in local commerce. Letters in support of the meeting's aim had been received from Councillor J. Smith, who mentioned that his staff of sixteen included nine of military age, of whom five had joined the Colours; from the local manager of the London, County and Westminster Bank, declaring that the question of sparing as many members of the staff as possible had received, and would continue to receive, sympathetic attention; and from Messrs Robins and Sons of Hove, brewers, stating that as far as their company was concerned everything possible was being done to encourage those eligible among their employees to join the forces and that forty per cent of all the men in their employ had already done so. The Mayor said that we had not come to the stage of compulsion yet but could not afford to wait a single day longer to take action. Mr Laurence Hardy, MP for Ashford, attending on behalf of the Parliamentary Recruiting Committee, emphasised the importance of the trades being organised to bring employers and employees together with a view to seeing who could give their services to the State in the Empire's need. At present, he said, recruiting was on a voluntary basis and as long as that was the State's policy, they had no right to use methods which practically amounted to compulsion. In any measures they took there should be cooperation and consultation with the employees concerned. It emerged at the meeting that there was now a definite demand for 300,000 men at once from Lord Kitchener. There were of course other calls on men: the Mayor mentioned that there was a shell factory at the railway works and nothing could be more useful than to supply that factory with hands. Mr Forbes, General Manager of the LBSCR, said they were urgently wanted. Robert J. Billinton, the Locomotive, Carriage, Wagon and Marine Superintendent of the railway, explained that the company could not only not spare any more men but urgently needed many more hands for the factory and if traders of Brighton could send such men it would be a great benefit – he was 300 men short at the works owing to men having gone to the war.

Mr J. Harry Gilkes (BHTPS) claimed that Brighton had already done wonderfully well in recruiting and instanced the case of one distributing firm which had given to the Colours twenty-three men out of a total of twenty-five, while another firm had to employ sandwichmen (workers hired to perform a specific job), as all their porters had enlisted. Alderman Colbourne JP, Chairman of the BHTPS, said he was connected with one establishment in which only two men out of twenty remained and the young ladies were doing the work. Sir John Blaker bore testimony to the patriotic action of virtually every trader in Brighton, and specially mentioned brewery firms like Tamplins and also the banks and Hanningtons. Having regard to the circumstances, he believed Brighton, which had sent 10,000 men to the Colours, had recruited more men than any other town of similar population in the whole country. It was agreed that a committee should be appointed, which Alderman Charles Thomas-Stanford believed would be a further step towards concerted action – of which there had been too little throughout this war.

Mr R.R. Tweed of Third Avenue, Hove, wrote a letter to the *Sussex Daily News* four days later railing against sporty individuals who had

*Brighton railway works played an important part in the production of munitions. These photographs appeared after the war (*The Engineer, *4 July 1920).*

not joined up to enlist. Referring to the parks, tennis courts and recreation facilities in Brighton and Hove being used by such characters, he declaimed: 'Every man in Brighton and Hove should now be drilling – those of 19-38 in the army, and all the remainder in the Sussex Home Defence Volunteer Corps. White flannels for men must give place, on our open spaces, to khaki and grey-green uniforms.'

A clever ploy on 3 July to attract interest in a recruitment exercise for the Royal Naval Division on 3 July was a flying exhibition in the vicinity of the Race Hill, graphically described in the local press. A meeting was also held at the Level, where the Mayor of Hove presided

On 20 November 1915, as a stimulus to recruiting, this captured 15-pdr German gun
was accepted for the town at the Town Hall by Mayor Otter from Major Pearce,
Recruiting Officer for Brighton. (Peter Booth collection)

in the absence of the Mayor of Brighton. He thoughtfully reminded his
listeners that 'we cannot live in watertight compartments in these days.
It is a time for sinking our individualities. We are fighting not only for
the liberties of the whole world but for our future happiness.' Other
speakers contributed to an exciting meeting at both places. During the
evening, the RND band from the Crystal Palace played selections.

A recruitment rally for the RND was held on the evening of 11
September in Queen Square. Although the Division had had recruiting
offices in the town for quite some time, many
more men were still required. The speakers
included the Mayor of Brighton, Commander the
Hon. Rupert Guinness RNVR, MP for Southend-
on-Sea, Lieutenant Frank Hughes, RNVR and
Mr Edward Gieve. At the rally, which opened
with a rousing welcome by the bugle band of the
Cadet Corps (RFA), Mayor Otter remarked that
in the matter of recruiting, Brighton was one of
the brightest spots on the map of England. He
was extremely proud of what had been done and

Efforts were made in
Brighton to recruit for the
RND. (Author)

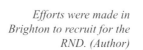

he was sure that it had done more than any other town of its size. Guinness remarked that Lord Kitchener had frowned on conscription, but if he said the word, it would have to come. If the slackers came forward it would never be necessary. To the women of Brighton, Guinness said, 'Make the greatest sacrifice you can. Give me the men who have not yet joined.' His wife Gwendolen (who, interestingly, would succeed him as MP for Southend) addressed a brief speech to Brighton's townswomen, demolishing the excuses that women used for being against their men joining up. At the close of the rally she was rousingly cheered.

Sir John Blaker was able to state, at a meeting and concert held in the Market Hall on the evening of the 25th to terminate the proceedings of the VTC Flag Day, that Brighton and Hove's response to our country's call had been magnificent – he estimated that in all branches of the Forces, the two towns had over 20,000 men. He nevertheless made an earnest appeal for recruits in this crisis in the face of the greatest menace that had ever threatened civilised mankind. They had to have the men and they would much rather get them by the voluntary system than by force.

October saw what was effectively the last major effort to obtain men by voluntarism. A great recruiting parade was ordered by the Army Council across the nation, and locally here and in Eastbourne, Worthing, Hastings, and Tunbridge Wells. It was planned for Saturday the 2nd, but in Brighton it was rained off. Officially postponed until Sunday the 10th, the occasion was nevertheless seized during the damp afternoon – on the initiative of Major William Wilson Grantham – to address the huge expectant crowds, as yet not informed of the cancellation. The Mayors of Brighton and Hove both spoke, the latter referring to the recent Allied victories on the Western Front, which, he felt, should encourage men to enlist and fill the places of men who had fallen. The Major, whose eldest son had left Harrow that very day to enlist, produced a brace of pheasants he had shot that morning and offered them as a reward to the person who secured the most recruits during the next twenty-four hours. Some marches meanwhile took place, as it had been arranged that various military units – regulars and volunteers, cadets, scouts, etc. – should, after passing through various districts in four columns, eventually assemble on Madeira Road and from there march behind the two Mayors to Hove Lawns for a mass meeting. This actually happened, in delightful weather, the next day. Thousands of people blocked the roadway at the Aquarium, where the police had difficulty in regulating the traffic. So long was the procession, which first headed east from the Aquarium to Duke's Mound then turned back along a packed Marine Parade, that when under way it took nearly half an hour to pass a given point. Once in Hove, the assembly was addressed by various speakers from four different platforms.

Alderman C. Thomas-Stanford MP emphasised the fact that the falling-off in recruiting had caused Lord Kitchener grave concern; Handel Booth, Liberal MP for Pontefract, said the time for talking was over and the best thing was for compulsory conscription by the government, while Mayor Otter repeated earlier publicly-expressed concerns about the situation in the Balkans. Brighton MP Captain Tryon declared that if 30,000 recruits did not come forward every week, the government would, in his opinion, have no alternative but to introduce conscription. Archdeacon Hoskyns, Vicar of Brighton, felt this was the greatest crisis our country had ever faced, with the prospect of our ancient history of 1,000 years being wiped out in blood (his son, a machine-gun officer, was wounded but recovering). The Mayor of Hove referred to the apparently impending change from voluntarism to compulsion, William O'Mally, Irish MP for Galway Connemara, dwelt on the glories of the British Empire and said he had been told this was to be the final call, a view echoed by the other speakers, including Sir Cavendish Boyle, KCMG, a retired British colonial administrator living in Brighton. To applause, Boyle called that day 'a sort of last dying effort of voluntary recruiting.' The Rev Charles Spurgeon, pastor of Holland Road Baptist Church, Hove, said his only son had been with the forces for fourteen months and two of his daughters were busy nursing the wounded. Mayor Otter had, since the postponed meeting, asked the Major if he had any more pheasants; Grantham hadn't but today made another offer – whoever got the greatest number of recruits before the government decided on conscription would be awarded a free day's shoot at Barcombe, where the Major had land.

Sadly, for all the fanfare, the *Sussex Daily News*' regular feature

The British Empire Union was established in 1916, replacing the Anti-German Union founded in April 1915. In 1960 it was renamed the British Commonwealth Union. Its political activities ceased from 1975.

'Current Local Topics' reported on the 18th the poor direct results of Sunday's recruiting parade but remarked that the experience, 'not over-flattering to Brighton, is regarded as having "cleared the air" of doubt and hesitations as to the future course of action.'

The first mentions locally of Edward Stanley, 17th Earl of Derby, better remembered as Lord Derby, appeared that October. Under his scheme, men who voluntarily registered their name would be called upon for service only when necessary. Married men had an added incentive in that they were advised they would be called up only once the supply of single men was exhausted. The scheme was also referred to as the 'Group System', since men were classified in groups according to their year of birth and marital status and were to be called up with their group when it was required. At the end of the month, the *Sussex Daily News* had the impression that the scheme was working; recruits were reportedly coming in without being approached.

The ominous term 'tribunals' seems to have been used first, by Mayor Otter, at a Town Council Meeting on 28 October. He stated:

> *'Certain tribunals had been formed who would decide in particular cases whether the men could be possibly spared or whether their services were of more importance to the industrial work of the country. It would be left to the tribunal to judge whether the excuse made was satisfactory.'*

These were established as part of the Derby Scheme in 1915, but were continued on a statutory basis under the Military Service Act (MSA) of 1916 which introduced conscription. Brighton Town Council appointed its tribunal, whose proceedings would feature so frequently in the local press until the end of the war, on 9 November (Hove had operated its own since 9 September). It held its first sitting on 14 December 1915 and by the end of December 1916, 132 sittings had taken place, dealing with 5,538 applications, both originals and renewals. Of the total, 2,957 had come from attested men and 2,581 from unattested. Absolute exemptions were granted in only five and thirty-nine cases respectively. The totals of other exemptions – conditional (certified occupations, etc.) and temporary – were 1,971 and 1,685, with temporary exemptions predominating.

Nationally, the Derby scheme of 'moral conscription' proved

unsuccessful and was abandoned in December 1915. While it was operational, 215,000 men enlisted, and another 2,185,000 attested for later enlistment. However, thirty-eight per cent of single men and fifty-four per cent of married men who were not in 'starred' occupations failed to come forward.

Officers and NCOs of the RSR 9th (Service) Battalion by the Aquarium. Formed at Chichester in September 1914, it moved to Shoreham in April 1915 and on to Woking in June. It landed at Boulogne on 1 September 1915. (Robert Jeeves/Step Back in Time)

One more recruitment exercise was held in Brighton on Saturday 13 November on behalf of the 4th Battalion of the Royal Sussex Regiment (RSR), The 1st/4th Battalion was on service in the East. Under Colonel W. R. Campion MP, it had taken part in the famous amphibious landing at Suvla Bay, Gallipoli, in early August. The location chosen was the Lower Promenade, west of the West Pier. The Battalion needed 700 men to fill the places of those who had died. The Battalion band rendered patriotic selections before and after the meeting. Although it was well attended, few eligible men were in evidence. Yet, within the week, there was a general rush of recruits. The *Sussex Daily News* noted:

'Recruiting is proceeding apace at Brighton and elsewhere and it is almost as difficult for the would-be soldier to go through the necessary formalities preparatory to taking the oath as it is to obtain a seat at the theatre when a national favourite is billed to appear. This is on account of the number of men who are coming forward. ... The best thing to do is undoubtedly to come early. ... Cases have been known of it being necessary to wait several hours.'

The recruiting officers and their staffs were kept at work very late each night throughout the week dealing with the batches of men who presented themselves for enlistment. On 29 November, a batch of fifty recruits left Brighton station for Chichester Depot – probably the largest draft of recruits for any one unit so far to leave the twin towns. Some twenty-five others had already gone. *Keep the Home Fires Burning* was splendidly rendered by the Home Counties RFA band as the party marched into the station. The men passed through a small crowd of passengers and friends, entering the western departure platform amid waving handkerchiefs, with the music from the band, which headed them right up to the train waiting for them, still ringing through the station. How many would return?

Volunteers for the war on the march. There was a ready response to enlistment in Brighton. (Trevor Cox collection)

People in Brighton were, courtesy of the local press, far from ignorant of the horrors of the war, either on the Western Front or in distant theatres such as the Dardanelles. Most of the combatants recounting their experiences, usually in letters home, had enlisted with the RSR. Among those who wrote of what they had gone through in France and/or Belgium were Corporal J.C. Clark, of the 9th Battalion. In a letter in October to his parents, who kept the New Ship Hotel, Ship Street, he described being suddenly rushed up to the firing line, after four days' hard marching, right into the strongest part of the German lines and fighting in the open, side by side with Scotsmen – Gordons and Camerons ('they are really wonderful men … their coolness and bravery are really astonishing'). They 'succeeded in driving the beggars back about a couple of miles, but we lost a good many of our fellows, chiefly wounded though.' He himself had a very narrow shave, with a bullet through his hat and his haversack violently torn from him by shrapnel. Drummer George Turner, attached to the 2nd Battalion, was the son by her first marriage of Mrs Langton of the Gas Fitter's Arms at 33, Tidy Street. He told the *Sussex Daily News* he had been through all the notable engagements – the retreat from Mons, the fighting at the Marne and the Aisne, at Ypres and at Givenchy, and had come through without a scratch, although on one occasion he had been up to his waist in water for forty-eight hours.

On the road to recovery at Dyke Road. (Author)

Time and again, however, the local press gave the names and addresses of the unfortunate parents, spouse or other family member who had received the news they had always dreaded. On 14 September 1914, Sergeant William Peters from the regiment's 2nd Battalion was killed helping a fellow soldier at the battle of the Aisne. A shell burst nearby and blew off both his legs. Son of well-known florist and gardener F. Peters of 2, Ladysmith Road, with whom he had tended the graves in the Brighton cemeteries before his call-up, he had served for eight years in India. Another victim from 1914 was Alfred Routhan, whose parents lived at 4, Baxter Street, Elm Grove. He was killed in action in the Ypres salient on 1 November. His brothers Mark and Thomas would lose their lives at the Front on 16 February 1915 and 25 September 1915 respectively. All of them were in the 2nd Battalion and all had served as Sergeants with the RSR in the South African War.

A remarkable pen and ink study drawn in 1915 by Fortunino Matania of action at the Battle of Loos, the largest British offensive mounted in that year on the Western Front during the Great War.

Thomas Routhan died in the Battle of Loos, the largest British offensive mounted on the Western Front in 1915. Among the other victims from his regiment on that fateful 25 September were Privates Walter Edwin Dapp, Harold Miles and Frederick James Gates. Dapp, the only son of Trayton and Ellen Dapp of 19, Viaduct Road, had been wounded on 10 September 1914 and returned to action. Miles was one of the four sons of Mrs A. Miles of 60 Springfield Road and his three brothers were all in the army. The parents of Gates, who was aged only nineteen, lived at 29, Lynton Street.

Earlier in the year, other RSR men had died. Charles George Colwell of 19, Islingword Street died on 15 March following wounds, while Privates Frederick Noyce and M.C. Waters, both of 2nd Battalion, died on the same day – 9 May 1915. Noyce had gone to France in November 1914, at which time he was employed by Reason and Co. in Lewes Road. His parents lived at 49, Upper Lewes Road. After serving seven years with the colours and nine with the Reserve, Waters had enlisted on 26 August 1914, after which date his wife and five little children never saw him again.

Describing conditions in the Dardanelles campaign, Lance-Corporal Iva James (RND Engineers) wrote to his parents at 74, Shaftesbury Road in the autumn of 1915 to tell them he had recovered from sunstroke in hospital at Alexandria and was back again on the peninsula. 'I have seen all I want to see … It is getting very cold … We are under shellfire all the time but we get so used to the projectiles that we don't take any notice of them unless one happens to come close to us, and then we make a dive for our dugouts.' He begged not to be sent any jam or rice, having had so much in hospital. Curiously, the mother of B.J.T. Webber, Sussex Yeomanry, also lived in Shaftesbury Road, at number 53. Writing on 24 October, Webber reported 'I went into the trenches at the beginning of the week for three days and spent a very enjoyable time doing a good deal of sniping myself, breaking two of Johnny Turk's periscopes. It is different here from France, for there are no YMCA huts or anything of that sort, and no parties of comedians come to sing to us.' In October, F.H. Triggs, who before he enlisted was in the service of Messrs Potts and Co, North Street, and whose parents lived at 9, Inverness Road, wrote from hospital in Liverpool of having been wounded in the head and knocked out cold for five minutes. 'Everywhere there were fires where the shells had caught the bushes alight; we seemed surrounded by fire … At last I managed to get up and ran to the reserve trench and made my way down to the dressing station on the beach. It was about 2 miles walk and they were shelling us all the way and we had to fall down flat every time they burst.'

Sergeant S.H. Hilton, 97th Battery, RFA, who had lived with his mother at 1 Wellington Place, worked for Mr Cowell, the bathing

Infantry from the British Royal Naval Division in training on the Greek island of Lemnos during the Battle of Gallipoli, 1915.

machine owner, when he left school. On first joining up he went to India and then to the Gallipoli Peninsula, where he was awarded the DCM for conspicuous gallantry. A distinction at Gallipoli was also earned by Gordon Leslie Broad of the East Lancs, the son of Mr and Mrs J.W. Broad of Brighton. Formerly employed by Messrs Clayton and Black, the architects, he was awarded the Military Cross for distinguished service. He was invalided home and was making good progress at Osborne House, Isle of Wight, when mentioned in the *Sussex Daily News*.

A number of Brighton men never returned from the peninsula and it was there that Private Leslie D. H. Raven died for his country. His parents, who lived at 35, Exeter Street, learned of their youngest son's death the next day. He had joined up at the beginning of the war and was a range-finder in a machine-gun section. Before the war he had been an employee of Messrs John Beal & Son in East Street for two years. The Keeping brothers, Horace and George, died on 17 August and 7 November respectively. Both were serving with the RAMC. They had gone out together in early August and before enlisting had both been employed by Messrs Cox and Co in the Lewes Road, George for fourteen years and Horace for thirteen. George was married and left a widow and one child but Horace was single and lived with his parents at 15, Aberdeen Road. The two brothers had been very keen footballers. Other deaths among Brighton men from July to September were those of Lance Corporal Frederick Ling (formerly with the Railway Works), Lieutenant Philip Clarence Williams (ex-Belvedere School and Brighton College, where he was a Sergeant in the Officers' Training Corps), Private Percy John Cane (died from enteric fever; formerly employed at Wingfield's, Market Street) and Private William Howard Speck (an old Lewes Road schoolboy). Speck's death was particularly poignant; on the night of 24 September, the trench in which he was sleeping was shelled and the sides of the dugout fell in, burying him alive.

In late 1915, the War Council decided to end the Gallipoli campaign and the troops were evacuated in December and in January 1916.

Brightonians killed in action much farther afield include old Harrovian Major Christian Franklyn Hales Rumbold, 42, of the East Surrey Regiment, whose father Charles, lived at 38, Sussex Square and

*Far from Brighton's tramways are these young Territorials. Back row: (L to R) Gunners Dumbrell, West, Preston, Tetters; Front row (seated): Gunner Gunn, Sergeant-Major Prior, Gunner Aukett. (*Brighton Graphic, *1 July 1915)*

who died at the Battle of Ctesiphon near Baghdad on 22 November 1915. Acting Bombardier Charles Barnard, RFA, of 82 Richmond Street died in India on 28 September 1915, leaving a widow and three children. He is buried in Mhow New Cemetery.

Back home, those too old or otherwise unable to enlist could become Volunteers. In mid-December 1914, the *Brighton Graphic* had carried a picture of men of the Home Protection Brigade, the prototype of the Home Guard. Brighton had the distinction of being, if not actually the first, one of the first towns in the country to raise a Home Protection Brigade on the principle of only enlisting men over military age for service in the Regular Army. The commander and founder of the unit was Major Campbell Fraser. They were depicted on parade at Preston Park, where they carried out regular training and exercises. They also mustered at Withdean from time to time, and had in fact held their first drill there. On 2 January, members of 'G' Company held a smoking concert at the spacious Unicorn Hotel in North Street featuring several speakers and many well-known local artistes. The Adjutant, Captain Heather, mentioned in his speech that some 200 of its members had volunteered for any service that might be required of them, and if they were called upon he was confident they would render a very good account of themselves.

On 12 February, the Major wrote an appeal letter to the *Sussex Daily News* jointly with Mayor Otter and the two Brighton MPs, G.C. Tryon and Charles Thomas-Stanford, which provides good detail about the force:

*Major Campbell Fraser inspecting the National Reser on the Level on 21 February 1915 (*Brighton Graph* 27 February 1915).*

'*Sir, - Most of the inhabitants of Brighton are aware that there exists in their midst a force of men organised for the protection of their lives and property in case of need. This force is known as the First Battalion of the Home Protection Brigade, and has been training since September. The men do not play at being soldiers. They have the keenest interest in the duties which they have voluntarily undertaken, and, by attendance at frequent drills, by taking part in route marches, and by carefully practising shooting, have become an efficient military body. This has been done at no small cost of time and energy. Almost all are engaged in daily work. Some actually begin at six o'clock in the morning.*

'The Battalion, which is over 1,000 strong, has its own excellent band, its ambulance corps and its signalling corps. We believe that the soldierly bearing of the Battalion has made a good impression on the public generally. Certainly it did on the minds of the experienced military officers, [Brigadier-]General Abbott, the Duke of Norfolk, and Lord Desborough [President of the National Association of Volunteer Training Corps], who inspected the Battalion in Preston Park on the 31st of January. The Battalion has now been affiliated to the Central Association of Volunteer Training Corps in London, has received the recognition of the War Office and become part of the Forces of the Crown. But the government are not prepared to render any financial support. Rifles, uniforms and other equipment must, therefore, be found by the men themselves or given by the generosity of others. The expenses up to the present have almost wholly been paid by the officers and men.'

An appeal to the people of Brighton to provide the above and other necessities followed.

Setting an example, the proprietor of the Palladium Opera House cinema on King's Road generously offered to give part of the takings on 1 July 1915 to the Battalion Fund. He showed a film of the Corps at work at 3, 6 and 9 pm on that day. The Major independently wrote a soundly-reasoned letter to the *Sussex Daily News* on the 15th making a strong appeal for recruits.

It was declared in the following month that the intention was to raise the Brigade's numerical strength as soon as possible to at least 2,000. One hundred recruits had recently been enrolled. Enrolling took place on Tuesday and Thursday evenings at Gloucester Road Drill Hall between 7.30 and 9 pm. The uniform proposed for the HPB was grey-green in colour. Also recorded in February were the HPB's Church Parade assembly (1,000 strong) on the Level together with the 9th Company of the Sussex National Reserve and the Boys' Brigade, and their march to Cannon Place to attend Divine Service at St Margaret's

Getting Fit for the Front at Breezy Brighton

Thousands of blue-clad recruits to Lord Kitchener's New Army are being trained in the art of war at Brighton. Parts of the beach are utilised for firing practice.

Rifle practice by keen recruits on the Brighton beach. The targets can be seen erected on the foreshore.

Other recruits learning to fire whilst standing. The eastern end of the lower parade is daily occupied by zealous soldiers anxious to qualify for the front. Inset : Practical shooting lessons from commissioned officers.

The War Illustrated *devoted a full page to Brighton's continuing preparations for the war in its issue dated 20 March 1915.*

Church. There, a stirring address on England's bounden duty to crush German militarism once and for all was delivered by the Vicar, the Revd. C.E. Wilson.

:: THE ::

ANTI-GERMAN UNION

(Head Offices: 346 STRAND, LONDON, W.C.),

Is holding a **CAMPAIGN** at **54 KING'S RD., BRIGHTON.**

¶ All patriotic Britons should call there and sign the Petition against a Premature Peace, which spells "Peace with *Dishonour*."

¶ All patriotic Brightonians should join the local branch of the Union (Hon. Sec., Mr. Holworthy).

¶ All patriotic Britons should help crush the enemy espionage system by joining the Union and reporting suspicious movements to its Intelligence Department.

¶ Our gallant troops are fighting at the front ; those who cannot go there should fight the enemy at home.

The Anti-German Union is the antidote for German Poison.

BRITONS, AWAKE!

Mark the Title, Anti-German UNION.

Union is Strength.

The Anti-German Union announces its vigorous local campaign and sets out its aims.
*(*Brighton and Hove Society *23 September 1915)*

Confusingly, the voluntary force headed by Campbell Fraser was variously referred to in the local press as the Home Protection Brigade and the Volunteer Training Corps, but they were the same, the VTC title being the one finally adopted. The official title of Sussex Home Protection Volunteer Brigade (1st Batt. Brighton) appeared in the Major's letter to the King dated 31 May humbly requesting that the prefix 'Royal' be allowed before 'Sussex Home', a request that was unfortunately declined.

In his *Sussex in the First World War* (Sussex Record Society, Lewes, 2004), Keith Grieves records that on affiliation to the Central Association of the Volunteer Training Corps in January 1915, the unit became the 1st (Brighton) Battalion, Volunteer Training Corps and in

May 1916 the 1st Battalion Sussex Volunteer Regiment. He additionally notes:

> *'Campbell Fraser was transferred to the RA in 1915 and was succeeded as commanding officer by Lt. Col. G.B. O'Donnell. Civic pride took the form of suggesting that Brighton was the first town to form a home defence corps in the Great War. The first parade at Home Farm, Withdean on 16 September 1914 was attended by 150 men over 35 years of age. Thereafter, the men undertook drill practice three times each week, rifle practice and manoeuvres on the downs. At Easter 1915 they marched to Worthing and back. In 1917 its home became the drill hall in Church Street.'*

Other points made are that the corps was not regulated by the Army Council until 1916 and received no government grants until June of that year. State funding then needed to be supplemented by members' subscriptions, flag day collections, concerts on the Palace Pier and a gift from the Council of £250 for the purchase of arms. In the last two years of the war the unit undertook guard duties at the Dyke observation post, Ford Junction and Littlehampton docks. It manned the searchlight at Brooker Hall, Hove and guarded German prisoners of war in Lewes. The VTC was suspended in December 1918 with a final parade taking place on 9 November 1919. It was officially disbanded in January 1920.

But that was in the future. In 1915, fellow-volunteers from the capital in the shape of the National Guard, or more strictly the City of London National Guard, chose Brighton as the centre of their Easter and Whitsuntide manoeuvres. The dates of the Easter visit were from Thursday 1 April to Tuesday the 6th. The *Sussex Daily News* reported on Saturday's proceedings. With a nasty drizzling rain falling, 1,036 men, including about 60 officers, paraded at the Aquarium and proceeded to Rottingdean Rifle Club's range in Saltdean on motor lorries. After they had gone through a course of manual and firing exercises, the Lord Mayor of London, Sir Charles Johnston, the honorary Commandant, inspected the corps and expressed his admiration for the men's general bearing and smart turnout. In the afternoon they went for a route march eastwards under the command of Colonel G. T. B. Cobbett, VD, Commandant, with some eighty men practising on the miniature and open ranges. A well-attended and very successful smoking concert was held in the evening at Brighton Cruising Club's headquarters.

On Easter Sunday the men attended Divine Service at Preston Parish Church, having paraded on Madeira Road at 9 am. Parading and manoeuvres continued on the following day, with a further visit to Rottingdean and Saltdean. A second smoking concert was held at the Cruising Club in the evening and there was a First Battalion dinner at the Queen's Hotel. The next day was the last of their visit. About 325 of the guard mustered at the Aquarium in the morning, of whom sixty went to the Saltdean range for musketry. The shooting there was of an exceptionally high standard, with one man on target with 39 out of 40 shots at 200 yards' range. When the National Guard, with whom London's Lord Mayor was 'deeply impressed', made its regretful departure from Brighton after their invigorating and enjoyable six days in the town, the *Sussex Daily News* commented:

> '*The visit of the National Guard has been a source of great attraction to Brighton and the inspiring spectacle of so many City men, all of them over 40 years of age and many of them filling responsible business positions, marching in uniform with shouldered rifles and with bayonets, haversacks and water bottles slung at their sides, made an immediate appeal to both residents and visitors.*'

Back at the beginning of the year, a very different civic duty from usual was performed at the Aquarium by Brighton's Mayor and Mayoress. On 13 and 14 January, they welcomed no fewer than 4,000 children of men on active service. The treat was laid on by the local branch of the Soldiers' and Sailors' Families' Association. The youngsters received gifts of toys from the American membership which were substantially supplemented by presents from local residents, notably the members of the Dames' Habitation of the Primrose League, who contributed no fewer than 700 toys and a sum of £35. The entrance hall, corridors and Winter Garden of the building were tastefully decorated with the flags of the Allies, towering palms and flowers, and presented a bright and inviting appearance, whilst the children were thrilled on the second day to receive, in the presence of a large and fashionable company, the toys from two huge Christmas trees, handed out by the Countess of March,

*Some of the thousands of 'children of Tommy and Jack' who gathered at the Aquarium for their great treat. (*Brighton Graphic*, 16 January 1915)*

President of the County Association. The boys and girls then enjoyed delicious cakes and sweets at a sumptuous tea and wondrously toured the Aquarium. When he addressed the children, the Mayor spoke of the noble part their fathers were playing in the cold, damp trenches and on the grey, rough sea. How proud they must be of them! The children themselves could do their bit for the war by seeing that things went well at home and helping their mothers in every way.

In dealing with the ongoing issue of aliens, Brighton took a hard line. In early 1915, a number of them were summonsed and received harsh sentences. Richard Greiffenhagen, 47, was charged on remand on 14 January with failing to furnish particulars under the Aliens Registration Act and with continuing to reside in Brighton without a permit, even though he was on the voters' list. Chief Constable Gentle said that although he had been living in the town for some considerable time, his conduct had been unsatisfactory. The 'restaurant' – if it could be called such – where Greiffenhagen lived in King Street was a rendezvous before the war for young Germans and was also used for immoral purposes. His business had been injurious to this country and he was a serious danger. The sentence was four months with hard labour. Edward Muchwitsch, 31, was likewise charged, on 23 February, with continuing to reside in the prohibited area of Brighton without a permit. Born in Germany, he had declared his nationality as Swiss (as Greiffenhagen had done). He had been trying to dispose of his hairdressing business. The Chief Constable said Muchwitsch had been 'in nightly association' with a German sentenced a few weeks earlier who had said he was an Irishman (no doubt Greiffenhagen, who had claimed Irish parentage). His sentence was six months' hard labour. Margaret Louise Wentzel, 40, was charged at Brighton Police Court on 14 March for failing to provide the licensing particulars required by the Act. She actually was a Swiss, who had come to Brighton in November from Hove. She did not register then, nor had she previously done so in Hove. When she refused to provide particulars after being summoned to the police station, proceedings had to be brought against her. She called the detectives liars and acted with bad grace throughout. Although she had worked in Norfolk Square, with excellent character, as a cook in the past, William Gentle told the Bench that she had been behaving in a very unsatisfactory manner for some time, frequenting public houses almost nightly, engaging soldiers in conversation and returning home very much intoxicated. Plus she was very familiar (far more so than even he was himself) with the details of local transport. Her sentence was imprisonment with hard labour for three months.

As the festive season approached, shopping early was urged by the newspapers, especially in order to ensure that goods posted to relatives or friends in the Services would be

Cartoon by C. H. Phelp illustrating the clampdown on aliens. Caption reads: 'The wily Turk: "Making an April fool of me are they?" (Brighton and Hove Society, 25 March 1915)

received in time. There were thus busy scenes at the parcel counters at post offices. The mountains of mail (at least thirty per cent down on 1914, however) were dispatched without undue delay, thanks largely to the postwomen, who tackled their tasks with characteristic cheerfulness.

The town had everything shoppers could want, but there were, of course, depleted staffs at many establishments. Soper's Bazaar in North Street was replete with every variety of useful, fancy and ornamental present and Father Christmas was there once again to delight the children. Among other stores featured in the local press were Anderson & McAuley, the well-known Irish linen and lace manufacturers; the outfitters Needham's, Burghope & Burghope and L. Phillips, the latter also selling travel goods. Two shops (Lyon & Hall and Messrs. Potts) sold music and musical instruments. Wines and spirits were available from, among others, the B. & H. Wine Co. and Edward Geere. Prominent food stores were Sands & Co; butcher, E.A. Rose, who sold fish, poultry and game; C.T. Norman, dealer in groceries, provisions and preserves and Hockley's, purveyors of provisions and meats.

An animated scene in North Street and by the Clock Tower a couple of years before war broke out. (Author)

On the 22nd, Christmas holiday visitors, arriving on fast trains from Victoria, were noted by the *Sussex Daily News* in the town, with a steady stream of traffic from the station. The large number of officers in khaki was remarkable. The enthusiasm of the crowds in the streets was in no way dampened by the rather grim and gloomy weather and traders reported brisk business. The paper recorded no 'perceptible diminution in the willingness of purchasers or the supply of money'. Bookings at all the hotels were encouraging, boarding houses were filling up and private apartments were in demand.

Shows were, of course, held on both piers and at other entertainment venues; the pantomime *Sinbad the Sailor* at the Theatre Royal was much enjoyed by young and old alike, as was *Cinderella* at the Grand Theatre. On Christmas Eve, carols were sung at the Grand Hotel from 9 pm, followed at 9.30 by a Cinderella Dance or, as an alternative, a Progressive Whist Party in the drawing room. On Christmas Day, a vocal and instrumental concert took place in the Lounge. At the Royal York Hotel, the resident orchestra, under J. Martin, performed as usual from 1-3 and from 7-9 and continued to do so at the same times on subsequent days. A well-attended Cinderella Dance commenced in the Lounge at 9.15 pm on Christmas Eve, followed at 10 pm by a selection of carols. Here too, on Christmas Day, a grand concert took place in the Lounge (from nine o'clock), with presents being drawn from the Royal York Christmas Tree in the course of the evening. A prominent feature of the yuletide festivities at the hotel was the usual Doll Sale, which realised £170 for local hospitals, making a total of well over £1,000 that the owner Harry Preston had raised in this way for those deserving institutions.

Boxing Day afternoon saw a bright and happy Children's Dance at the Grand Hotel, while in the evening at the nearby Metropole the glittering Boxing Night Ball was held, attended by crowds of well-known society dancers. The long corridor and lounge at the end of the ballroom were decorated with flowers and palms, while the platform was bedecked with exotics and tender greenery, flanked by high palms. Here, the Metropole Orchestra, led by Sidney Hemming, played a splendid programme of the latest music. For a time, the war could be forgotten.

The Grand Hotel was a splendid venue for Christmas celebrations. (Robert Jeeves/Step Back in Time)

But beside many hearths, it could not. The Christmas Eve edition of the *Sussex Daily News* expressed this poignantly:

'There are faces and forms that once brightened the home at Christmas that will never more be seen. They are lying in shallow graves on friendly or hostile soil, their work done, their sacrifice made. But the sorrow that enters the heart at the thought of them is tempered by pride and gratitude that they have done well in the eyes of their country, that they have won the most glorious wreath of honour which man can confer. They have not died in vain, though the victory be still far off for which they struggled and fell.'

No fewer than 427 wounded survivors were treated on the 28th to a monster tea party at the SEGH in Dyke Road. The splendid entertainment, organized into five sections which included invited guests from other local hospitals, was arranged by Mr and Mrs Walls, the local Superintendents of the Soldiers' Christian Association. All the sections began tucking in to the ample festive fare at the same time – 4 pm. Entertainment was provided until 8.30. Bernhard Baron, the noted cigarette manufacturer, generously distributed 400 packets of Black Cat cigarettes.

The Walls mustered their large body of helpers again two days later for the second of the great tea parties for wounded soldiers organised by the Association, this time at the Stanford Road Hospital, where the colourful Christmas decorations had almost all been produced by the patients themselves. Here the numerous guests were divided into two sections, with the remaining soldiers eating in Victoria Ward; this afterwards made an admirable concert hall which accommodated everyone for the varied entertainment offered.

The wounded and their carers looking moderately happy at their Christmas dinner in Stanford Road Hospital. (Trevor Cox collection)

In the town, many dances were held to welcome in the New Year. At a lively ball in the Assembly Rooms of the Old Ship Hotel, fancy dress was worn in many instances, mixing colourfully with the abundance of khaki. At the Grand Hotel, 1916 was ushered in by a Cinderella dance to the splendid music of the Ladies' Orchestra. The large attendance was swelled by the hotel guests bringing in numerous friends. At the Metropole, the crowds of elegantly-dressed dancers paused at midnight, standing by as the dying year passed. The lights were then lowered, and as the last stroke of twelve struck, a blaze burst forth to welcome in the New Year. Rousing cheers resounded as *Auld Lang Syne* was played and sung. The colour and richness of the scene were enhanced by many spectacular gowns, while jewels flashed and shimmered under the glow of the electric light. 1916 had arrived.

CHAPTER THREE

1916 – Tribunals, Hospitals and Holiday Crowds

When 1916 dawned, the outlook for Brighton as a resort was bright. The *Gazette* remarked:

> *'... the number of people who will accept the pleasant and diverging elements of the Sunny South is almost certain to increase, provided Brighton keeps up those innocent allurements that have appealed to so many as the correct antidote for depression.'*

The spring, summer and autumn seasons would be remarkably successful, notwithstanding the suspension of cheap travelling facilities. Seldom, the paper recorded, was the town better patronised. Casual visitors flocked in week after week, with hundreds of families choosing to stay in Brighton because wartime conditions here were more agreeable than elsewhere. The introduction of the new daylight saving scheme in May certainly helped. Receipts from the letting of deckchairs on the front reached a record high, while the volume of railway and tramway traffic was a further indicator of the prosperity enjoyed by the town despite the curtailment of the former at the year's end.

Notable events during the year included the emergence of the food question, the departure of the Indians from Brighton and the visit by Canadian troops in June.

Service personnel and civilians mingle in this busy scene. The tall building in the distance is the Hotel Victoria at the bottom of West Street which opened in 1898. It is today's Umi Brighton Seafront Hotel. (Author)

While visitors enjoyed all that the resort could offer, for working residents 'business as usual' was often a struggle, not because of economic conditions – for trade was everywhere brisk – but because the army's net was closing in. Conscription, introduced by the first Military Service Act in January 1916, came into force on 2 March. It applied to men of military age, namely those between the ages of 18 and 41. Married men, widowers with children, those serving in the Royal Navy, ministers of religion, or anyone working in one of a number of reserved occupations were exempted. However, a second Military Service Act extended liability for military service to married men (a third Act in 1918 raised the upper age limit to 51). Men or employers who objected to an individual's call-up could apply to the local Military Service Tribunal, a body established in each Borough and District Council which could grant exemption from service, usually on a conditional or temporary basis. There was right of appeal to a County Appeal Tribunal.

MILITARY SERVICE ACT, 1916

Every man to whom the Act applies will on Thursday, March 2nd, be deemed to have enlisted for the period of the War unless he is excepted or exempt.

Any man who has adequate grounds for applying to a Local Tribunal for a

CERTIFICATE OF EXEMPTION UNDER THIS ACT

Must do so BEFORE

THURSDAY, MARCH 2

Why wait for the Act to apply to you?
Come now and join of your own free will.
You can at once put your claim for exemption from being called up before a Local Tribunal if you wish.

ATTEST NOW

Poster setting out the March 2 deadline for a Certificate of Exemption under the 1916 MSA.

The reports of applications to the Brighton Tribunal and appeals to the East Sussex Tribunal make absorbing reading. They reflect the extraordinary variety of occupations in the district and the impact of enlistment on businesses and provide snapshots of local family life and circumstances; they also illustrate the demands of the military prevailing in most cases over pleas for understanding and sympathy from those beset by seemingly insurmountable domestic and business difficulties. The majority of the applications appeared genuine, although some were patently untenable. Very few full exemptions were granted and by the autumn the strict decisions ordering limited postponements, generally two or three months, became predictable almost to the point of monotony. In Middlesex, for example, an appeal was, in the vast majority of cases (nearly 7,000 out of 8,791 considered), either dismissed or a short period was granted for the man to get his affairs in order before heading to the trenches.

The tribunals nationally were regarded as being harsh and Brighton's was no exception. Sir John Blaker, the chief military representative, although at times not devoid of humour and no doubt innately compassionate, had his targets to reach. Applicants were normally represented by a solicitor, with their cases being brought by their employer if applicable or, less usually, a close relative. Names and addresses were never disclosed in the press, but ages, being critical, always were. The first of a multitude of column inches reporting tribunal proceedings appeared in the *Gazette* on 1 March 1916. There followed a report of cases heard by Brighton's Tribunal on 28 February.

Although no total exemptions were granted, the majority of the applicants were allowed a temporary postponement. Sir John, chairing the proceedings, urged that there should not be too great a display of leniency. 'We must get men immediately,' he said. 'The delay to the army is appalling.'

In many applications there was a pathetic note of threatened domestic and/or business upheaval. An old lady of 66, with a crippled husband, one son killed on active service and another serving, appealed to the mercy of the Tribunal not to throw her onto the parish. Her husband, she said, was unable to either dress or undress himself. She kept a large apartment house and if her other son were to be taken, there would be nothing left for her but parish relief. Two months' temporary exemption was granted. The managing partner of two grocery shops, one of which was described as the most important in a poor district of Brighton, sought exemption on the ground that all his assistants and his managing partner were at the Front and that his home was dependent on him. Being a manager, he considered himself in a reserved occupation but Sir John argued that he could not be manager to himself. Temporary postponement for six months was granted, conditional on the applicant remaining at his post. Exemption for three months was allowed in the case of a youth whose mother appeared on his behalf. She had run a confectionery business for twenty years. Three of her sons were serving and, being ill, she was not able to look after the shop. The second application of a fruiterer, greengrocer, coal and coke merchant working for himself was heard. He had been in business for eight years and if he had to go he would lose everything. At the last application, postponement had been allowed to enable him to sell his business but he had not done so. His father and mother were both living and were aged about 45. The father was ruptured and could not carry on the business. Two months were allowed, conditional on his making arrangements to dispose of it. 'This means ruin to me!', exclaimed the applicant. 'And a good many more are being ruined too', was the rejoinder from Alderman Colbourne.

Conscientious objectors represented, contrary to popular perception, only a small proportion of applications. To compare with Middlesex again, only five per cent of the total 8,791 cases considered there came from pacifists. The reports of proceedings in Brighton reveal a high success rate in achieving exemption from combatant duties but some, especially later on, were required to perform military duties and action was taken against those who failed to comply. In March 1916, an 18-year-old student teacher of art put forward his case in dry, forceful tones:

'Where individual conscience is concerned, no amount of cross-questioning or argument can prove anything. I beg leave to remind the Tribunal that it is not necessary for me to justify my conscience. The act simply requires me to prove that I am sincere. ... If I fail to get absolute exemption – and I should like to remind the Tribunal that as a sincere conscientious objector I have the legal right to such exemption – I shall appeal. If I then fail to get the exemption required, and I am not allowed to go any further with my claim, I cannot abandon my convictions and must take any consequences which may arise from refusing to comply with the Military Service Act.'

Exemption from combatant service only was granted.

The same exemption was granted to a young man aged 21, who said all men were brothers and he could not kill them. A list of Biblical quotations was cited in support of his claim. He was expecting shortly to travel as an evangelist. He agreed he had a duty to the state but his duty was to God first. Other exemptions from combatant service granted during the year included a pacifist who declared he was not a patriot and did not care whether he lived under King George or the German Emperor; a man employed as an evangelist who 'couldn't see his way clear' to assisting the wounded but admitted that he was helping the war by paying taxes with his house rent; a Roman Catholic tailor; a lithographer associated as a children's worker with the Society of Friends; and a man engaged in laundry carting who was also a member of that Society. Disallowed were the claims of a grocer who turned out to be Dutch, with five years service in the Navy behind him, a factor which rather negated his conscientious objection, and those of a clerk who was 'terrified out of his life by the sight of blood'. Three town missionaries were given three months' exemption in September on the ground that they were doing useful work where they were – one of them had even applied to join the VTC without knowing what the duties might involve. When asked what he thought the volunteers were training for, he answered 'I didn't think they hardly knew themselves at the time.'

Elderly Gentleman (alone in a compartment with fully-armed soldier, next stop one hour). "EXCUSE ME, MY MAN, BUT YOUR FACE IS STRANGELY FAMILIAR TO ME."
Soldier (with meaning). "QUITE LIKELY, SIR, SEEIN' AS YOU WERE THE GENT IN THE TRIBUNAL WHO MADE GAME OF ME BEIN' A CONSCIENTIOUS OBJECTOR. BUT YOU'LL BE GLAD TO 'EAR I'VE CHANGED MY MIND, AND I AIN'T NOW GOT ANY OBJECTION TO TAKIN' 'UMAN LIFE."

A tribunal member at the mercy of an objector. From Punch, *14 June 1916.*

Exemptions on economic grounds were usually conditional, the condition being a time limitation and/or the requirement to remain in the certified occupation. Trades which qualified were generally food-related, such as baking, butchery and fishing. Indeed, the ease with which one baker secured exemption prompted Sir John to declare that he intended having 'a night out one of these fine nights and visiting all the bakehouses in the town so as to investigate the different claims.' But it was an important trade; one 25-year-old was the only baker in the business and his daily output of loaves was 200. Another applicant, after a tussle, secured total exemption, although Sir John found it 'ridiculous' that the young man – producing no fewer than 500 loaves a day – worked sixteen hours a day for 28s a week and he severely cross-questioned him, having now become, he humorously remarked, 'an expert in breadmaking matters.'

Turning to the meat trade, a rare instance of total exemption occurred when the manager of a retail butcher's shop appealed. He made three points: first, that he was of more use in his present employment; secondly, he would suffer serious hardship; and thirdly, he was engaged in a certified occupation. The Clerk to the Tribunal pointed out that if the last point were agreed on the others were unnecessary. The man's employer stated that the applicant had been in his employment since leaving school and had been a manager for six years. Sir John admitted the man was in a certified occupation although he did think he would be of more use serving the country.

Absolute exemption for a manager and salesman in a wholesale meat company was claimed by the employers on the grounds of indispensability owing to a depleted staff, and also that the business was performing a national service. Sir John Blaker did not oppose temporary exemption in this case and six months conditional was granted. A slaughterman/gut dresser and a master butcher, who also worked at Newhaven on transport work, were both awarded conditional exemption, although a pork butcher with two shops, appealed for by his employer, was only allowed time; despite Sir John's view to the contrary, he claimed there was still a demand for his products.

Certain other trades and professions received relatively sympathetic consideration. Conditional exemption was allowed, for example, in the cases of – among others – a foreman and shoeing smith; a wharfman; a wharf manager solely engaged in the coal business; a grocer's manager and a dairy utensil maker, the occupation being a certified one.

Among professional people whose applications were heard were the secretary of a 'well-known Sussex hospital', whose work was 'of a very intricate nature and took years to grasp.' Many of the patients were military ones and the point was made that the man was of a great deal more use to the country where he was than he would be in the army. Twelve months' postponement was granted, conditional on his remaining in his present employment. An unexpected decision which can only be understood because of the medical grounds was one arrived at on 29 May when a father applied for his son, who was his assistant in fine arts. The son also pleaded. He had one brother in the Sussex Yeomanry, and two sisters were nurses. The son did most of the buying. The Medical Board had passed him for sedentary work only. Six months' conditional exemption was granted on his continuing as a fine art expert.

The fishermen of Brighton merit separate consideration. As a body they faced more pressures than others. Attention was called to their plight, owing to the stringent Admiralty restrictions, at a meeting of the Local Relief Committee chaired by Mayor Otter at the Town Hall on the evening of 28 February. Councillor Mansfield, in moving the adoption of the Relief Sub-Committee, pointed out that the Sub-Committee had considered forty-six applications for relief and stated that this figure was due to the restrictions placed on the fishermen. They were able to fish only in the daytime and then go out only a short distance. Most of them were not able do transport work and were thus greatly distressed. An editorial on the fishing season in the *Gazette* of 3 May painted an equally gloomy picture:

> *'Brighton beach life is no longer what it was. For some years there had been perceptible decline in the fishing industry. The war would seem to have reduced this old institution to vanishing point. It is rather unfortunate for several reasons. ... The most serious consequence however, is the loss of a valuable article of food. It is one of the ironies of the economic situation that has arisen in this country out of the war that the vast resources of the Channel in the way of fish supplies have been placed "out of bounds" in more than the military sense of the term.'*

The activity at Brighton's fish market always fascinated passers-by. (Author)

Overall, the reports indicate that applications from fishermen themselves (whose occupation, like that of bakers, was a certified one) received more favourable consideration than fish traders. In a typical case, a fisherman applied for his son who, he said, had worked all his life on the sea. At present they were engaged preparing nets for the next voyage out. Sir John agreed as to the occupation, and the man was exempted. To make his point, one fisherman turned up at the tribunal attired in his fishing garb and claimed 'our name is one of the greatest in England in fishing circles.' Fishing was his sole occupation and he had been 'born to it'. Conditional exemption was allowed. More than one fisherman was informed that he would be exempt from service in the army as long as he remained in his present occupation, although he was liable to be called up for service with the Navy.

On the processing and distribution side, more conditions were imposed; a master fishmonger received three months on condition that he joined the Special Constables, a stipulation also applied to a fish salesman who was granted six months. Others were less 'lucky' – the case of a fish dealer who applied for absolute exemption was heard *in camera* and his claim was not allowed, but the military representative undertook that he should not be called up for three weeks. A poulterer and fishmonger asked for absolute exemption for two employees, a fish curer, aged forty, and a blockman, aged thirty-two; he explained that a blockman was one who prepared the fish. The curer had been with him since boyhood and had been a member of the VTC from the inception of the movement. He had lost forty-seven men, who had either gone into the army or into munition factories and had had to refuse contracts with the military on account of shortness of labour, with the result that the contracts had gone out of the town. 'The business is running us; we are not running the business,' he added. Each man was allowed six months conditional exemption. Three months were granted to a fish fryer aged 30, appealed for by the owner of a large fish business which he urged was a 'necessity to the nation. The man was the manager of the business and was married, with four children dependent on him. Three months postponement was also allowed for a fish curer who cured fish at an average of 2,000 a day. Curers and fishmongers came together at a well-attended meeting at the beginning of July held at the King and Queen Assembly Rooms to discuss the best ways and means of meeting with the wishes of the Appeal Tribunal. Sir John Blaker attended in a supporting role as Recruiting Officer and stated he was greatly impressed by their difficulties. One point discussed was how many shops were necessary for any particular neighbourhood but it was at once agreed that every one of them was necessary locally. The meeting came to no decision, except to send a three-man deputation to the Appeal Tribunal to discuss their problems.

Some fish trader appeals were disallowed, such as that of a fish salesman; a considerable number of military hospitals were being supplied by his firm and it was claimed that the man was engaged in a certified trade and also that he was indispensable. It was elicited that the business was a retail as well as a wholesale one. The appeal was dismissed, with the man not be called up for a month. A fishmonger was treated likewise. A fish salesman, whose appeal was dismissed, was passed for garrison duty abroad, as was another rather unfit individual with bad toes, varicose veins and partial deafness. He had to look after his father's 'house property'. Under examination, he said the fish business had fallen off and he had not done anything in it since the war broke out. The Military Representative, Ernest Wyon, remarked that they would put him into a special battalion, being deaf. Alderman Colbourne humorously suggested an artillery regiment, especially where large howitzers were used.

The Skylark, *a name carried in succession by several pleasure boats on Brighton beach, was a favourite attraction among holidaymakers. (Author)*

Fishing was not the only way to make a living with one's boat. Visitors flocked to go out on the waves in pleasure craft, Brighton's most notable being undoubtedly the *Skylark* in its various versions down the years (Charles Dickens wrote in a letter on 8 June 1867 that he had enjoyed 'a trip in the famous *Skylark* and it was a lark'). The *Brighton and Hove Society*, in its issue of 10 August 1916, enthused 'A good deal of interest always centres round the dear old *Skylark*, the yacht which has been an institution on the Brighton beach for sixty years.' A small line drawing was reproduced of the late Fred Collins (he had died in 1912), the famed boat operator, which was loaned by his son Captain Fred Collins II. Captain Fred senior had at first been only a Deputy Captain but had gone on to acquire a monetary share in the boat and gradually, through sheer hard work and strength of personality and determination, made himself the leading owner of this particular kind of craft on the South Coast.

Brighton-born Fred Collins (1832– 1912) was a true local 'character'. He introduced the original Skylark *to the resort. (Author)*

The decision taken by the War Office in late 1915 to move the majority of the British Indian army from the Western Front to Mesopotamia and Egypt meant that no more of their wounded would be sent to Britain. Brighton had certainly played its part in caring for these troops, for between their opening on 1 December 1914 and their closure as an Indian hospital on 15 February 1916 a total of 4,306 Indian patients had been admitted to the three buildings on the Royal Pavilion estate. Patients unable to return to their military units for active service went back to hospitals in India. Some units of the Indian Cavalry remained in France throughout the war and their wounded were treated in hospitals there. Sadly, Mesopotamia would see the highest number of Indian casualties in the war: nearly 30,000 dead and 32,000 wounded.

Mayor Otter received the following letter from Lieutenant-Colonel J. N. Macleod, I.M.S., latterly in command of the Indian Hospital at the Royal Pavilion:

'Princes Hotel, Brighton,
16th January, 1916.

'Dear Mr. Mayor,—Having been temporarily ordered off duty for a rest, I have had to give over charge of the Pavilion. In doing so I wish to express to you my warm thanks for all the support and assistance you have given me during the past year. Will you also kindly convey the same to the members of your Corporation and to the Pavilion Committee?

'The Indians I know have greatly appreciated all that has been done for them by the people of Brighton, and the name of Brighton will be blessed by them in India for many years to come.

'Believe me to be,
'Yours very truly,
(Signed) J. N. MacLeod, Lieut.-Col., I.M.S.
Late O.C. Pavilion Indian General Hospital'

Indian wounded enjoying their leisure hours in the grounds of the Pavilion. The low wall was removed in 1921 and the roadway widened. (Peter Booth collection)

At the end of January/beginning of February for a limited period, the vacated Pavilion and Dome were thrown open to the paying public. This attraction proved an even greater success than had been anticipated. On the Monday of the first week of February the entry charge was 2s 6d, while on the Tuesday to Thursday, when 737,709 and 695 visited respectively, it was one shilling. On the Friday, when the charge was reduced to sixpence, no fewer than 2,675 people queued right through Castle Square to the Steine to get in, entering the buildings at the rate of fifteen a minute. But even this record was broken on Saturday the 5th when the queue stretched right round the grounds inside the gate as people stopped to take in the details of arrangements of the nine different kitchens. The total number of visitors following the weekend, when the pipers of the Black Watch again played in the Pavilion grounds in the afternoon, reached 10,641. Picture postcards showing the wards and scenes in the grounds were available for twopence each and two official publications, both written by Henry D. Roberts, Director of the Public Library and Art Galleries, were on sale. One, priced sixpence, was entitled *The Story of the Royal Pavilion, Brighton, including a description of it as a Hospital for Indian Wounded Soldiers*, while the other, with 120 pages and 35 illustrations, cost one shilling. Since it included translations of the text into Urdu, Hindustani and Gurmukhi, the India Office purchased 20,000 copies for distribution in India. The proceeds - only a few pounds short of £330 – went to the Mayor of Brighton's war charities.

On 29 January, the *Gazette* reported that the decision to send no more wounded Indian soldiers to the town released the buildings appropriated for their benefit for the use of British soldiers. Kitchener's Hospital in Elm Grove and the York Place school buildings had now been completely evacuated and would soon be receiving their new tenants. Of the three Indian hospitals in Brighton, two – 'Kitchener' and the York Place Schools – would re-open shortly as hospitals for British troops from the Expeditionary Forces and together they would accommodate well over 2,000 patients. In view of this great influx,

COUNTY BOROUGH OF BRIGHTON.

By kind permission of the Military Authorities,

THE ROYAL PAVILION

AS USED FOR AN

INDIAN MILITARY HOSPITAL

WILL BE

ON VIEW TO THE PUBLIC

For One Week from Monday, 31st Jan., 1916,

From 2 till 5 p.m.

The following Charges for Admission will be made, the Proceeds being given to the Mayor of Brighton's War Charities :

Monday, January 31st = **2/6**

Tuesday, Wednesday and Thursday, **Feb. 1st to 3rd** = 1/=

Friday, Saturday and Sunday, **Feb. 4th to 6th** = 6d.

ENTRANCE by the SOUTHERN GATEWAY.

HUGO TALBOT,
Town Clerk.

8292—28/1/16—3,000, The Southern Publishing Co., Ltd., 130, North Street, Brighton.—Q8,79s

Visits to the vacated Pavilion during the interval before it became a hospital for the limbless were hugely popular. (Royal Pavilion &Museums, Brighton & Hove)

the Mayoress of Brighton issued an appeal for music to be provided in the wards and recreation rooms, for the loan of pianos and for the gift of gramophones and records. Even mouth organs gave enormous pleasure. Games of all sorts – draughts, cards, dominoes, etc. – were required in large numbers. A library should be provided and books of every kind, plus newspapers – or funds to purchase them with – would be gratefully accepted. Flowers and fruit, large quantities of cigarettes, tobacco, and pipes – or funds in lieu –, free passes to theatres, concerts, and cinematographic shows, these, and many other things, would be acceptable. Gifts of all sorts, in kind or in cash, would be gladly accepted by her at her depot at 14, North Street, where she would also be willing to receive personal offers of help, or by Lady Seton at the Kitchener Hospital, where they could either be handed in at the guard room or left at the gift house outside 'K' block. This message was reinforced on 5 February at a meeting held at the Kitchener Hospital itself. Colonel Sir Bruce Seton, the officer in command, presided and among the persons of note present were the Mayor and Mayoress of Brighton and the Mayor and Mayoress of Hove. Sir Bruce briefly explained the needs of the hospital, which at present, he said, possessed nothing at all except what the government supplied. They wanted the 'amenities of life,' such as those requested by the Mayoress. The hospital would have 145 wards, and the number of beds in each ward would range from eight to forty or forty-five. An Amusement Committee, supported by Mr W.H. Boardman and Mr Harry Preston, would meet and consider the ways and means of entertaining the men. Mayoress Otter reported that as an immediate result of her appeal in the Press, subscriptions of more than £6 had been received, while various other offers of help had been forthcoming. Mrs Thomas-Stanford had also handed Sir Bruce a cheque of £2 2s from Mr W. H. Abbey and mentioned that Lady George Nevill, who had sent apologies, would be sending books regularly once a week, while Mrs Herbert Jones, who was not well enough to be present, would provide regular gifts of fruit. The Mayor of Brighton, speaking in support of the schemes, mentioned how anxious the people of Brighton were to do all they could for our wounded soldiers, while the Mayor of Hove promised to receive gifts at Hove Town Hall and to do anything in his power to help. Bernhard Baron of Hove promised to send 5,000 Black Cat cigarettes every week to the hospital.

After the meeting, the visitors formed into groups and were conducted by Sir Bruce and five of his officers through the whole of the building. The operating theatre in 'H' Block (No 3 Division), with its magnificent view over the Race Hill and its slanting white tiled floor, exemplified the thoroughness of the preparations being made for the treatment of the wounded heroes.

A rare glimpse of medical facilities inside the Kitchener Hospital. Here, the X-Ray Room is shown in use. (Chris Horlock collection)

On the very next evening, at 10.30, the first contingent of wounded brought to Brighton that year arrived at the station. There had been something of a break since the battle of Loos in September, but with the advance in France there was the inevitable resurgence in the incoming stream of disabled warriors. They were from various British regiments. No fewer than 100 of the 180 cases were 'cot' or stretcher cases, some rather serious, hence the train took a considerable time to clear. Thankfully the sitting patients were only slightly injured. Many of the men had come straight from the trenches, with the mud of Flanders still caked to their boots. They had crossed the Channel to Dover and travelled to Brighton in a suitably appointed Great Eastern ambulance train. Mrs Pollak was in attendance as usual and was soon busy distributing cigarettes among the men. A fleet of military ambulances from the North Road depot stood waiting, and the majority of the patients were conveyed in these to the Dyke Road hospital, the remainder being dispatched to the Royal Sussex, to Third Avenue, Hove, to the Sussex Eye Hospital (Queen's Road) or to Hove Hospital. The sitting cases were dealt with in a few minutes and most of the slightly wounded left in cheery spirits, puffing their cigarettes with keen enjoyment. The stretcher cases, however, required careful and tender handling, and it was only at ten minutes past midnight that the task was finished.

VADs (Sussex 53) at Brighton Station. The ambulance evidently accommodates four stretcher cases. (Trevor Cox collection)

Not until 15 April was the first batch of wounded, composed of eighty sitting cases and eighty cot cases, conveyed to the Kitchener Hospital. By then there had been three convoys, in February, March and April respectively, totalling 320 men, who had been placed in other hospitals. Just over half were cot cases. On 17 May, men from a great number of regiments (English, Scots, Irish, Canadians, and Australians), most of whom had seen fighting around Ypres, were all taken to Elm Grove and thenceforward that was the main receiving establishment. The others were the SEGH, the RSCH and hospitals in Hove, although some contingents were placed in Lewes Crescent.

The arrivals situation changed dramatically from July, when the great offensive on the Somme began. This First Battle, waged on a 21-mile front north of that river, continued until 13 November and resulted in a total of around 420,000 British casualties, with nearly 60,000 (20,000 dead) on the first day of the attack.

When the first convoy of 189 wounded British from that battleground arrived at Brighton Station on 4 July, an extraordinarily large crowd had assembled and gave the heroes a heartfelt welcome, according to the *Gazette* of 13 July. The number of casualties rose to around 200 on the 18th while on the 26th there appeared one of the largest trainloads of wounded to have come to Brighton: 220. All the sufferers, who included a hundred cot cases, were taken to the Kitchener Hospital. In all, some 1,536 wounded in eleven trainloads were brought into Brighton that July. That worst of months was followed by 1,093 in September and a drop to 772 in November.

The injured men brought to Brighton had almost invariably been welcomed by Mrs Frances Pollak of Hove. After she had met the first train on 1 September 1914, except for the one or two Red Cross trains arriving in the early hours of the morning, she had been there for twenty-two months to greet the arrivals with gifts of cigarettes, matches and stamped postcards; some of these were written on by the men there and then for posting. She also hosted tea parties for the wounded and took them on outings during their convalescence. In mid-July, however, she was obliged to leave for a spell in the North, on doctor's orders, having been unwell for a while but would soon return to resume her good work.

The home of 'the soldiers' friend' in Hove (18, The Drive). Inset, Frances Pollak. (Trevor Cox collection)

None of the wounded was allocated to the Royal Pavilion, since from 20 April 1916 until 21 July 1919 the building was designated the Pavilion Military Hospital for Limbless Soldiers. During that period, over 6,000 British amputee patients were admitted. The Officer Commanding the new hospital was Colonel Sir R. Neil Campbell, who had been the Senior Medical Officer of the Royal Pavilion and York Place Indian Hospitals. On 19 April he held a reception at the Pavilion for the many guests, military and civilian, who had been involved in setting up the building for its new use.

Nine days later, Princess Louise, Duchess of Argyll, a daughter of Queen Victoria, visited Brighton. Few people were aware of her arrival. She was there primarily to inspect the Patriotic Housekeeping Exhibition at the Municipal Technical College, although the first place she visited was the Royal Pavilion (which she had previously visited in mid-January). Colonel Campbell received the royal guest and they toured the building with other members of the staff. The Princess, to whom several presentations were made, was most interested in all she saw and asked many questions about the historic building. She later visited the Kitchener Hospital, where Colonel Sir Bruce Seton, Bt. and Lady Seton greeted her and personally escorted her through the establishment. She greatly admired all the arrangements and after tea, warmly cheered by the wounded occupants, she left to return to London.

In mid-July, another illustrious visitor, Viscount French, formerly Field Marshal Sir John French, inspected the hospital. The purpose of his visit to the town was threefold: to take the chair at a meeting at the Hippodrome at which Ben Tillett – a founder member of the Labour Party and the *Daily Herald* newspaper who would from the following year until 1924 serve as Labour MP for Salford North – was to deliver a war speech; carry out a postponed inspection of volunteers; and give the wounded heroes at the Pavilion Hospital a personal assurance of his interest and his sympathy with them. At the Hippodrome, Tillett gave a rousing speech intended to demonstrate the critical need for every able-bodied man to put his weight into the struggle, if not as a fighter, then as a worker. His powerful words included an impressive eulogy of the First Army, dubbed 'contemptible' by the Kaiser.

At the Pavilion, Viscount French spent over an hour, against the

background of music played most of the time by the wounded soldiers' band, inspecting the hospital arrangements and sympathetically greeting the limbless heroes being cared for there. He then crossed over to the Dome and Corn Exchange, 'probably the greatest and grandest hospital wards in England' (*Gazette*), and there also spoke to the invalids.

Field Marshal John French, 1st Earl of Ypres (1852-1925). C.–in–C. of the BEF for the first eighteen months of the war before serving as C.–in–C., Home Forces.

The Pavilion Military Hospital proved to be a great success and the patients integrated well with the town and townspeople. The new occupants soon settled in and scarcely a week passed without a description in the local press of the entertainments held for them in the building, often featuring performers from among their own number, especially the Blue and White Concert Group.

On 9 August, Queen Mary's Workshop for training and rehabilitation

*The original Blue and White Pavilion Military Hospital Concert Group. (*The Pavilion Blues, *July 1916)*

was formally opened in the grounds by Lady Falmouth on behalf of Her Majesty. In an article on the Pavilion Hospital published on 16 September in the *British Medical Journal*, which mentioned that other hospitals on similar lines had been established at Bray in Wicklow, Belfast, Glasgow and Kelso, it was stated that the Brighton hospital contained 610 beds, all reserved for limbless soldiers and its primary function was to prepare them to be fitted with artificial limbs at Roehampton (the Queen Mary Convalescent Auxiliary Hospital at Roehampton Lane, SW London, founded in the previous year). The Workshop was described as a 'very special feature of the hospital', a place where the patients could prepare during their stay for a future career by gaining a knowledge of skilled trades. The whole cost of maintaining it was met by charitable persons, who either subscribed money, provided material or gave their services. The men appreciated the classes and were diligent and assiduous in their attendance. It was indeed 'wonderful to note how skilful they became and how cheerful they remained.' Attendees would, when moving to Roehampton, be enabled to complete their training in the workshops there while waiting for their artificial limbs and being instructed in their use.

Queen Mary's Workshop on the North Lawns of the Royal Pavilion Gardens was intended to provide the limbless men with new skills, such as carpentry, for use in civilian life. (Royal Pavilion & Museums, Brighton & Hove)

Interior of the workshop showing carpentry workbenches. The building was later presented to Hollingbury Golf Club as a clubhouse. (Royal Pavilion & Museums, Brighton & Hove)

Four special departments had been opened: the Motor Department; Electrical Department; Carpentry and Woodwork Shop; and Educational Classes. A number of employers had expressed their willingness to engage all those men who attained the necessary degree of proficiency.

The 1917/18 *Brighton Season* magazine also devoted several pages to the work and staff of the hospital and workshop, commenting that 'In all there are 526 beds in the Pavilion, Dome, and Corn Exchange [rather less than the *BMJ* figure], eight isolation wards, with a staff of ninety-one doctors and medical attendants, thirty-three nurses, thirty-three general service women, class 1 and forty-seven class 2. This is for the Hospital alone, and does not include the staff of Queen Mary's Workshops.' The review concluded with a last look at the Pavilion as a whole, noting that it contained everything, including the most up-to-date appliances, that could contribute to the well-being of the inmates.

A canteen was attached, run by ladies who attended daily for the purpose.

The article in the *British Medical Journal* noted that of the cases admitted to the Pavilion it was found that some seventy per cent required further treatment, the average duration of which was two months. The men, ever cheerful, were strongly advised to take up one or more courses, thus lessening the handicap due to the loss of a limb.

The townspeople of Brighton naturally had the greatest respect for these heroes but this would, sadly, be put to the test in December 1916 through an episode described by the magistrates as 'disgraceful'. Two one-legged ex-soldiers, 24-year-old Thomas Burns and 21-year-old Harry Smith, were brought before Alderman Colbourne and other Magistrates at Brighton on Saturday the 9th charged with having been drunk and disorderly and with using obscene language on the previous evening. In addition, Smith was charged with assaulting Sergeant Edward Hall. Both the ex-soldiers admitted being drunk. Burns was fined 20s or nine days' imprisonment, Smith 20s or nine days for being drunk and disorderly and 20s or nine days for the assault, both sentences to be consecutive.

Public house opening hours had been restricted since 1915 in an effort by the government to reduce alcohol consumption. The Central Control Board (Liquor Traffic), set up under the Defence of the Realm Act (DORA), limited opening hours to 11 am till 3 pm and 6 pm till 10.30 pm; before the law was changed, establishments could open from five in the morning to half past midnight.

William Mead of the Dreadnought beerhouse in King Street fell foul of the regulations in February 1916. He pleaded guilty to unlawfully keeping his premises, which had been kept under observation following complaints, open on the morning of Sunday 13 February and to unlawfully selling beer to Harry John Parker of Kemp Street on that date. Parker likewise pleaded guilty. Mead was liable to a fine of £10 but was fined only 40s. Parker, described by his defence solicitor as 'in poor circumstances' and 'a hardworking man', was fined 10s.

Regulations infringed far more frequently were those relating to lighting. During 1916 no month passed without cases before the courts in varying numbers (September to November inclusive were bad). The public perception of the absence of lighting in the town was well set out in a feature in *The Brighton Season* of 1916/17:

> *'The lighting restrictions make it unpleasant to get about in the evenings. There are dangers to chauffeurs and coachmen, and they ... must be considered. ... Brighton is getting quite complacent about the dark streets by now, and greets as an old friend the kerb that is not there, rising also to the occasion when its presence is unsuspected.'*

It was, notes the periodical, a sign of the town's adaptability that it arranged all its important society functions in winter in the afternoons.

*Another Phelp cartoon. The caption reads: 'More stringent lighting regulations have been introduced this week in Brighton and Hove.' (*Brighton and Hove Society, *13 January 1916)*

The regulations were tightened up at the beginning of 1916, prompting a review of the situation from the *Brighton and Hove Society* magazine, which stated:

'The new lighting orders for the district have been received with excellent temper by the people of Brighton. It is realised that a coast-town is more exposed to the chances of war than an inland one, and that certain precautionary disabilities have to be endured. It is not pleasant to have to grope about in streets as dark as those of the most benighted of hamlets; to be slipping off kerbs, colliding with lampposts, and walking into walls. ... from all we hear, the shops are busier during the daylight hours than they have ever been before. People, in short, are doing their shopping in the morning and the early afternoon.'

Many of the prosecutions brought related to vehicles of various kinds, whether motorised, horse-drawn or two-wheeled. The absence of correct lighting on them was as much an offence as the showing of too much light from a residential or commercial property. With no red light on even his hand truck, Henry Collins of Hove was fined 5 shillings. Double this amount was imposed on Ephraim Felday of Southwick because the light on his motor car in Preston Road was too bright. Bicycle offences were often reported; Harold Wright of Camelford Street pleaded guilty to riding a bicycle on 8 January in the Old Steine at 8.50 pm. without a red rear light. He was fined 5 shillings. Only half that amount was imposed on Henry Wood of Totland Road who was summonsed for having no lights on a bicycle in Duke Street on 22 January. He pleaded guilty.

The fine on Wood was among the lowest imposed; the sums generally ranged from 5 shillings to 20 shillings but these were sometimes substantially exceeded. On 1 February, charges were, by coincidence, brought against two laundries. Gladys Long, manageress of the Harrington Model Laundry in Hollingdean Road, did not have the blinds down on her packing room, which had only just been cleared. The penalty was 20 shillings or 6 days. But Frances Steer of the Caledonian Laundry, Hollingdean Place, was hit harder. A bright light came from a window on the ground floor facing south. A piece of sacking had been placed over the window but there was a large hole opposite an unshaded incandescent light close to the window and it did not shade it in any way. There were also other unshaded lights. The penalty was 40 shillings or 9 days. A worse case still was that of William Robinson of Glenside, Grand Parade, who pleaded guilty to an offence committed on 30 January. The illumination came from the rear of the house from electric lights and the whole of the garden was lit up. The defendant said it was the fault of the maid. He had, however, been previously fined for a similar offence. The Borough Bench, declaring it a serious case, fined him 60 shillings or 7 days.

For all their precautionary benefits, restricted lights posed a danger to the public in certain cases. On the evening of 27 September a regrettable incident occurred involving a bus and two pedestrians, one of whom was killed and the other injured. The accident happened at the bottom of North Street, near the refuge in the middle of the road between the London County and Westminster Bank and the corner of East Street. The bus was travelling slowly and the driver sounded his horn, although this point was disputed by the injured pedestrian, William Milson, of 54, Bread Street. The bus collided with Rebecca Redford, 48, who lived at No 34 in the same street. By the time Dr E.C. Maguire, the police surgeon, reached the porchway of the bank, to which the woman had been taken, he found her dead. The cause was shock, due to severe internal injuries and broken ribs. It was subsequently suggested to the Coroner, who exonerated the driver from all blame, that there should be a little more light at this particular corner. It would be quite easy to extinguish it in case of a visit from

Thomas Tilling Ltd began the operation of motor buses in the Brighton area in February 1915 on a route between Portslade Station (seen here) and Castle Square, Brighton, using five vehicles transferred from London. (John Roberts)

Zeppelins. Superintendent Wood promised to forward the suggestion to the proper quarter. The jury returned a verdict of 'Accidental death'.

Thomas Tilling Ltd, whose bus was involved, had begun operating motor buses in the Brighton area in February 1915 on a route between Portslade Station and Castle Square using five vehicles transferred from London, where the company was running an extensive network of buses. It also operated in other parts of the south east and had set up a garage in Holland Road, Hove. In 1916, it took over the Brighton, Hove & Preston United Company and replaced all the remaining horse buses in the town with motor buses with the Tilling name on their sides.

Early in the year, Brighton suffered the heaviest snowstorms it had known for many years, resulting in traffic and social and business life generally being greatly dislocated. Yet Tilling's buses battled heroically through the conditions, putting the 'resident' company to shame. The *Brighton and Hove Society* magazine recorded the widespread disruption in its issue of 2 March and remarked 'There has not been much snow in Brighton this past seven or eight winters, but the downfall of February, 1916, has raised the average very handsomely indeed.'

In the Tilling bus accident, a conductress, Mary Jackson, had been on board. By this time, women had also been serving on Brighton's trams for well over a year and had given a very good account of themselves. On 22 April 1915, the first batch of six began conducting and the number was gradually increased until at the end of March 1916 it had risen eightfold. Brighton was one of the first towns in Britain to have female conductors, although Glasgow had already led the way. Their starting wages were set the same as those of male conductors, namely 4¾d per hour, with the hours of work set at eight per day. In mid-July 1915 we find the *Sussex Daily News* enthusing about the new labour force:

> *'The experiment in the employment of women tram conductors in Brighton has given entire satisfaction to the authorities and the public. During the past week, the young women have appeared in the new regulation uniform. ... The young women are doing their work admirably on several of the busiest routes. Their manner is strictly correct and businesslike. Passengers treat them with respect and freely recognise their efficiency.'*

The Corporation's new Tramway Employees. L to R - Back Row: G. Taylor, B. Wicks, M. Johnson, E. Bannister, C. Johnson, D. Parrack, A. Lee, E. Parsons. Second Row: E. Fletcher, L. Knight, C. Munnery, N. Burrows, A. Stamford, K. Zolner, C. Spencer, E. East, E. Dudman, F. Johnson. Front Row: A. Hobden, M. Ruben, F, Smith, A. Howe, M. Harwood, L. Barnard, C. Humphrey, L. Scriven, K. Allen. (Brighton Gazette, 24 February 1916)

Brighton – and Britain – was being forced to recognise woman power. Just two days after publishing the above, the *Sussex Daily News* proclaimed 'WOMEN AND WAR WORK – 50,000 ALREADY ENGAGED IN THE FACTORIES' and went on to describe how, despite heavy rain affecting the proceedings, women marched in procession in London on 17 July to demonstrate their readiness to take a greater part in war work. Lloyd George received a deputation headed by Emmeline Pankhurst and told her the Registration Act gave women complete statutory recognition. 50,000 of them were already engaged in munitions factories and obstacles to their further employment were being removed.

In September, the paper reported that ladies in Brighton were getting used to postal rounds, albeit so far only on light distribution on the outskirts of the town. 'Householders', it stated, 'are impressed by the quiet, unobtrusive way in which the post-women perform their work.'

A splendid record of the virtually all-female staff, holding wing sections, at the Fiat aeroplane assembly works located at the bottom of Devonshire Place, behind St James's Street. (Chris Horlock collection)

Also on their 'rounds' were the Women Patrols. In that year, Helen Fraser, in her *Women And War Work* (G. Arnold Shaw, New York, 1918), recorded that the Patrols wore an armlet with badge and number and mentioned how successful their work in London had been. A Patrol was 'generally a woman who is busy in her own home or profession

A study by portraiture specialist/postcard publisher Henry T. Edwards of Lewes Road of a stalwart group of munition workers in 1916. (Robert Jeeves/Step Back in Time)

all day, but who gives some hours one or two evenings a week to this work.' They had done the work faithfully and well and in their success had exceeded all anticipations. There were then about 3,000 Patrols in the country, of whom eighty-five were engaged in special work in London and paid by the Commissioner of Police. In many big towns admirable work had been done, and praise had been forthcoming from the military, Admiralty, police, and civil authorities. At the first Annual Meeting of the Women Patrol Committee in Brighton, held on the evening of 10 April 1916 at Christ Church Schools, Brighton's Chief Constable, William Gentle, thanked the ladies in the name of the Corporation and the whole of the police force for the quiet and unostentatious manner in which they had carried out their work and hoped that other municipalities would benefit by their example.

The Women's Auxiliary Force, launched in London in 1915 by Miss D Sparshatt and Miss D Walthall, under the presidency of Lady Milman, was a uniformed, voluntary organisation. Based at 82, Victoria Street, it soon opened branches in Essex (Walthamstow and Leyton, Braintree and Southend-on-Sea); Middlesex (Hackney and Stoke Newington, Highbury and Islington); London (St Pancras and Kensington); Surrey (Croydon and Forest Hill) and in many other districts. A branch in Brighton, based at 17, Compton Avenue, opened in the spring of 1916. Non-political and non-sectarian, the Force had as its main object the training of women

The local WAF. Back row (L to R): Privates Clarke, Ryman, Campbell, Wynne, Ellis, Coates Slater. Front row: Col. Sparshatt, Capt. Carson, Lt. Dugdale, Major Walthall. (Brighton Graphic and South Coast Illustrated News, 1 May 1916)

in useful subjects in their spare time and the utilising of their abilities for the service of their country. They assisted in hospitals, sewing and making comforts, helping in soldiers' canteens, of which there were eight (their largest London one was at 8, Waterloo Street), giving concerts to the troops or the wounded, collecting for war charities, keeping order in times of emergency or danger, and making themselves generally useful to their local authorities. The drill and discipline taught rendered each company fit to obey orders and keep their heads on such occasions as air raids or fires and tended to promote good health. Marches were undertaken and camps arranged, as were social evenings. Companies, when trained, acted as escorts to municipal authorities, important visitors on state occasions, and so on. Officers could be promoted from the ranks. One such was Miss Gladys Carson of Rottingdean, a daughter of Sir Edward, who had a large house there. By June, however, she had been called up to work on a farm, ridding the land of deeply-rooted dock. The *Gazette* remarked that 'the muscular strength developed by drills and exercises with the W.A.F. will doubtless find her equal to the task.'

On 2 May, Harry Preston kindly lent the large drawing room of the Royal York Hotel for the purposes of a sale in aid of the local branch. After the summer, we next hear of the Force in November when Miss Julia Smith came down from London to speak at a meeting. She remarked that the WAF was a help spiritually and mentally to shopgirls and other working girls from the age of seventeen and over.

Advertisements were run locally for training in munition-making. On 20 May 1916, a letter was published in the *Gazette* from W. Beckit Bernie at the Municipal Technical College, who pointed out that the College was now in a position to take women as well as men. There was currently no difficulty in finding places in factories for women who had

Bomb testers, 1915-16.
Their work was dangerous
but necessary. (Author)

completed a short course in machine tool work. The wages started at £1 per week and, as soon as the worker got onto piece work, rose to some 30 shillings or 35s per week. No fee was charged for the course.

By the end of November 1915, women in Brighton were also engaged in reading gas meters. Scarcely any two houses were alike in their internal gas arrangements and accessing the meters was often challenging.

In a report submitted to the monthly meeting of the Brighton Relief Committee, it was recorded that during the four weeks ended 12 November 1915, 444 females had registered for employment at the Labour Exchange as compared with 361 in October and 244 in the corresponding period in the previous year. In spite of the large number of women already engaged in various occupations, the supply of willing candidates was evidently still in excess of the requirements. No fewer than 78 of the applicants were anxious to secure situations as postwomen. A number of men working in the transport service had been discharged.

Looking back on 1915 from the perspective of female employment, the *Gazette* of 1 January 1916 remarked that

> '*Next to the patronage of Royalty, perhaps the most striking development of the year was the substitution of female for male labour in many important local industries. The public see it in the women tram conductors, women ticket examiners at the railway station, women postmen, women gasmeter readers, and women distributors of parcels; but the change has really permeated almost every place of business in the town. Lady clerks are to be seen at the banks, electricity offices, insurance offices, and grocery establishments.*'

One enterprising and skilled lady, we are informed by the 1916/17 *Brighton Season*, was Miss Dora M. Basley NSPE, the town's 'most popular exponent of physical education and fencing' who held classes at 6, Norfolk Terrace. She was also a keen motorist and, what was more, worked with the well-known motor agent, Mr George Hill, in the establishment of a School of Motoring at Duke Street. She was, he declared, competent and painstaking. Her pupils at Hill's School of Motoring included many young officers, and these were in her opinion 'amongst the most apt of learners'. The periodical urged: 'One should call and see Miss Basley at 7, Duke Street, and learn to drive a car – a very useful thing to know in these times – for "one never knows".'

Miss Esme Fennings, described in the *Brighton Season* as 'the bright daughter of Dr Fennings of Kemp Town' was clearly also skilled as a driver since she had her name down as a chauffeur for the RFC. She was one of the first society girls to take the wounded out in her car. After carrying out this good work regularly for a year, she joined the Land League, working on a farm and private estate and was now helping at the 2nd Eastern General Hospital, Kemp Town. The same periodical featured (with photographs) Mrs Maguire, wife of Dr E.C. Maguire – who attended at the accident involving a bus – of the Old Steyne [sic] and Miss Sylvia Bright, the daughter of Dr Bright of Kemp Town; both 'represent two ladies who set a splendid example of whole-hearted war work.' Mrs Maguire had learnt to drive a car and, as all their menservants had enlisted, had taken the place of chauffeur to her husband, while Miss Bright had learnt to drive a car and had 'lately driven one on its daily rounds for a business house.' In several of the spacious avenues in the Hove district, handsome motor cars were seen driven by women in smart liveries, while on Hove Lawns, females were employed in attending to the chairs. Elsewhere in the Borough, it was 'no uncommon experience to see women performing the work of furniture removers' (*Gazette*, 2 August 1916). Some ladies turned their hand to assisting chemists, although not in the dispensing side of the business.

*Ticket-punching staff in front of a tank engine. (*Brighton Graphic and South Coast Illustrated News, *23 June 1916)*

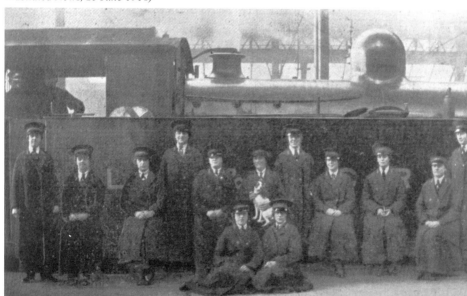

On the railways, women were performing much useful work. At the 137th Ordinary Meeting of the LBSCR Company held on 23 February 1916 at London Bridge Terminus, the Earl of Bessborough, KP, Chairman of Directors, stated 'we have been supplying some of the vacancies in the staff by employing women, and at the present moment we have nearly 650 women working in various capacities. So far they have proved themselves quite fit to perform certain classes of work, and we see no reason against adding to their number for duties suitable to them as and when occasion may require.' He also mentioned that the number of men who had responded to the call of duty was 2,884, being a little over 17% of the total staff. Of them, 118 had given their lives and 237 had been wounded, were prisoners of war or were reported as missing.

A revealing survey of the rise in female employment nationally, by trade, since July 1914 was provided in the October 1916 issue of the Board of Trade's *Labour Gazette*. The estimated numbers of women and girls employed in all trades in July 1914 had been 3,219,000 and the estimated increase in that figure by April 1916 was 583,000. All trades shared in this increase, except agriculture, which since July 1914 had suffered a decrease of 14,000. Among Brighton women, some reluctance to take up farming work was evident. The *Gazette* commented on 6 May:

> *'It has been again noted that of hundreds of women who have registered for employment in Brighton none seek agricultural work. Judging by what can be seen every day in the streets of the town, young women are willing enough to undertake almost any laborious occupation in urban life. As yet they do not appear to be drawn to rural pursuits. It is said that the sex have been rather piqued by the slighting tone in which farmers have referred to female assistants.'*

On the 26th of the month, a meeting was held under the auspices of the East Sussex Women's Agricultural Committee (in conjunction with the Board of Trade) at Abinger House, King's Road, where Kingsley Court now stands, the residence of Mr Gerald and Lady Louise Loder, to promote the employment of women in agriculture during wartime. It was chaired by the Countess of Chichester, who was president of the movement for East Sussex. She wanted to impress on all types and sorts of women the importance of the work they were now called upon to do. Thousands of women were needed if a severe food shortage was to be prevented, and an organisation had been formed in various counties to inaugurate the scheme. Britain's food production was considerably reduced and this was a serious matter.

It is highly likely that while the Countess was speaking, passers-by, many of them, one would imagine, visitors to the town, were soaking up the sunshine with hardly a care in the world. The 1916/17 *Brighton Season* commented:

> *'The attractions of Brighton for those who seek rest and recuperation from the worries of wartime have resulted in an extraordinary influx of visitors this year. Not only to its vitalising air and freedom from Zeppelin scares, but to the all round efficiency with which it prescribes for the health, happiness, and entertainment of its huge floating population, is this desirable result to be attributed. There can be no question but that its great popularity is to be largely attributed to the variety and quality of its distractions and the smart enterprise of its business people, for Brighton entertains its visitors right royally. The best of musical attractions are regularly to be found here. The Municipal Orchestra, under Mr. Lyell-Tayler's direction, has transformed the Aquarium into a veritable home of melody. The beautiful Palace Pier, too, is second to none in its provision of first-class bands, military and otherwise.'*

The West Pier was not mentioned but elsewhere the West Pier Company reported good results despite the war and the 'lights out' order that went with it. At its half-yearly meeting in April, it noted that visitors during the six months ended 29 February had been 405,765 as against 297,017 in the corresponding half of the previous year. The Chairman announced that the new Concert Hall would be opened on 20 April, and as evidence of the stability of the structure said the recent great storm had not displaced a single bolt or bar. He also referred to the engagement of female labour and to the depletion of the pier's staff through enlistments; by the next meeting, the Assistant Secretary and seventeen of the employees would have been called to the colours. At the 53rd Ordinary General Meeting, held at the Hotel Metropole on 6 October – the exact fiftieth anniversary of the opening of the pier – the

Chairman of Directors, W. H. Gibson PCS, stated that the Report he had to submit to them that day was the best for half a century. This, he believed, was largely due to the splendid new concert hall – probably the finest of its kind in the United Kingdom. It had proved an unqualified success in every way.

Postcard publisher Alfred Wardell has admirably captured the holiday scene in this view from Brighton's West Pier. (Robert Jeeves/Step Back in Time)

The number of visitors for the six months had been 1,100,000, and for the whole year 1,503,810, as against 785,150 in the corresponding period the previous year. That was almost double. These figures did not include the many thousands of invalid soldiers who had had a free pass to the pier during the whole year. A letter of congratulation from Sir John Howard, unable to attend, was read out. The military bands this year had been a great success, especially the King's Royal Rifles, with the new Concert Hall repeatedly filled to overflowing. The splendid results had been achieved despite the absence of lighting on the pier. The large crowds who patronised the Theatre and Concert Hall had had to grope their way on and off the structure in the dark. Plus, there had been no railway excursions, which made an enormous difference, because when they ran they brought patrons down in thousands. The prohibition of a Bank Holiday in August had substantially affected receipts, nor had there had been any steamboats, which in past years had been a considerable source of income. Finally, there had been the false reports circulating in London and other places to the effect that Brighton had been bombed and the sea front partly destroyed, and that everyone had therefore deserted the town. However, they had it on the authority of Brighton's Chief Constable – who made the statement before the Magistrates – that not a single bomb had been dropped in the whole county of Sussex. As long as that continued 'Brighton would remain Brighton still, and receive its full amount of patronage.'

The West Pier's sister must not be forgotten. The *Brighton and Hove Society* enthused, in early August:

> *'Now that summer has come again, people are appreciating more than ever the numerous attractions of the Palace Pier. One of the handsomest structures of its kind on the South Coast, if not the handsomest, it certainly affords exceptional opportunities for passing the time in the pleasantest, but not necessarily the idlest, way possible. Naturally it is round the band stand that the crowd very largely congregates, and the comfortable deck-chairs are quite at a premium when a performance is going on. This week the band of H.M. Royal Garrison Artillery, under the baton of Mr. P.F. Battishill, is giving bright programmes of popular music, and the listening crowd is characteristic of the place. There are "flappers" in dainty frocks, soldiers in hospital uniform or in khaki, spruce business men on holiday, and elderly spinsters, reading, crocheting or strolling about listening to the music. And, through the constant hum of conversation and laughter, the persistent chug-chug of fussy little motor-boats beats its regular rhythm and, occasionally, an aeroplane will pass overhead with its whirring buzz of sound. ... There is a whole colony of shops at the Pier head and a really excellent restaurant so that both inward and outward comfort are catered for. Altogether, it is, as the Americans, say, "Some Pier"!'*

While there were no Americans in Brighton in any number, there were Canadians here at that time. The *Sussex Daily News*, in a piece also

An untypically quiet day on the deck of the Palace Pier. (Peter Booth collection)

extolling the delights of the pier, remarked on 19 June that 'during a lull in the afternoon performance the band of the Canadian contingent visiting the town could be seen and heard, followed by the men along the front from the very successful drumhead service on the Brunswick Lawns.' Just a few days earlier, on Friday the 16th, the mayors of the twin towns had in fact welcomed at Brighton Station a contingent, from Shorncliffe, of the 12th Battalion Canadian Infantry – a unit of the First Expeditionary Force which had fought so gallantly in France. The visit, scheduled to last until the Sunday evening, was the highlight of the Allies Week organised by the Mayors of Brighton and Hove to raise money for the relief and Red Cross funds of our brother nations in arms, especially those whose countries had been devastated by the enemy. A number of streets in both towns were decorated with flags and bunting and thousands of people, waving hats and handkerchiefs, stood at the Station and in Queens Road, North Street and the Old Steine, where the visitors, some 120 strong and under the command of Major H.G. Deedes, were officially welcomed by both mayors. The Canadians' two bands, one brass and one bugle, had processed behind mounted police from the station, where the men had been met by a guard of honour; the bugle band was thought by many to be one of the best ever heard in Brighton. In the afternoon and evening, both bands gave performances on the Palace Pier and drew very large and enthusiastic audiences to the central enclosure. The officers were allotted quarters at leading hotels while the men were billeted at a number of private houses as guests.

After playing on the bandstand in front of the Bedford Hotel, the entire contingent was entertained to luncheon at the Clarence Rooms, Hotel Metropole, as guests of the two mayors. In the afternoon, the Canadians competed in athletic sports with other military teams at Preston Park Cricket Ground and their bands played. There the spectators watched with great interest the professional baseball match between Montreal City and St. John's City. It was an entirely new game to many of the watchers. Oddly, however, no result of the game was kept and no one could be found to claim the prize at the prize-giving ceremony. In the evening, at St Anne's Well Gardens, Hove, there was a grand concert, including recitations, a sword dance, ventriloquism and a monologue, all supported by the Canadian bandsmen. On the following day the drumhead service was held on Brunswick lawns with an address by the venerable Archdeacon of Hastings, the Vicar of Brighton. Also in Hove, thanks to an extension in the duration of the visit, Mrs Pollak gave a tea party on Monday the 19th in honour of the visitors. She also invited along a number of wounded Canadians from

ALLIES' WEEK,

(BRIGHTON, HOVE & DISTRICT)

Organised by the Mayors of Brighton and Hove to raise Funds to he our Allies, especially those whose Countries have been devastate

Commencing Whit-Monday, JUNE 12th

THE MAIN FEATURES WILL BE :

Whit-Monday - - - Preston Pa

Military Day—Parade **11** a.m. March Past **12** noon
Sports 3 p.m.

Admission **6d.** Morning and Afternoon. (Soldiers and Sailors in Uniform, an Children Half-price).

Tuesday - - - - Hove Town H

" **Legends of the Allies.** "

Afternoon, **3** p.m.—Table for **4**, One Guinea, or Single Seats, **6** - (including Tea)
Balcony, **2 6** : Unreserved **1** -. Tea Tickets 9d.
Evening, **8** p.m.—Table for **4, 7 6**, or Single Seats, **2** - (including Refreshments)
Balcony, **1** - (Unreserved).

Wednesday - - St. Ann's Well Garde

Country Fair, Maypole, Bands, Booths, White Elephant Sale, etc.
2.30 to **9** p.m. Admission : Afternoon **6d.** Evening **3d.**

At **7.30** p.m., **Grand Whist Drive**
at the South Coast Creamery (Opposite West Pier).

Tickets 2|- including Refreshments. The Mayor of Brighton will distribute the Prize

Thursday - - - Hove Town H

Reception—followed by
Sale of Pictures and Works of Art.

Friday - - - - Palace Pi

Fête : Gala Performances ; Bands of H.M. Royal Marine Artillery and
12th Canadians ; Swimming Competitions, etc. **Pier Toll 6d.**

Saturday - **OUR ALLIES' FLAG DA**

12th Canadians **(Sports) & Bands** at County Cricket Ground, Hove, **3** p
,, ,, **(Military Concert)** at St. Ann's Well Gdns., ,, **8** p
Admission **6d.** (Sailors, Soldiers and V.T.C. Members, in Uniform, **Free**).

Hon. Organising Secretaries for Allies' Week :
Ald. E. J. BUTT-THOMPSON (for Brighton), Mr. W. S. MARCHANT (for Hove)
to whom all communications should be addressed at the respective Town Halls.

Cliftonville Press, 119 Blatchington Road, Hove

Programme of Allies' Week events from 12 to 17 June 1916. (Royal Pavilion & Museums, Brighton & Hove)

the various Brighton military hospitals, some of whom were known to the Shorncliffe men, so that the merry party seated around the tea tables included gallant young soldiers from almost all parts of Canada.

The Canadian band at Preston Park in Allies' Week, 1916. (Tony McKendrick Collection)

The soldiers were sorry to leave. One sturdy sergeant had cracked jokes on the difficulty of finding where Brighton ended and Hove began and suggested the granting of an extra day's leave in the two towns so that the difficulty might be solved! Although there was no formal send-off, there was a large crowd to bid them farewell; in fact, hundreds of people could not get onto the platform. As the train steamed out of the station, the Canadians gave hearty cheers amid bugle calls. How many would see their homeland again?

A number of appeal letters on behalf of the wounded were published in or near the festive season. Two were published on 25 November calling for funds to provide extra comforts in the Pavilion Military Hospital and the Kitchener Hospital respectively. The former was from both Mayors and Col. R. Cecil Campbell, Officer Commanding, while the latter was from 'A Visitor', who explained:

'I have been staying in Brighton a few days in order to visit a wounded relative in the Kitchener Hospital. The patients have plenty of good plain food, but none of those little luxuries that mean so much to them, such as fruit, flowers, cakes, sweets, magazines, &c. No doubt it is because the hospital is out of the way, as there always seems plenty of these things in other hospitals in the town. A convoy of wounded men came in to-day, and I am sure if your readers knew what was needed there would be an abundance of good things for them.'

As Christmas approached, a public appeal was made on behalf of the 2nd Eastern General Hospital to make the occasion a merry one for the wounded. A committee had been formed to raise a fund for providing festive teas and entertainments for some 1,000 patients. The response from the townspeople was magnificent and made it possible to extend the celebrations beyond the central hospital to all the men under Lieutenant Colonel Rooth's command, numbering between 1,000 and 1,400. The celebrations also extended Christmas, since the series of teas was held as from 27 December. The first gathering took place in the new YMCA hut at the Dyke Road Hospital. Although not yet formally opened, the building had been kindly lent for the purpose. Here the tables, charmingly decked with flowers and crackers, were laden with good things all beautifully served, ham sandwiches nicely cut, bread and butter and jam, cakes galore and plenty of fruit. Among those seated at the top table were the Mayors of Brighton and Hove (the former, since the previous month, was Alderman Herbert Carden) and Mrs Pollak and her son, Jack Cleugh.

Some weeks earlier, festive cheer had been brought to the Kitchener Hospital. On 29 November, a crowded audience of British wounded and the Australian contingent greeted Maurice Goodger and the artistes of the Morriston Concert Party. A few days later, an unusually large number of Tommies filled the concert hall for a concert party taken by A.W. Parkin. Everybody thoroughly enjoyed both the varied programme and the cigarettes handed round by a guest of the party. Nearer Christmas, 19-year-old Miss Pearl Sortain met with an enthusiastic reception when she gave a delightful concert. At least half of the nearly 1,000 men then in the immense hospital filled the Recreation Room. The artiste's gift of song had been put to good use during the war, for in the previous year she had sung at over sixty concerts for the soldiers and for war relief. Mrs Sortain, as usual, supported her gifted daughter as accompanist throughout the evening. On 27 December, in the festively decorated Recreation Room, an entertainment was held in which the members of Hove Dramatic Club gave a short playlet while the variety part of the programme consisted of songs, recitations, and dancing. At the end of the proceedings, Miss Maud Longden's distribution of eleven hundred cigarettes among the audience was greatly appreciated.

In the town, Christmas and the New Year followed much the same course as in 1915, despite the fairly severe curtailment of rail traffic due to the demands of the war and the hint of rationing to come. Two interesting editorials in the *Gazette*, one published on 23 December and the other on the 27th, reflect prevailing thoughts and feelings. In the former, Christmas is described as being regulated by economic conditions and the government. The market had already imposed restrictions upon the quality of the pudding, the weight of the turkey and the consumption of seasonable beverages, while under DORA, the principal meal of the day was to consist of three courses only. Among the people, however, there was a new resolve. 'Thank goodness,' stated the paper, 'Christmas sees us united as never before in this war. It has taken us two years to learn the lesson. The answer we shall send Germany to the Christmas message will be the true proclamation of lasting peace on the only terms that give us security.' The editorial on the 27th recorded 'the restraint of the public, the subdued atmosphere in every home, the tension of public emotion' and observed:

> 'there never was a Christmas at which there has been more sincere individual effort to minister to the happiness of kith and kin at home and abroad. For weeks greetings have been dispatched to the four quarters of the earth and in this way the English had put a girdle of love round the world. It was a comfortable fireside thought, this strange Christmas.'

The town was full for the festival, just as it generally had been in other years. Business was very brisk throughout Christmas week, with shop assistants working at high pressure for three days and far into the nights. The crowds in the shops late on the night of Saturday the 23rd

*Soper's Emporium at the top of North Street offered a wide selection of gifts for Christmas. (*Brighton Graphic and South Coast Illustrated News, *16 December 1916)*

presented a remarkable scene. The nature and size of the festive dinner was affected far more by what was available than by its regulation, with 'the apparent shrinkage in the bulk of the Christmas pudding [being] due more to the difficulty in obtaining currants, sultanas, and spices than to the edicts of the Food Controller.' Some people went in for a goose instead of a turkey. There was, indeed, quite a run on geese, and an amusing tale was told of how the Quartermaster-Sergeant of a Canadian regiment raided certain shops in the north of the town and 'commandeered' thirty of the birds. All in all, there was 'plenty for everybody, within reason and without extravagance'. And enough is as good as a feast.

On that Saturday, the first performance of the pantomime *Aladdin* took place in the theatre on the Palace Pier, with the traditional second spectacle, *The Babes in the Wood*, premiering on the same day at the Theatre Royal. Both shows were greatly enjoyed by children and it was for them that a colourful Boxing Day party was laid on at the Grand Hotel. Here, in the seasonally adorned ballroom, the attraction was the pupils of Miss Egerton Welch who all appeared in fancy dress, including the children of Madame Cloquet – Belgian refugees who had escaped from their beloved homeland in a rough coal van. Germany, buffeted, beaten by the Allies and thoroughly driven back, was depicted by Miss Marjorie Sandals, who was followed by 'Peace', personified by little Sabe Torua, with a white dove on her shoulder and an olive branch in her hand, while the 'dance of triumph' was vivaciously performed. It symbolised, simply yet graphically, what the town – and the entire nation – yearned for.

CHAPTER FOUR

1917 – Prosperity against the Odds

The winter of 1916/17 was the harshest for over twenty years, with near-Arctic conditions on the coast ushering in the new year. Brighton shivered its way through January yet, remarkably, visitors continued to arrive. By March the weekends were witnessing large gatherings at the hotels, thanks to the arrival of some spring weather and encouraging war news. Visitors poured into the town and a large number of residents who had taken up allotments (for food was becoming a pressing issue) were at last able to devote some time to their plots.

Yet winter was a long time dying, with persistent cold winds and low temperatures characterising part of that month and early April. Internationally, the big news in the latter month was America's declaration of war against Germany – a huge morale-booster for Britain. Oddly, however, Americans here were deemed to be aliens, as evidenced by the 10 shillings fine imposed on barmaid Gladys Inwood of the Cricketers Arms Hotel, Black Lion Street, for failing to notify the presence of an American guest.

In May, summer suddenly burst upon the town. From then on, crowds flocked to the beach and piers. The spell of calm seas encouraged bathing, angling and boating, although trips on pleasure steamers were still unavailable. Lawn tennis was played in the parks and on the bowling greens many a match took place. The local economy benefited immensely from the circulation of huge sums of

*Hanningtons store in North Street/East Street was a shopper's paradise. Closure sadly came in 2001 after nearly 200 years of trading. (*Brighton and Hove Society, *19 July 1917)*

money, representing the high wages now being earned by most workers. Not put off by the curtailment of rail services, an increase of fifty per cent in fares or the unprecedented difficulties faced by boarding-house owners in catering for them, visitors came and liked what they saw. Many were also attracted to the shops, where the summer sales were in full swing.

July ushered in six weeks of encouraging weather. Among visitors in the second week were doubtless a number escaping the capital for respite from air raids. One had taken place on the 7th which had resulted in fifty-seven deaths and prior to that attack there had occurred the tragedy of 13 June, when 162 civilians had been killed – the highest death toll from a single air raid on Britain during the war.

On the night of Monday 30 July and the early hours of Tuesday, bad weather returned. Heavy squalls of wind and rain caused problems for three boats of the Brighton fishing fleet (*Violet*, *Jenny Lind* and *Emily*) but none were lost. Come rain or shine, however, Brighton remained a magnet for visitors from all over, but especially London.

Writing in the *Evening News* in early August, W. McCartney, who had made a 'sardine journey' to the resort, reported:

> 'In all its history Brighton has rarely been so tightly packed. Hotels are full; boarding houses rammed and stuffed and overflowing; and from small furnished holiday flats to the big furnished houses on both ends of the immense white stone front everything is taken.
>
> 'The piers are filled with a happy and sun-browned London crowd. I have never seen so many women bathing at Brighton.
>
> 'All over the beach there are picnic parties from morn to night.

As for the promenade you either move slowly or sit down and stay there.

'Restaurants and cafes – packed again. It is a huge, hot, careless, jolly London crowd, for the most part. But wherever you turn, there are sick and maimed and blinded soldiers, whose quiet suffering runs as a note of pain through the careless mirth of Brighton.

'Brighton seems to specialise in ample matrons with large followings of children, and this year there are more than ever, and in the same highly decorative costumes. For example, I saw one formidable lady in a blazer sports coat that could be seen from here to Madagascar.'

*Head Waiter. "Sorry, Sair—can't help it. Full up! No room for a long time. After all, dere is a war on." (*Punch, *5 December 1917)*

A great gale in the Channel, such as had rarely been witnessed before in summertime, struck the town on 24 August. Howling throughout the night, the winds beat against window casements and whistled among the telephone wires. At dawn, a plate glass window on the premises of Freeman, Hardy and Willis at 16 Queen's Road was blown in, the shutters of an empty shop in Edward Street were brought down and several panes of glass in the window were broken. Many houses in both Brighton and Hove had their chimney pots or tiles blown off. As if all this was not bad enough, a second gale, the most violent for twenty years, hit the town just four days later, with wind speeds at one point reaching sixty-four miles an hour.

Yet nothing could halt the rush to the south. As the season waned in September, the *Gazette* marvelled at the influx:

> *'People have fought their way into crowded trains in the sheer determination to reach the town. They have endured almost pathetic discomforts in searching for lodgings, well content to find recompense in any sort of shake-down. ... The war has produced many startling surprises, but it may be doubted whether any have made such an impression as the rush for Brighton. It seems to have infected all classes. Apparently having reached Brighton the masses fancy themselves in a worldly paradise.'*

In London, Brighton's success was too much for some. Among the extraordinary rumours was a fantastic report about Russian Jews hiding in the town; this was followed by a suggestion that food hogs were flocking to the south coast to 'dodge the Food Controller'. But the alarming claim that Brighton had been 'bombarded from the sea' which spread across the capital on Saturday the 8th was, the *Gazette* thought, 'much too serious to be ignored'.

The summer as a whole, despite July and August being mainly responsible for making it the wettest for ten years, had been successful, not to say astounding given the circumstances:

> *'... it is marvellous that Brighton should be flourishing as it is after three years of devastating warfare which has convulsed Europe. Once more fact is stranger than fiction. If the scene of a seaside resort at the height of its prosperity within the sound of the booming of the greatest war in the world had been presented in a romance, it would have been deemed absolutely incredible.'*
> *(Gazette, 29 September)*

Even after September, the crowds remained, continuing to bring wealth into the town. Remarkably, the reinstatement of racing in the following month had little impact on the numbers on the promenades. Encouraging war news on the 20th buoyed people's spirits; the French had shot down four Zeppelins returning home after a raid over London which had left twenty-seven dead. There was a spontaneous outburst of enthusiasm at the Hippodrome when the first news of the airships' fate was flashed upon the screen.

The autumn/winter season was soon in full swing. On the weekend of 4/5 November, the town was crowded to capacity, with members of high society predominating. Costly furs were worn by many women.

Crowds of visitors – and doubtless residents too – throng the wide promenade opposite the Metropole and Grand Hotels in this view from the West Pier. (Robert Jeeves/Step Back in Time)

Brighton's two piers offered not only the enjoyment of the open air by way of a healthy and relaxed stroll or the strains of bandstand music but also first-class dramatic and concert entertainment on elegantly-appointed premises under cover.

On the Palace Pier, where plays were normally performed for a week, the theatrical year of 1917 began with the farewell performance of the seasonal pantomime *Aladdin*, an event so popular that hundreds were turned away. Plays during the rest of the year ranged from Ibsen's *Ghosts* to *Sherlock Holmes*, a collaboration between Conan Doyle and William Gillette, which involved the strange case of Alice Faulkner, 'a hitherto unpublished episode' in the life of the great detective. Hubert

William Gillette in Act 1 of Sherlock Holmes. The play premiered in New York in 1899.

Henry Davies, who died in the August of 1917, had four plays in the town over the year – *Outcast, Doormats, Molluscs,* and *Mrs Gorringe's Necklace.* Horace A. Vachell, the most prolific playwright of the war years, gave the delighted audiences *The Case of Lady Camber, Searchlights* and, in collaboration with novelist Thomas Cobb, *Mrs Pomeroy's Reputation.*

On the musical entertainment front, the honours were shared mainly between Henry Lyell-Tayler, the conductor of Brighton's Municipal Orchestra and well known to audiences at the Aquarium, and James 'Jimmy' Sale and his Hippodrome Orchestra.

As in 1916, the West Pier was also hugely popular. Between March and August inclusive it received more than a million visitors while in the

*Poster advertising concerts at the Aquarium's Winter Gardens. (*The Brighton Season *1917/18)*

period 1 September 1916 to 31 August 1917 the number was 1,582,000 – an increase of 208,000 over the corresponding previous year. At the 55th OGM of the West Pier Company, held at the Metropole on 26 October, it was revealed that all records in the Company's annals had been eclipsed during the previous half-year.

In town, at the Theatre Royal, a wide variety of entertainment was on offer throughout the year. As on the Palace Pier, Ibsen's *Ghosts* was shown, the single performance taking place on 25 May. Equally controversial plays by another major European dramatist, Eugène Brieux (1858-1932), were also performed. The only war play that seems to have been put on at the theatre during the year was *Seven Days' Leave*, by Walter Howard (1866-1922). Its action centred on the unmasking of a couple of German spies who, in the guise of Belgian refugees, had taken up residence in a village on the East Coast and, dramatically, the luring of a submarine to her doom. First shown in late April, it returned in October.

At the Hippodrome, the war got comic treatment in late September in a sketch by Ralph Roberts entitled *In the Trenches*. In May, another sketch had been performed, *The Johnson 'Ole* (full title: *Bairnsfatherland or the Johnson 'Ole*), co-written by Basil Macdonald Hastings (grandfather of journalist and author Max Hastings) and Captain Bruce Bairnsfather (1887-1959), famed for his cartoon character Old Bill. With his pals Bert and Alf, Bill featured in Bairnsfather's *Fragments from France* cartoons published weekly in *The Bystander* magazine during the war. *The Johnson 'Ole* was a highly amusing episode of life in Plug Street Trench around Christmas, 1914, which had featured in the revue *Flying Colours* at the London Hippodrome since September 1916. 'Johnson' refers to a 'Jack Johnson', the nickname used to describe the impact of a heavy, black German 15-cm artillery shell. In November, the Hippodrome presented, for one week, *The Better 'Ole*, which Bairnsfather had co-written with Captain Arthur Eliot.

The many big names who entertained at the Middle Street venue during the year included Seymour Hicks (husband of Ellaline Terriss),

*Old Bill, the much loved fictional character created in 1914–15 by cartoonist Bruce Bairnsfather. (*Brighton and Hove Society, *21 November 1918)*

Harry Tate, George Formby, Ciceley Courtneidge, Phyllis Dare (who sang a war-time ballad, *Somewhere with you in France*), Harry Weldon, Gertie Millar and Marie Lloyd. When Miss Lloyd appeared on 28 July, the theatre was packed from floor to ceiling.

From the Hippodrome we return to the seafront area, where, across the road from the Palace Pier, stood the Aquarium (now the Sea Life Centre). The Conservatory (renamed the Winter Garden) was from 1907 to 1918 the home of the Municipal Orchestra, in later years under Lyell-Tayler, and was dubbed the Kinema for a time. Films were shown there until 1939. During the Great War, the complex's fortunes were decidedly on the wane, with a loss of £3,294 being reported in 1917, for example, for the year ended 31 March. A Councillor Lewis even proposed closing the Aquarium altogether and disposing of the contents. Disbanding the orchestra was discussed as one economy measure, but this did not happen.

The 'Queen of the Music Hall', Marie Lloyd (1870-1922). (Author)

Lyell-Tayler, as Musical Director, naturally fought to retain the concerts, which had always been greatly appreciated by the public. He wanted Brighton to be 'the premier position musically outside London'. His plea was received sympathetically, with re-engagement being agreed for the year ending 30 September 1918.

In the autumn, a new YMCA building, mounted on the roof, brought in crowds of soldiers from local hospitals and Shoreham Camp for refreshment, socialising and entertainment. At perhaps the earliest concert to be held

Mᴿ LYELL-TAYLER

A clever caricature of conductor Henry Lyell-Tayler. (Author)

there, on 13 October, the place was packed. One week later, the hut was officially opened by HRH Princess Helena Victoria, the President of the YMCA, Ladies Auxiliary. An address was given by Sir Arthur Yapp, YMCA National Secretary, in which he expressed great pleasure and gratification at the splendid work Brighton and Hove were doing for the Association.

The work of the organisation had likewise been praised on 17 June at the Hippodrome by the celebrated evangelist Rodney 'Gipsy' Smith (1860-1947) when recounting his experiences in a talk titled 'Just behind the Firing Line in France'. Everywhere on his national tour, big crowds gathered to hear him – in some cases he had audiences of over 3,000 and in every case the largest halls available were packed.

British evangelist Rodney 'Gipsy' Smith (1860-1947), who conducted evangelistic campaigns in Britain and the USA for over 70 years.

Another new YMCA hut had been opened on 6 January at the Dyke Road Hospital, the gift of Bernhard Baron. He had given away over 12 million cigarettes while the war had been on and had sent a million cigarettes to the defenders of Verdun. The new building, a replica of the hut at Fulham Military Hospital, would enable the wounded soldiers to be taken out from their wards in the SEGH into different surroundings and enjoy a little recreation.

Returning briefly to 1915, we see wounded soldiers at St Anne's Wells Gardens, Hove, entertained courtesy of Mr and Mrs Bernhard Baron (Trevor Cox collection)

The facility of a hut was also enjoyed at the Kitchener Hospital in Elm Grove. At the end of January 1917, the hospital housed over 1,100 soldiers, mostly Australians, the majority of whom were convalescing. Entertainment was important to them, as it lifted their spirits.

Regrettably, the former workhouse continued to be one of the main recipients of the freshly wounded from Brighton Station. The returns listed in David Sheldon's St John Ambulance history, *In The Service Of Mankind* (CreateSpace Independent Publishing Platform, 2014), reveal that arrivals at the terminus during 1917 totalled 11,393 giving an average monthly figure of 949. There were spikes in April (1,039, Battle of Arras), August, October and November (1,539, 1,689 and

A company of VADs, plus a Boy Scout and young lad, surround a casualty at Brighton Station (Robert Jeeves/Step Back in Time)

1,276, Battle of Passchendaele) and December (1,445, Battle of Cambrai).

On 14 April 1917, a Great Central Railway ambulance train brought in, via Dover and direct from the scene of action, 123 'cot' cases, the largest number ever to have reached the town. One week earlier the figure had been 122 and on the 19th the figure would be 115.

The ambition of the ladies of the Brighton Nursing Division of the St John Ambulance Brigade to install a permanent canteen at the station was achieved in December 1917, thanks to a successful appeal for funds. The Night Convoy Workers' Canteen, to give it its official title, was opened on Platform 5 on the 16th by Sir William Gentle, Chief Constable and Superintendent of the Brighton and Hove Corps of the St John Ambulance Brigade, who was handed the first cup of coffee served from the bar.

Tales of service abroad were sometimes recounted in letters sent to residents or by townspeople themselves. An unlikely combatant was Lieutenant the Revd W. Stanley Blunden, home on leave after some months in hospital. From the pulpit, on 29 November, he gave the members of Norfolk Road Wesley Methodist Church a vivid account, lasting an hour and a half, of his experiences at the front. A member of the Warwickshire Regiment, he had been wounded in France in April. He spoke of the indescribable state of the communication trenches through which men had to make their way – often literally up to their necks in mud. He then went into detail about the routine of watching and working in the dreadful wintry weather, work that went on day and night. He asked his listeners to remember that although the weather had been dead against our men in the summer of 1917, 'they had simply done miracles'.

Some, however, became captives of the enemy. In one of only a couple of accounts from prisoners of war to appear in the local press during the year, a Private William H. Hickman, whose parents lived at 49, Brading Road, wrote reassuringly, but probably untruthfully, to his wife at 156, Upper Lewes Road (his home address is given in another source as 28, Viaduct Road):

> *'You will be pleased to know I am going on well, and am being very kindly treated and very well fed. I am fairly comfortable as regards my wound, which was a bullet through the thigh. I think it is going on favourably. I have had a trying time of it, being wounded on 25th April, and lying on the field till the 30th. So you can guess I was a little delirious, having had no food at all for three days, and being reduced to eating the grass. But I must tell you more about that later on, for I hope that it will soon be over. You can rest contented that we are being kindly treated.'*

Hickman, who was in the Hampshire Regiment with the Salonikan Expeditionary Force, had joined up twelve months previously. His father had been on the staff of the Royal Albion Hotel, where William had also been employed some years before. A brother, Albert, had been killed in France about a year earlier and another brother was still serving at the Front. William died at the Military Hospital, Skopje (Macedonia) on 12 November 1917, two or three days after his left leg was amputated.

On the afternoon of 10 January, Brightonian Henry C. Mahoney lectured to a very large audience at Hove Town Hall on 'Sixteen Months in Four German Prison Camps and Prisoner of War Camps'. His talk was in aid of the local branch of the British Empire Union and Prisoners of War Funds and was illustrated by lantern slides of photographs which he succeeded in taking during his enforced stay in Germany. Mahoney, a civilian internee, drew a harrowing word picture of the brutal and inhuman treatment of British prisoners, particularly during the first part of the war, and while admitting that in some camps the treatment had considerably improved, he was very sceptical about it in others. When war broke out, he was passing through Germany on his way to Russia on business and was arrested as a spy, thrown into a dungeon, tried for his life and, narrowly escaping with it, had long personal experience subsequently of the horrors and discomforts of camp life. The barbarities he witnessed included men being trussed up to trees (he showed photographs of this) and being confined in stables like cattle; in one instance, thousands of men were turned into an open field and left there without anything but the ground to sleep on throughout a stormy night. Soldiers captured in the retreat from Mons had been penned in cattle trucks for four days and nights on the journey without food or water and their gaping wounds had not been attended to. This neglect proved fatal in a number of cases. Were it not for the parcels so generously sent out by the British public, many men would have starved. He himself had received parcels sent out by the Mayoress of Brighton. In conclusion, Mahoney appealed warmly for support of the British Empire Union, whose aim was to fight against German influence – social, financial, industrial and political – and on behalf of the Sussex Volunteer Regiment, in whose second battalion he was now serving in Hove.

Ex-Mayoress, Lady Audrey Otter, had been, and was still, hard at work on her regular consignments to POWs in Germany. She had first opened her War Work Depot just over a week after war had been declared, initially at 14, North Street and later at 82-83, Grand Parade. Between that time and mid-July 1917, over 30,000 articles had been made and dispatched to various hospitals, troops at home and abroad and to the Navy and, up to 13 July, £3,200 had been subscribed. In October, 1914, a contract for making shirts, by poor civilian women of Brighton, had been obtained from the Royal Army Clothing Department. Over 60,000 had been made and passed, and up to 13 July, £2,314 had been paid to the workers. In May 1915, a department for dealing with Brighton men who were prisoners of war was started. Over 4,000 parcels had been sent, and more than £1,400 had been spent. This was now an authorised Association. In January 1917, a depot for waste paper, to be sold for the benefit of local war work was opened at 25, Market Street and all sorts of paper and books were gratefully received there. The 'hospital dressings' branch at 9, Chesham Place had been opened in May 1915 and had been amalgamated with

The 'Kemp Town Depot for Hospital Dressings' at No 9 Chesham Place, Kemp Town, approved, according to the board outside, by the War Office. (Peter Booth Collection)

the Brighton depot in September 1916. Nearly 90,000 articles had been supplied to home and foreign hospitals and £473 had been spent.

On 4 August 1917, the third anniversary of the start of the war, Lady Otter's Forget-Me-Not Day for the War Work Depots and Prisoners of War Fund was celebrated in the town. The fundraising event was blighted by downpours of rain yet the proceeds of the collections and sales of flags and mementoes totalled no less than £400.

Money was raised in other ways, especially collections at entertainments. Lady Otter herself wrote to Brighton Town Council's General Purposes Committee ahead of its meeting on 27 September on behalf of her POW fund and was successful in obtaining a grant in aid of £100. At the meeting, Sir John Otter explained that the prisoners of war supplied from the fund were all Brighton men and a regular supply of parcels containing food was sent to them. After responsibility for the Royal Sussex Regiment's needs was taken over by the Regimental Committee, Brighton's list was reduced to about fifty-five. A list of recipients, members of many different regiments, was published weekly in the *Gazette* and the number averaged thirty-forty. Each was sent six parcels per month.

Prisoners of war and the wounded, although casualties in varying degrees, at least survived. The fallen, through battle, injury or disease, paid the ultimate price. The names and some details of a few of these many victims and their families or association with the town appeared with unfailing regularity in the local press. Exactly where they died was not generally disclosed nor, usually, was the exact date, but research reveals that, as in the case of the wounded arrivals at the station, the figures for 1917 reflect the intensity of fighting at Arras in the spring offensive and – in nearly half of the reports in the *Gazette* – at Ypres and area in the latter part of the year.

Families in which two brothers were lost in 1917 (unless otherwise indicated) included the following:

CHAPPELL, Frederick W. (10 May 1915), George W. (12 October); CLARKE, Alfred E. (14 September 1914), Thomas C. (7 May); JOHNSON, Ethelbert (31 July), Ernest E. (22 September); PETERS, William J. (14 September 1914), Lewis A. (11 October); RICHARDSON, William G. (23 June), Frederick J. (1 October);

1914 1918
LEWES ROAD BOYS SCHOOL BRIGHTON

IN GLORIOUS REMEMBRANCE OF THE
OLD BOYS WHO GAVE THEIR LIVES IN
THE GREAT WAR

THEIR NAME LIVETH FOR EVERMORE

ERECTED TO THE MEMORY OF
HERBERT F. HEDGCOCK
ASSISTANT MASTER 1880-1916
HEAD MASTER 1916-1924
DIED OCTOBER 13th 1924

memorial tablet at Lewes Road Boys' ool lists sixty names, including four dgers, presumed to be brothers. evor Cox Collection)

SPENCER, William (20 September), George (4 October).

Remembrance of the fallen was important to Brighton's townspeople. Among the forms this took were church memorial services; shrines in churches and the streets; and assemblies at schools and elsewhere remembering pupils, comrades and colleagues.

A remarkable local hero was Brighton and Hove Albion goalkeeper Robert W. Whiting (1884-1917), dubbed 'Pom Pom' on account of his powerful kick resembling the force of the rapid-firing naval gun of that name.

Transferred to the Albion in 1908 (previous clubs included West Ham United and Chelsea), he played for them for seven seasons (320 appearances) until the outbreak of war. In December 1914, aged 30, he enlisted as a Private in the 17th (Service) Battalion (1st Football) of the Middlesex Regiment. However, his military career was blighted in 1916 when, to remain with his wife who was pregnant with their third child, he took 133 days of absence without leave when receiving treatment at the SEGH, Brighton for scabies contracted in the trenches. Arrested for desertion, Whiting was sent for trial in December 1916. At his court martial he was demoted to Private and sentenced to nine months' hard labour. Since, however, the rate of losses at the Front were so high, his sentence was suspended and he returned to his unit.

He was killed in action on 28 May 1917 near Arras. His remains were never

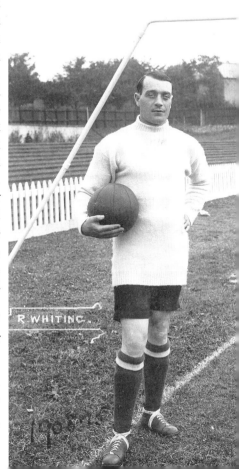

Robert 'Pom Pom' Whiting (1884-1917), who at one stage put family before country but died a gallant death on the battlefield. (Brighton & Hove Albion Collectors' and Historians' Society)

recovered. In Brighton, unfounded local speculation that her husband had been shot for desertion forced Nellie Whiting to have a letter published in the *Evening Argus* from his commanding officer attesting to his courageous end. Another appeared in the *Sussex Daily News* on 3 September 1919 on that paper's own initiative.

On Sunday 11 March, a solemn and impressive memorial service for men of the parish who had given their lives for their country was held in St Peter's Church. Many relatives of the gallant dead attended and were given seats near the chancel. Among the large congregation were a great number of men in khaki. Sixteen heroes were specially commemorated, of whom one had been killed in 1915, twelve in 1916 and three in 1917. Archdeacon Hoskyns conducted the service and read out the names of the fallen. Their sacrifice, he said, would leave an

A tram heads south to the Aquarium. In the background stands the parish church of St Peter. (Author)

indelible mark upon our race and upon the character of generations to come.

At the end of April, a memorial service was held at Preston Parish Church. The Vicar, the Revd A. Garry Copeman, conducted the first part of the service, shortened evensong, after which the Revd J. E. Preece read out a list of forty-three names of those who had given their lives for England. Death, he declared, did not stamp out victory. Death

✠TO THE GLORY OF GOD AND
IN PROUD AND GRATEFUL
MEMORY OF THE MEN OF
THIS PARISH WHO GAVE THEIR
LIVES IN THE GREAT WAR :
1914-1918

NOEL ROWLAND ABBEY	WILLIAM FRANK JAMES
FRANK ADCOCK	WILLIAM THOMAS JUPP
FREDERICK J. ALLEN	WILLIAM STUART KENZIE
GEORGE HENRY ALLEN	BASIL H.BARRINGTON KENNETT
RICHARD FREDK ALLEN	VICT A.BARRINGTON KENNETT
FRANK AUGER	AUBR H.BARRINGTON KENNETT
THOMAS BARNES	WILLIAM KILLICK
RICHARD BARNSDALE	WILLIAM KING
ALFRED GRENVLE BISHOP	REGINALD WILLIAM KING
FREDERICK BOUGHTON	THOMAS LOCK
FREDERICK BRAINES	EWART A. MACKINTOSH
WALTER BRAYBON	HERBERT MARTIN
ALFRED BRISTOW	WM C. KENNEDY MEGAW
PERCY C V. BURROUGH	SIDNEY C. MOPPETT
STANLEY BURSTOW	ALBERT JOHN NOBLE
ROBERT H.BURTENSHAW	HERBERT E.PEMBERTON
JOHN READ CATER	FREDERICK PETTITT
REGINALD B.CHARSLEY	CECIL HERBERT PROCTER
EDWARD COWELL	ALFRED QUINTON
JOHN ANTNY C. CROFT	ALGERNON L. REEKIE
PERCY ROWLEY DAY	ERNEST ROBINSON
HUBERT B DIXON	EDWIN JOHN ROFT
FREDERICK DOWNS	KENNETH C SANDEMAN
JOHN DUNN	WILLIAM BERNARD SHAW
GEORGE GOODWIN	ALBERT SUMMERS
ARTHUR DOWSON GREEN	STUART L. THIRLBY
ALFRED HENRY GRIFFIN	HARRY E. TOOGOOD
CYRIL THOMAS HARDING	LEONARD TOOGOOD
VICTOR CECIL HYDE	RALPH J. WOOD-HIGGS
EDGAR WYATT	

THESE NAMES ARE HERE
RECORDED TO BE HELD IN
HONOUR FOR EVERMORE

The fifty-nine names on this memorial tablet in St Mark's Church, Eastern Road, Kemp Town, photographed on 14 January 2015, include those of a number of brothers and of the poet E. A. Mackintosh. (Author)

led us to victory, and so all the heroes who had died had made a great step to victory.

In mid-September came a dedication service at St Mark's Church, Kemp Town, to commemorate a war shrine, a gift from a bereaved resident in honour of a son and of others who had made the great sacrifice. On the base of the memorial stood the inscription: 'To the dear and honoured memory of William Bernard Shaw, Lieutenant, 9th Royal Sussex Regiment. Vimy Ridge, April 12, 1917. Hubert Bradshaw Dixon, Captain, 1st Sherwood Foresters. Neuve Chapelle, March 12, 1915. And all others who have laid down their lives for their country.' The Vicar, the Revd B.M.C. Browne, read out all the names and solemnly dedicated it to their memory.

Another dedication service, one at which the Bishop of Chichester, Dr Charles Ridgeway, officiated, was held on 4 November at the now lost church of St Anne in Burlington Street. The shrine had been given by the St Anne's branch of the Mothers' Union. Above the crucifix were the words 'The Great Sacrifice' and beneath it the prayer 'Rest eternal grant to them O Lord and let light perpetual shine upon them.' The panel on the left hand side was inscribed 'Blessed are the brave, who died for God, King and Country'; then followed the names, twenty-four in all.

A well-attended valedictory service in memory of the fallen in connection with the Brighton Secondary and Technical Cadet Corps, R.E., took place on the afternoon of Sunday 22 July in the school playing field at Preston. It was attended by the Mayor of Brighton, Alderman Carden JP. Some of the old boys were present in service dress and received a hearty welcome. The climax of the annual assembly came when the roll of honour of masters and seventy-seven boys who had made the supreme sacrifice was submitted by the Officer Commanding, Major W. J. Stainer.

Back in October 1916, a shrine and roll of honour – doubtless one of several unveiled in that year – had been dedicated in Brewer Street, a small street off Lewes Road comprising forty-one houses. Its contribution to the armed forces was reported to have reached a total of no less than forty-five, although the list printed in the *Gazette* contains only forty-four names, thus giving an average of more than one man per house. Two of the men, Charles Hunt and George Woodnutt, had already been killed. The memorial had been provided through the efforts of the ladies connected with St Martin's Church, Lewes Road. In this instance, 'Roll of Honour' denoted men on active service, not war dead, the latter being named below the heading 'R.I.P.' Similar shrines were erected in 1917 in Park Street (February), Elder Row (May), and Crown Gardens, Centurion Road, Upper North Street and Providence Place (August). In the case of both Elder Row and Providence Place, Brewer Street's record of more than one name per house was matched.

Yet the insatiable war machine demanded ever more replacements for the heroic dead. With the loss of Russia as an ally, the defeat of Italy and the shortage of ships to bring American armed forces to Europe, the government needed to step up the process of 'combing out' the protected industrial workforce – actually in breach of pledges given to the trade unions in 1916 – to put more men onto the battlefields or wherever else they were needed. Unsuitability on medical grounds was to be critically re-assessed; the Clerk of Brighton's Tribunal stated in April that he had received notice of the War Office's intention to call up all men medically rejected for re-examination within 30 days of receiving an intimation from the military. In June, he reported receiving a new list of certified occupations, which came into force with immediate effect. In it, the age limit had been raised and therefore a number of men who had hitherto been exempted as being engaged in such occupations would automatically lose their exemption certificates.

*Cartoon captioned 'THE ARMCHAIR CRITIC'S CHANCE. The Call for Volunteers for the Army up to the age of Fifty has given our omniscient critics the chance of doing something in place of finding fault.' (*Brighton and Hove Society*, 17 May 1917)*

They had the right, however, to go before a tribunal on their own behalf.

Reporting on the crisis, the *Gazette* had noted on 7 February:

> *'Now the tide of low categories as "safe" has turned. The Brighton Tribunal met on Monday, and had before them a very formidable list. It contained the names of nearly 60 men. This was the longest list yet presented to the Tribunal for an afternoon sitting in one Court.'*

At the end of the month, the newspaper presented its readers with a grim picture:

> *'From what one gathers from the employers who come before the Brighton Tribunal, it seems that Brighton is getting seriously short of men. Seventy-five per cent of employers are appealing for their last men. Women and girls are taking men's places, it is true, but*

when it comes to the last man in a big office it is not easy to put a woman in his place. Such are the laments of the employers.'

The numerous column inches in the local press recording cases at the Tribunal reveal how the apparently most deserving, and sometimes most pathetic, applications left the Chair and members unmoved; an extension of exemption of three or four months, and more rarely six, was the generally predictable decision reached. Among those granted six months' renewal was a 41-year-old market gardener in February who was doing great work in producing food – so much so that the Chairman congratulated him. He told the Tribunal that he had been working seven days a week ever since he had had the land. All his help was one boy of fifteen. In addition to several acres, he had fifty-one pigs. Other six-month extensions during that month were granted to a rag, metal and general merchant; a barrister; a demonstrator and seller of motor vans; a steam laundry proprietor; a market gardener's foreman; a flour delivery carman and two grocery assistants. A valet, now a munition worker, was allowed six months (conditional). Surprisingly, a solo cornet player in the Municipal Orchestra, 41, was in October allowed the same amount of time.

At the other end of the spectrum, short shrift was given to a 36-year-old watercress wholesaler, whose legal representative had argued that 'watercress was necessary for the troops'; he was allowed six weeks (final), i.e. no further extension would be allowed thereafter. The Tribunal clearly deemed he was not doing work of national importance. A dental surgeon was allowed just fourteen days (final). One man who had not kept his word had his exemption withdrawn, making him immediately eligible for the army: this was an 18-year-old confectioner who had been granted six months on condition that he joined the VTC but he had not done so. Another 18-year-old told the Tribunal he was earning 30 shillings a week as an assistant electrician at a Brighton theatre and apparently had been receiving this amount for some time at another theatre. He gave 25 shillings of his earnings to his parents. The members decided, however, that he must serve his country.

The hearings provide a valuable insight into the prevailing labour situation and social conditions in Brighton. The chief cashier of a large Brighton hotel (allowed three months) stated that over one hundred men from the hotel had enlisted and since his previous appearance an assistant cashier had also enlisted. Workhouse staff totalled fifty-nine before the war, of whom no fewer than forty-nine had joined up. Eight had been exempted by the Tribunal and there was one young man of eighteen who had been rejected. At the water pumping stations, the shortage of staff was acute. The men were working seven days a week, with some of them putting in as much as 105 hours. There was, stated the waterworks engineer appealing for seventeen members of his staff, an enormous waste of water going on in the town – and some of this was due to the gross carelessness of the public. At the Brighton and Hove Gas Company Limited, they were not only producing gas for public utility but were under orders from the government. The Company had released 120 men out of the available 180 of military age. The total number of men employed before the war was 876 but now, including boys and women, the total was 723. At the Black Rock branch, there were 329 men employed before the war – 207 were now in the army. In the case of a corporation tramway motorman, the manager gave particulars of the depleted staff, a relatively larger number having joined the army from the Brighton system than from any other tramway system in the country. He also dealt with the great difficulty of getting drivers. The motorman in question was a conscientious objector, one of only a few to lodge a claim during the year. On 9 March, one, a combed-out railwayman, raised all the old arguments against serving and had to go through the usual cross-examination from Sir John Blaker representing the military:

Sir John Blaker: What you object to in the war is killing? – Yes.
You object to even killing Germans? – I do
You know how the Germans treated the women and children in Belgium ? – Yes.
Well, supposing the Germans landed on Brighton beach, what would you do and what attitude would you take? –I would take no part at all in anything; as a civilian I could not.
Would you protect the women and children? – Yes.
In other words you would fight then? – I would never use force.
I suppose you would trust to argument!

The man had at least expressed his willingness to do work of national importance, so his case was referred to the Pelham Committee, which was the body charged with trying to find suitable occupations for conscientious objectors during the war, for this to be arranged. Just over three weeks later, two young conscientious objectors recently discharged from the railway company because of their objection to military service came before the Brighton Tribunal. They were prepared to undergo imprisonment rather than yield to the military authorities. When examining one of them, Sir John Blaker, exasperated, exclaimed 'We are fighting for the freedom of Europe, while he is doing nothing at all.' The man was utterly uncooperative regarding any form of work and even objected to being referred to the Pelham Committee, as that 'would be making a compromise'. He was referred to it regardless, as was the second man, who for his part had refused even to be medically examined.

Food economy and food production became critically important in 1917. A claim for renewal was put before the Tribunal in June by the employers of a Brighton market gardener. The man was employed 'at a local institution for the education of clergymen's daughters', probably St Mary's Hall, in cultivating a garden which provided vegetables for 180 people. All his time was spent on this in the day and in the evening

St Mary's Hall today. Opened in 1836, it was the oldest girls' school in the United Kingdom before closure in 2009 when it was taken over by Roedean. Many senior girls were transferred to the latter. Its junior section became Roedean's junior school from 2009 until 2011. (Author)

he was stoking furnaces. Three months' further exemption was allowed.

At St. Mary's Hall in Kemp Town, founded in 1836 as a School for the Daughters of the Clergy, the girls did their share of war work, helping refugees and some poor families in St Alban's Parish, off Lewes Road. They also produced knitted items, both for the school's own sales and to send to those in need; about £50 was earned or saved for home and foreign missions and for war funds. Younger pupils knitted some five dozen stretcher pillows and 200 cup covers for the War Depot in Hove. A concert held in the spring term yielded £5, which was sent to the Brighton Home for the Queen's Nurses. The school joined the Brighton and Hove War Savings Association, the School Branch of which numbered forty-nine members. By 1917 it had invested about £90 in small amounts.

At Roedean, not far away, there had been 361 pupils in 1914. In her centenary history of the school published in 1985, 'Miss Butcher' records:

'During the first World War the School continued. It was full and business as usual in lessons, games, examinations was the theme. Such traditional celebrations as the Summer Half Term for O.R.s [Old Roedeanians] were of course abandoned and problems of wartime restrictions and the black-out of the windows facing the sea must have caused some anxious moments. Chapel collections were made for various good causes: five beds could be named Roedean in the British Water Ambulance Hospital at Cherbourg. Wounded men from the Brighton hospitals were entertained, many knitted comforts were despatched to the forces and the carpentry enthusiasts produced invalid requirements in great quantities – bed tables, bed-rests, crutches, walking sticks, splints, fracture boards, massage stools and sundry other equipment. P.L. [Co-Principal Penelope Lawrence] kept the letters she received from her "adopted" prisoner of war [Private Ward of the King's Royal Rifle Corps] among her papers.'

The Water Ambulance Fund, for a hospital barge flotilla established in 1915, received a gift of £100 from the school in June of that year subscribed for the beds.

The sign on the left-hand side of the ambulance reads: 'THE ROEDEANIANS, Presented by the pupils of ROEDEAN SCHOOL, BRIGHTON'. (Roedean School archives)

When 500 motor ambulances were appealed for by the British Red Cross Society, the Old Roedeanians' Association, meeting in October 1914, chose a 16-20 Wolseley fitted with four stretchers, or capable of seating twelve. On 2 November it was delivered and handed over to the Society and on the 7th, just five days later, word was received that it had left for the Front for use by the British Ambulance Contingent. A Captain Tarbutt wrote from the Vosges to say that the car [sic], with 24 others, was doing very good work, much of it in the mountains at night, close to the Front with all lights out. A second ambulance was given to the French in the following year and was reported to be working in Alsace.

From 1915 onwards, the carpentry workshop was very busy, working chiefly for the hospitals; the School sent large numbers of wooden items, as mentioned by Miss Butcher, for wounded soldiers. Their work was greatly valued. Chief Scout Sir Robert Baden-Powell, visiting in the summer of 1915, remarked that he 'had no idea that schoolgirls could show such skill'. In her history of the school, Dorothy de Zouche gives detailed figures of what the pupils produced and noted:

'Most of it went to the 2nd Eastern Hospital in Dyke Road, but a special appeal was received – and answered – for the hospital

opened in Brighton early in 1917 for paralysed and nerve-affected soldiers [the Lady George Nevill Hospital, actually in Hove]. A dozen collecting-boxes were made for the Chichester Hospital for Women. The French Red Cross too received bed-rests, splints and other things in the summer of 1917.'

Another important girls' school, located centrally in Montpelier Road, Brighton, also did its bit for the war effort. Brighton and Hove High School, founded with just some 30 pupils in 1876, was affiliated to the War Savings Association and, since 1914, the Girls' Patriotic Union of Secondary Schools, of which Princess Mary was Patroness. It sent frequent parcels to 'its' torpedo boat and to a division of the RFA at the Front. Subscriptions were sent to the Belgian Relief Fund, the Red Cross and the French Red Cross, and weekly parcels were regularly dispatched for soldiers and sailors. The number of garments made and brought by the girls for distribution in 1916 exceeded that in any previous year. Every form joined in – even the kindergarten. The girls knitted squares to be made into rugs for the wounded, and the third

Roedean's pupils showed remarkable skills in carpentry. (Roedean School archives)

square finished and brought in was done by a boy of six. As at other local schools, there was much pressure on places.

Brighton College was relatively unaffected by the war. In his 1995 history of the school, Martin D.W. Jones writes that 'In essence, the story of Brighton College and the First World War is one of "business as usual". The war barely disrupted school routine.' The Officers' Training Corps stood ready to man trenches dug locally by the boys against possible invasion. More digging followed in 1917, this time on 3.5 acres rented by the College for the purpose of growing potatoes and other vegetables. This 'allotment' was extended by an acre within a year.

In 1914, four masters joined up, as did the head porter, and they were followed by four more in 1915. The December 1914 issue of the Magazine printed a list of 349 Old Boys known to be in the forces. By the end of the war, some 976 were recorded as having served in

Brighton College schoolhouse. Nearly 1,000 Old Boys served during the War, of whom 146 made the supreme sacrifice. (Author)

British, imperial or allied forces, three-quarters of them in the army. Many who enlisted were decorated, with thirty DSOs, two DFCs, two DSCs and fifty-two MCs being awarded. Of those who fought on land, roughly one in seven was killed. The names of all the fallen from the college, totalling 146, were published in 1920 in *The Brighton College War Record*. Three brothers named Belcher lost their lives, one of them, Gordon, both pupil and master, in 1915. The names of all three may be seen on a stained glass window in the chapel. Two poets were among the casualties: Second Lieutenant Francis St Vincent Morris (Chichester House 1910-14) and Lieutenant Ewart Alan Mackintosh (Hampden House 1905-9). Morris had transferred from the Sherwood Foresters to the RFC and died in France on 29 April 1917 from injuries sustained some weeks earlier when his plane crashed during a blizzard at Vimy Ridge. His poems were published in that year, as was Mackintosh's *A Highland Regiment*. Like Morris, Mackintosh, of the Seaforth Highlanders, met his death in France in 1917, being killed in action on 21 November. In one of his poems, he achingly recalls a childhood memory from Scotland when he sat on a stone in a glen, his leg dangling in a stream:

Well, the glen is empty now,
And far am I from them that love me,
Water to my knees below,
Shrapnel in the clouds above me;
Watching till I sometimes see,
Instead of death and fighting men,
The people that were kind to me.
And summer in the little glen.
(from Anns An Gleann 'san Robh Mi Og
[My Bonnie Native Glen])

Mackintosh had been born in Brighton (his parents lived at 16, Sussex Square), although his father's roots were in Alness in Ross and Cromarty. He had learned Gaelic and considered himself Scottish first and British second. A second volume of his verse, *War, The Liberator, and Other Pieces*, was published in 1918.

The extension to the chapel, designed by Sir Thomas Jackson and completed in 1923, stands as the College's War Memorial. In it, the names of the dead are carved into the north-west wall.

Not far from the College stands Queen's Park, purchased in 1825 by wealthy solicitor, Thomas Attree, dubbed the 'King of Brighton'. His grand

Poet and former Brighton College pupil, Ewart A. Mackintosh (1893-1917) was killed in action in France.

The chapel was built as the College's war memorial.

villa nearby, completed in 1830 to the design of Sir Charles Barry, was opened as a College in 1909 by the Xaverians, a Roman Catholic religious order. Speaking at a garden fete and sale of work held in the grounds on 30 May 1917 in aid of the Brighton branch of the Catholic Women's League, Brother Cyril, referring to the Cadet Company, said that although the College was hardly eight years old, 'a great many of its students had joined the forces, and many had made the supreme sacrifice'. Speaking forcefully about the current issues besetting the nation, Father Bernard Vaughan, the Principal, said he was glad to see the Cadet lads there, 'although looking, of course, somewhat pulled down for the want of proper rations.'

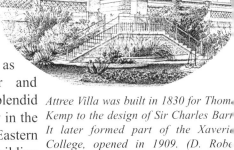

A great sacrifice made by Brighton's Grammar School, founded in July 1859 at Lancaster House, 47, Grand Parade, as the Brighton Proprietary Grammar and Commercial School, was giving up its splendid new premises on Dyke Road very early in the war for their conversion to the Second Eastern General Hospital and returning to the building it had vacated in Buckingham Road.

Attree Villa was built in 1830 for Thoma Kemp to the design of Sir Charles Barr It later formed part of the Xaveri College, opened in 1909. (D. Robe Elleray)

It was reported in 1917 that a list had been prepared and published of over 800 boys who were serving in His Majesty's forces. Over seventy had laid down their lives for their country. A War Savings Association had been started and had over 150 members, the sum collected up to the time of writing totalling just over £938, of which £724 had been paid in by the boys on their own behalf. Allotments had been marked out and cultivated, with over one hundred boys helping.

The figure of over seventy former pupils of the Grammar School who had died for their

WAR LIST

DECEMBER, 1915,

The Roll of Honour in the Grammar School's War List, compiled to November 1915, comprises 14 names. (Author)

country was matched, in 1917, by the sacrifice made by Old Boys (and three staff members) of the Municipal Secondary School for Boys in York Place. At a Cadet drumhead service held on Sunday 22 July in memory of the casualties, the Headmaster, Major W.J. Stainer, stated that the total was seventy-three. The school playing field furnished a large number of gardens during the year, fifty-six boys each having a plot measuring thirty-six yards, and many masters and mistresses had gardens averaging two acres each, while thirty gardens of two acres or slightly larger had been lent to residents living near the field.

All the schools were thus very much aware of the national food crisis Britain faced. To survive, the nation had to produce more and eat less. In February 1917, Rowland Prothero, President of the Board of Agriculture, addressed an appeal to headmasters, headmistresses and teachers in elementary schools throughout the country for help in the general scheme of increased food production. He pointed out that there were about 3,200 school gardens and asked the teachers to make each one 'every foot of it – a prize kitchen garden'. The actual addition which each individual child or separate school could make to the national food supply might well be small but 'added together it may come to something substantial'. He was convinced that every child would be proud to think he or she was doing national work.

For its part, the people of Brighton rose to meet the challenge. In a letter to the *Gazette* written in the spring, Mayor Herbert Carden gave instances of this:

> 'Sir,—A few weeks ago Mr. E. Moreau, of Withdean, very kindly offered me five acres of land in Surrenden-road, rent free, for the purpose of allotments, and also sent me a cheque for £10 towards the cost of seed. I am very pleased to say we let the whole of this land to 75 allotment-holders, and it has been a remarkable sight for the last two week-ends to witness the very large number of men, women and children at work on this ground.
>
> 'I have to-day had a similar generous offer made to me by Mr. S.C. Witting, of Hollingbury Copse, who has offered me five acres of very good land in Ditchling-road, adjoining his house, rent free, and has sent me a cheque for £10 towards the cost of seed.
>
> 'We have obtained from the Curwen Estate three acres of land at

Varndean Farm, between Surrenden-road and Ditchling-road. This is very good arable land, and should produce good crops.

'The Corporation also have some other land available, on the Race Hill and at the top of Bear-road, and applications for any of the land should be made at once to the Superintendent of Parks, Lodge Gates, Preston Park, Brighton.

'Yours, &c, H. Carden, Mayor.
Town Hall, Brighton, 15th March.'

Just three days earlier, he had reported:

'We have let some hundreds of allotments during the last few weeks, and I am anxious to let a great many more. I am hoping to get about eight acres of land at the top of Balfour-road, and I am going to ask the Corporation to allow the Level and a portion of Preston Park to be dug up. There are also some very good plots still available on the Race Hill and at the top of Bear-road. I invite immediate applications for these plots to the Superintendent of Parks and Gardens, Preston Park, Brighton. The Corporation have power to take over any land occupied or unoccupied and if anyone can suggest suitable plots for allotments, I shall be glad to hear from them. There is going to be a great shortage of food throughout the world, and it is the duty of everyone to take an allotment if he can possibly spare the time.'

A couple of months previously, the Town Council reviewed local land use or, more strictly, non-use, in the light of the emergency. Before its meeting on 25 January, the Town Clerk had presented to the Parks and Gardens Committee a Report on the principal provisions of the Cultivation of Lands Order, 1916, made by the Board of Agriculture and Fisheries under DORA Regulations towards utilising unused ground to increase the supply of food. On 29 December 1916, allotment holders and representatives of certain allotment and horticultural societies had attended a meeting convened by the Mayor at which the question of the steps to be taken with a view to increasing food production in the borough area was discussed. There were plots of vacant land in Cornwall Gardens, on both sides; Preston Park Avenue; Arundel Road; and at the back of Exeter Street, and notice of intention to enter upon the land referred to under the powers of the Order had been served on the respective owners.

One new land tenant at this time was the Revd F.J. Gould, who set up a Food Producing Guild in connection with Lewes Road Congregational Church. He took up from the Corporation two and a half acres located behind the Sanatorium at the top of Bear Road. He launched the venture on 18 March 1917 by cutting the first turf in the presence of some seventy or eighty members of the congregation. The main produce grown would be potatoes and other vegetables. The ground, divided into forty-five separate allotments, had been taken by the members in lots of about ten rods [a rod measures roughly a quarter

The Sanatorium (renamed Bevendean Hospital in 1948) was originally used to treat patients with contagious diseases. Opened in 1898, it closed in 1989. The site is now occupied by housing (Fitzherbert Drive) and the headquarters of the Sussex Beacon charity. (Peter Booth collection)

of an acre], though some had less. Negotiations were ongoing for more land.

The *Gazette* remarked in March that 'allotment fever' in Brighton and Hove had attained the proportions of a respectable epidemic and that it should produce wonderful results. Certainly demand for plots was outstripping the supply. At a Council meeting on 22 March,

Councillor Southall reported that the Parks and Gardens Committee had about 37 acres of land for allotments in 478 plots, of which about 347 had been let. They had also let about 50 acres to Sidney Hole, who had built up a large milk distribution business in Brighton and ran farms in and around Brighton and Lewes. Alderman Griffith believed every bit of convenient land which had been offered for allotment had been taken up, although some of the more outlying land had not. He moved that the Committee be instructed to place portions of Queen's Park and Preston Park at the disposal of those wishing to cultivate allotments, and that they continue to deal similarly with these and other enclosures if they found demand continuing.

For the nation to survive, increasing food production was not enough. Consumption had to be reduced, and this meant economy and moderation, initially voluntary but later controlled. For now, rationing was on the horizon. An urgent government appeal by Lord Devonport, Britain's first Food Controller, appointed in December 1916, appeared in newspapers in early February 1917. He wanted to avoid compulsory rationing but there was a very urgent need to economise. Bread, meat and sugar, which he described as 'the three most important staples of daily consumption', were focused on. People were asked to restrict their eating to no more than 4lb of bread, or 3lb of flour used to make bread, 2½lb of meat (including bacon and sausages) and 12oz of sugar a week. There was no shortage, people were told, of fish or eggs.

To reduce the consumption of bread, a 'war loaf' was imposed on a reluctant nation. However, it was perhaps not so bad, since the *Gazette* remarked on 6 January 1917:

> *'Well, the war loaf has come. There is so little difference between it and the old style that positively hundreds of households had been eating it with relish for some days without knowing it! Really, one feels that the sensation mongers ought to be compelled to offer reparation for unnecessarily alarming timid people.'*

Bakers were forbidden to sell bread until it was twelve hours old; no stale bread could be exchanged; only 'regulation' flour could be

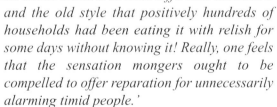

THE NEW LOAF. Mr Lloyd George:
"LUCKY RHONDDA! BUT I TAUGHT HIM THOSE NUMBERS" (The subsidised quartern loaf was made from flour at a standardised price and was thus affordable by the poor). (Punch, 11 July 1917)

used, with millers preparing flour from such grains as the authorities provided, and under their control. Even the shape of loaves was controlled, and all fancy pastries were forbidden. No sugar could be used in the making of bread, and currant bread, sultana bread and milk bread could not be sold. Cakes and pastries could not be covered or coated in sugar or chocolate.

Voluntary abstention from meat was introduced in the spring. At a meeting of the Brighton Hotels Association on 28 February, it was unanimously resolved to observe a meatless day once a week in all the hotels associated with the organisation, and Friday was selected as the most convenient day. The arrangement commenced on 9 March. Menus would thenceforth consist mostly of soup, fish, omelettes, with dressed vegetables, and salads in season. The idea met with ready support from guests and in the wider community. By early May, however, the *Gazette* noted that 'it is now admitted that the meatless day experiment, though successful in one way, really precipitated the evil of the greater consumption of bread.'

In 1917 and beyond, the humble tuber was king. Following the poor harvest in 1916, the paper reported in January that 'sugar scrambles in Brighton have given place to potato hunting.' On the nearly 1,000 plots being brought under cultivation, potatoes were the principal crop grown. Some of the excellent results achieved were displayed towards the end of the year at an exhibition at the Aquarium organised by the Brighton, Hove, and Sussex Horticultural Society. Unused land all over the town was made to yield its bounty.

*'The Links being devoted to Allotments, Mr. and Mrs. Bunker-Browne practise approach shots, with the idea of filling their basket with potatoes at the same time.' (*Punch, 11 July 1917)*

Measures to reduce consumption that spring included the introduction of potato-less days. The supply situation would ease before long, however, so that over the last weekend in June it was reported that new potatoes could be obtained at comparatively moderate prices. The 1917 harvest was the best ever, with a considerably increased output also of other root crops and cereals. In September there were even references in the local press to a glut.

Sugar became a commodity of great concern to the general public in 1917. The members of the Brighton and Hove Grocers' Association were told at their January meeting that the Royal Sugar Commission had decided that for that month the amount allocated to distributors was to be half of the monthly average of 1915. In February the supply would be based on the actual percentage supplied in January and for each succeeding month it was to be as nearly as possible based on the amount supplied in the preceding month. Housekeepers, therefore, had to realise that if they could not obtain their usual quantities, it was not the grocer who was to blame but the Royal Commission's decision to cut down supplies to one half of the amount available in 1915. By March, the public was having great difficulty in obtaining even small quantities. On 23 March, Mr G.C. Anderson of Ship Street raised an interesting point in a letter to the *Gazette*:

'In view of the sugar restrictions it will be interesting to know what we are to do with the rhubarb, gooseberry and other such crops which will be arriving in due course. For instance, I have just had a quantity of rhubarb sent me, but, being unable to obtain sugar to cook the same, have been compelled to waste valuable food.'

Advice would be forthcoming at the end of April, when Mrs. C.S. Peel, Director of Women's Service, Ministry of Food, addressed a crowded audience in Hove Town Hall on the subject of food economy. She recommended that rhubarb leaves be used as a substitute for spinach. Yet in May, press reports appeared of a hidden danger. There were deaths in Middlesex (and doubtless elsewhere) due to oxalic acid poisoning attributable to cooking rhubarb leaves, although the use of the

THE NATION'S FOOD

BRIGHTON WAR SAVINGS COMMITTEE.

A

PUBLIC MEETING

WILL BE HELD IN THE

BRIGHTON AQUARIUM

ON

WEDNESDAY, 25TH APRIL

At 8 p.m.

CHAIRMAN:

THE MAYOR OF BRIGHTON.

SPEAKER:

MRS. C. S. PEEL

(Director of Women's Service, Ministry of Food).

Admission FREE. Questions.

N.B. Mrs. PEEL will also Speak at the HOVE TOWN HALL at 3 p.m. on the same day.

Mrs Peel's talks on food preparation and consumption attracted large audiences in Brighton and Hove in late April 1917. (Royal Pavilion & Museums, Brighton & Hove)

stalks as fruit was safe. The Mayor of Hove was in communication with Mrs Peel on the matter.

Mrs Peel spoke at Brighton's Aquarium that same evening. Her lecture was preceded by an address by Mayor Carden, who forcefully reminded his audience that the food problem was the most important question before the country at the present time. Were we going to sit down and allow the Germans to starve us? They were making very determined attempts to do so. They were sinking something like 500,000 tons of our shipping every month. Mrs Peel, who was enthusiastically received, remarked that it was no exaggeration to state that upon the question of the food supply of the nation depended the winning or the losing of the war. She also dealt with the subject of sugar, claiming, strangely, that the more sweets big boys and girls ate, the less likely they were to crave alcohol, and of public kitchens, which she said they might well consider in a place like Brighton. This the town actually did in 1918.

This well-known poster featuring a critical message was published by the Food Controller under the auspices of the Ministry of Food (1916-21). (UBC Library)

Another important lecture on food economy was held at the same venue in late October at which Sir Arthur Yapp, Director-General of Food Economy, addressed a huge audience. He warned his hearers that the U-boat menace, although diminished, was still serious. He therefore urged every man and woman present to practise the economy in food for which the government was appealing and to avoid waste in any form. 'If we can save one slice of bread each a day or do with one ounce of meat less it may make all the difference between victory and defeat', he said. There was at least a fine crop of potatoes, but none to waste, and the greatest care should be exercised in storing them. His appeal was firmly supported by the mayors of the twin towns in their own speeches.

Rationing, like it or not, was inevitable but would not be introduced until 1918. Food production and distribution, meanwhile, continued to be subject to strict and multiple controls, while consumption was shaped by constant exhortations to moderation, calls for economy and the avoidance of waste. These were observed, on the whole, by the local population with good-humoured cooperation and adaptability.

In a letter to the *Sussex Daily News*, the Vicar of St Nicolas, Portslade, the Revd Vicars Armstrong Boyle, expressed the view that

HOW TO LOSE THE WAR AT HOME.

*A trenchant comment from Britain's favourite humorous magazine (*Punch*, 31 October 1917)*

we had had it too good for too long. We had been 'petted and pampered in the past with cheap "luxuries" and the sweetness of gratifying every impulsive whim and fancy.'

Mayor Carden, at a public meeting on 10 December of the War Savings Association connected with Lewes Road Congregational Church, deplored the rate of expenditure that was going on throughout the country. He alluded to the scenes he had recently witnessed in Oxford Street, London, where shops were 'packed to the doors with people spending their money on useless objects', and said the same thing was happening in Brighton. A leading tradesman in the town, who sold luxury articles, had told him he had never known such times and that he was 'almost ashamed to see people entering his shop'. The Mayor appealed for moderation in spending and food consumption and also for economy in paper, mentioning that he even saved his tram and bus tickets.

Shortly before Christmas, Lord Rhondda made an Order giving Local Food Control Committees the power to control supplies of margarine within the areas for which they were responsible and to make arrangements for the fair distribution of that product among the various provision shops of the district. If necessary, they could take it from any shop whose supplies they regarded as excessive and distribute it to others. Every retailer of margarine was obliged to be registered with the Local Food Office for his district. By the end of the year, margarine was on sale in Brighton in forty-eight shops in conveniently chosen distributing centres in various parts of the town, instead of at only about five as previously. The news soon spread, and there was a brisk demand at all the shops, but nothing like the long and tedious waits in a queue, often only to end in disappointment when the counter was reached, that had previously been the experience of many shoppers. The situation would change again in early 1918, however.

In November, it was reported that another Brighton food casualty had been added to the list; no Christmas pudding for the town's paupers. This disheartening prospect was aggravated by the assurance of mince pies for the officials. With eggs costing five shillings a dozen, Brighton's households faced the same daunting no-pudding prospect but would no doubt adapt. The *Gazette* commented: 'They tried to shock us on Good Friday by proscribing hot cross buns; still the buns survived in another form, and the Christmas pudding may still appear, even though slightly changed in the making.' Sure enough, the puddings materialised.

Advertisements appeared in Brighton as usual on behalf of various outlets, such as Hanningtons, Lyon & Hall, the Irish Linen Shop, Tom Smith (for Xmas crackers!) and R. Potts and Co. of North Street and Western Road, which stocked records and gramophones. At number 201 in that road, Messrs Smithers had as good a selection of Christmas beverages as was possible. Also in Western Road stood Messrs Diplock's, purveyors of exquisite china and glass. For jewellery, one could go to Terry's, a long-established shop at 2 and 3, Gardner Street. As far as Christmas fare was concerned, the roast beef of old England was on sale at Messrs Sands and Co. of 19 and 20, Kensington Gardens, while the Christmas turkey could be obtained at S. Porter's, with branches at 21, Prince Albert Street and 10, Preston Street. Prices across the town seemed to be no object: turkeys at half-a-crown a pound were snapped up quite joyfully and it was reported that one woman in moderate circumstances unhesitatingly paid 17/6 for a leg of pork.

Busy pre-Christmas preparations were in hand at the hotels, with every effort being made at the Grand, for example, for the day to pass pleasantly, in spite of the sadness of war. On Boxing Day, a dance was held for adults in the ballroom. Although the annual children's party did not take place during the afternoon, they were entertained to a conjuring performance in the lounge. The Royal York Hotel, under the genial Harry Preston, held its annual sale of dolls on the day, raising a total of £250 for the RSCH and the Royal Alexandra Hospital for Children.

With the brilliant weather, visitors came in droves:

'... *the gathering of people in the town was almost without precedent. Both on*

*The World's Stores had three branches in Brighton, one in Hove and one in Portslade (*Brighton and Hove Society, 6 December 1917)

Christmas and Boxing Day the front was literally alive with promenaders up to the lunch hour, and celebrities and well-known local folk were numerous.' (Gazette, 2 January 1918)

Just as the third summer season in the war had brought record crowds to the town, so the fourth Christmas witnessed a massive influx of all classes. The strollers in the sunshine brought to mind the crowds on the sea front in the middle of the August holiday:

'It was certainly a most extraordinary display. A great concentration had been expected, because the town had been inordinately full for several months, and it was certain that many distant acquaintances would be invited, to make up pleasant house parties for the holiday; but apart from these elements there was a large influx of casual visitors. It is satisfactory to know that this happy consummation was possible notwithstanding many difficulties. It was another proof of the esteem in which Brighton is held – an appreciation which each successive period of the war seems to enhance, so that the town is building a super structure of popularity.' (Gazette, ibid)

In the old days, commented the paper, the huge gatherings were easily understood. Liberal railway facilities, the wonderful organisation of excursion traffic – which sometimes transported 10,000 people in a few hours – plus the development of motor traffic by road, made the arrangement workable and easy. But none of these conveniences existed during 1917 and still the crowds in Brighton grew to a record level. As for food supplies, this multitude was sufficiently provided for by various trade organisations and there were no reports of any serious shortage. Looking back over the year, one editorial saw it as a milestone:

'There is certainly no reason why inhabitants of Brighton should be downhearted. The year now closed has been perhaps the most remarkable in the history of the town for one hundred years. Conditions that produced that prosperity appear to be likely to continue. The demand for residences at Brighton is as brisk as at any period during the past twelve months. The inflated population may conduce to difficulties in the distribution of supplies, but so long as the congestion lasts it means a big addition to the potential wealth of the borough. ... From the purely local point of view, the

inhabitants may well be prepared to face the new year with a feeling of optimism. War influences are inevitable in many departments of life, but the situation is immensely relieved for residents by the evidence of prosperity and the sense of peace and security.' (Gazette, 2 January 1918).

Dense crowds on the lower and upper promenade absorbed in watching a show or musical performance. A Brighton View Company postcard. (Author)

With this year of phenomenal prosperity, the unexpected had continued to happen:

'Who would have imagined when the shock of the war first fell upon the world that in the third year of the struggle, Brighton, essentially a pleasure town, would have been fuller than ever? Fate has been very kind. The position of the town has so far enabled it to escape the terrors that have afflicted places not many miles away. It has basked in an atmosphere of comparative peace and security. Of course that is the real explanation of the remarkable influx of people.' (Gazette, 29 December 1917)

In that same issue, the comment was made that 'the longer the war lasts the greater Brighton seems to be in favour.' As on previous holiday occasions during the year, visitors were not deterred by the inevitable restrictions on traffic, planning their trip 'in the firm determination to carry it through by hook or crook.'

A sobering note, however, was struck in the *Brighton and Hove Society* on 20 December. The magazine stated there were few signs at home or abroad of festivity this yuletide.

> *'How could there be with so many of our people mourning the loss of brave husbands, fathers, sons, lovers and kinsmen? ... Day after day the newspapers publish their tragic lists of those who have fallen in this gigantic struggle of Right against Might, and every name means the breaking of some heart at home. Day after day, our nation is being impoverished by the loss of some of the most splendid of its manhood, and the more we consider the circumstances of the times the less sign we see of any recovery from these dreadful losses. ... And when we look around at some of those who remain – the slackers, the shirkers, the Conscientious Objectors, the grossly selfish – the tragedy of those who are left seems almost as great as that of those who are gone.'*

Patriotism, it claimed, was where the strength of Germany lay. That nation was enduring far worse things than England had hitherto had to put up with and was doing so with a Spartan courage which it is 'impossible not to admire and infamous not to emulate'. All readers were urged to do so over that Christmas and in the fast-approaching New Year.

When Christmas Day did arrive it was, therefore, celebrated with mingled emotions but everyone made a brave effort to live up to the spirit of the occasion. No end to the war was yet in sight at this, its fourth Christmas. The festival was not, of course, just about food. More than one poem celebrating Christ's birth was published in the local papers and the churches across the town held their traditional worship and carol services. At Norfolk Road Wesleyan Church, the Revd. E.A. Spear, after heartily welcoming the servicemen present, begged them to remember their comrades still 'out there' in prayer. He then asked the congregation a profound question: 'Do we really realise that the brave men at the Front are enabling us to sing our Christmas songs of praise?' It was then, with the fine organ simulating church bells and the choir singing 'Peace on earth, goodwill towards men', that the realisation dawned on all those present.

In its last issue of the year, the *Gazette* noted that the dying days of 1917 were a time for review and introspection, a time for the people to take their bearings for the pilgrimage ahead. On the threshold of each previous new year of war, there had been a fervent prayer that it might be the last. If that prayer was going to be made now, there was one condition; everyone should make a new year's resolution to do his or her utmost to contribute towards bringing the war to an end and securing victory and peace.

*'Father Christmas wears unusual clothes this year, but he does not forget the Boys at the Front'. (*Brighton and Hove Society, *20 December 1917)*

CHAPTER FIVE

1918 – Holding Fast

The year began with prayers and commemoration across the twin towns. Sunday, 6 January was designated Intercession Sunday, or the National Day of Prayer – not by the Church but by the State. In the proclamation to his people, the King called on them to devote a special day to prayer 'that we may have the clear-sightedness and strength necessary to the victory of our cause.' Offertory collections were to be given to the Red Cross.

At St Peter's in Brighton, the vast congregation included civic leaders and representatives of other denominations. The Vicar, Canon Dormer Pierce, read out the proclamation, in which it was declared, 'We have yet to complete the great task to which more than three years ago, we dedicated ourselves … and in a spirit of reverent obedience ask the blessing of Almighty God upon our endeavours.' He added 'Let us remember also in our prayers the Mayor, Aldermen, Councillors and the rulers of this borough' and 'our own town, that it may continue to take a high place as an example to others in endurance and sacrifice', adding 'We remember in our prayers the people of Belgium, and the children of that country' and also included the disabled among the wounded and sick. One of the responses from the congregation

Lewes Road Congregational Church, on the west side of Lewes Road, dated from 1868. It is seen here as the United Reformed Church in 1975. It has been partially demolished, with the facade retained. (Royal Pavilion &Museums, Brighton & Hove)

related to all those who had laid down their lives for their country.

During the following week, Lewes Road Congregational Church celebrated its jubilee, the first services there having been held in a small building seating 200 on 5 January 1868. A public meeting in connection with the occasion was held in the building, with the Mayors of Brighton and Hove among the speakers. At the crowded special services on Sunday the 6th, attention focused on the landmark date as well as on national prayer and thanksgiving.

The Treasurer of the church's Jubilee Debt Extinction Fund was John W. Beal of 55, East Street, at which address he ran a long-established stationery business. On 22 March, he would suffer the loss of his 35-year-old son, Ernest Frederick, in battle. Yet his grief must have been tinged with tremendous pride when the temporary Second Lieutenant, who had worked in the family business following his

Oil on paper portrait of Second Lieutenant Ernest F. Beal VC painted (possibly over a photograph) in 1919. (Royal Pavilion &Museums, Brighton & Hove)

education at Brighton Grammar School, was posthumously awarded the Victoria Cross.

Towards the end of June came the first civic recognition of the young man's heroism, when the Town Council's General Purposes Committee passed a resolution recording 'their great admiration of the heroic conduct of their fellow townsman Ernest Frederick Beal, and their satisfaction that it has been recognized by the award of the Victoria Cross.'

Four months later, on Wednesday 23 October, striking tributes were paid to the courageous officer at the Lewes Road church where, in the presence of a large congregation, the Mayor of Hove, as Boys Brigade President, unveiled a large portrait of him surmounted by a replica VC. Below it were Beal's full name and regiment and the following citation:

'For most conspicuous bravery and determined leading. A gap existed between his Company and the neighbouring unit. This gap

was strongly held by the enemy, and it was of vital importance that the gap should be closed. Second Lieutenant Beal organized a small party of less than a dozen men, and with revolver in hand led them against the enemy. Proceeding up the trench, he encountered the machine guns one after another, overwhelmed the gunners and captured four guns. Later in the evening, regardless of danger, he walked up close to an enemy machine gun and brought in a wounded man on his back. Second Lieutenant Beal was killed by a shell on the following morning.'

For a considerable period before the war, young Beal had been a keen, able and enthusiastic officer in the 13th (Lewes Road Congregational Church) Company, Brighton and Hove Battalion Boys' Brigade, and had done a great deal to establish it and to maintain its leading place in the Battalion.

Further civic recognition followed in late November at a ceremony held at Brighton Town Hall, where Lieutenant Beal's parents were presented with the resolution, on vellum, of congratulation and sympathy adopted by the Council at the June meeting.

In late June 1918, the local press reported the award of a second VC for Brighton. The recipient, also a Second Lieutenant, was John James Crowe of the Worcestershire Regiment. Although born in Devonport, his home was in Brighton, at Dudley House, Dudley Road, to which address he and his family had moved in 1916.

Crowe's award was announced in the *London Gazette* of 28 June. The citation read as follows:

'For most conspicuous bravery, determination, and skilful leading when the enemy, for the third time having attacked a post in a village, broke past on to the high ground and established a machine gun and snipers in the broken ground at the back of the village. 2nd Lt. Crowe twice went forward with two N.C.O.'s and seven men to engage the enemy, both times in face of active machine-gun fire and sniping. His action was so daring that on each occasion the enemy withdrew from the high ground into the village,

Captain John James Crowe (1876-1975), acknowledged as Brighton's second VC holder when his award was conferred in 1918.

where 2nd Lt. Crowe followed them and himself opened fire upon the enemy as they collected in the doorways of the houses.

'On the second occasion, taking with him only two men of his party, he attacked two enemy machine guns which were sweeping the post, killed both the gunners with his rifle, and prevented any others from reaching the guns and bringing them into action again. He then turned upon a party of the enemy who were lined up in front of him, killed several, and the remainder withdrew at once. He captured both the guns, one of which was the battalion Lewis gun which had been captured by the enemy on the previous day. ... The valour and zeal displayed by 2nd Lt. Crowe were of the highest order.'

On the outbreak of the First World War, father-of-four Crowe was Regimental Quartermaster Sergeant. He landed in France with his battalion on 15 August 1914. Throughout the conflict he was frequently in the thick of the fighting and although twice blown up and once buried, he lived to go home at the end of the war.

On 14 April 1918, just two weeks after being appointed Adjutant, he was awarded his great distinction. On 26 May (*London Gazette* date) he was given the rank of Acting Captain. Three days after the Armistice he was promoted to Captain.

In its issue of 3 July 1918, Brighton's *Gazette* reported, 'Another VC has been brought to Brighton' while the next day the *Brighton and Hove Society* magazine proudly announced that this was 'the second Victoria Cross awarded to a Brighton soldier.' After the war, he worked

locally in education, moving with his family to Woodingdean in 1931. He died in 1965 at the age of 88. Crowe had not only brought a VC to the town but had further helped the war effort by purchasing, with his wife, 200 war savings certificates. In War Weapons Week (8-13 July), he had donated £100 to that cause.

During that Week, Brighton was asked to raise £250,000, in return for which it

Scottish music hall and vaudeville theatre singer and comedian, Henry 'Harry' Lauder (1870-1950), raised vast amounts of money for the war effort, for which he was knighted in 1919. (James Marturano collection, the Harry Lauder Online Museum)

would have the honour of sending a tank named after it to the Front. The target was easily reached. Hove, asked to make a similar effort, ultimately achieved a figure of £289,621.

On Monday 8 July, the first day of 'the Week', the star turn at the Hippodrome was the famous Scottish comedian and singer, Harry Lauder. After his act, he made a fervent appeal for public support for the local 'Tank' collection being made and also for the following Saturday's great matinee at the theatre on behalf of our limbless heroes. The response from the audience was overwhelming. In a written appeal, Mayor Carden pointed out that 'we are not asked to give, but only to lend our money, and at a very satisfactory rate of interest.'

After many refusals, Brighton, jointly with Hove, had a visit from a tank. For the last three days of War Weapons Week it was stationed on the Esplanade at the King Edward Memorial, astride the boundary line of the two towns. Named *Egbert*, it was one of six machines touring nationally, the others being named *Julian, Old Bill, Nelson, Drake* and *Iron Ration*.

Residents and visitors alike were enthralled by the manoeuvres performed by Egbert the tank on Brunswick Lawns. (Judy Middleton collection)

The bystanders are more interested in the photographer than the tank Brighton*, here pictured in Preston Park on presentation day, 12 January 1920. (Tony McKendrick collection)*

The *Gazette* commented that the local population and visitors, many of whom had arrived from the metropolis in packed trains, could now understand that

> *'... there is a direct connection between banks and tanks. ... That curious monstrosity on the sea front spoke to the people as no platform orator can ever expect to plead. Without uttering a sound, in its veritable dumb ugliness it breathed a message: "...rush to your bank and help ... to bear the name of Brighton or Hove into the battle line!"'*

On the afternoon of Saturday the 13th, *Egbert*, to the wonder of thousands – and especially Mrs Toyne and Mrs Harm who made the trip inside it – twice lumbered to the western end of Brunswick Lawns and back to the eastern end, on each occasion effortlessly surmounting piles of pre-stacked sandbags. It gave a repeat demonstration in the evening. The tank made an ideal and unusual platform for various dignitaries. There Alderman Colbourne presented Mayor Carden with a cheque for £50,000 from the Corporation – which had already invested over £350,000 – for investment in War Bonds. Further massive input into Brighton's collection came from the Oddfellows, representing the Manchester Unity, whose investment of £100,000 made such a difference to the town's total.

War Weapons Week was a brilliant fundraising success for the twin towns. Brighton raised no less than £407,020 and Hove, as mentioned, £289,621. Tanks therefore went into action representing both places. After the war, each town received one as a war relic. Hove's was christened *Hova* on 23 September 1919 when it took up its station in Hove Park, where it remained until 1937, while Brighton's was officially received in Preston Park on 12 January 1920 by the Mayor, W. J. Wellman and christened *Brighton* by the Mayoress, Miss E. R. Palfrey. It remained in situ for over twenty years.

The main contributors to this great cause had been bodies and institutions, such as banks, which could expect a good return on their investment. In the case of numerous other war and non-war causes and charities, it was the townspeople, whether individuals or groups – and no doubt many visitors – who made the difference. Collections and causes relating to the war alone included the following: Appeal for gifts for trawlermen; Children's Welfare Fund Collections for European Allies (Belgium, France), the Canadians and other countries (e.g. Poland) and places (Salonika); Duchess of Marlborough's Soldiers' and Sailors' Children's Welfare Fund; Eccentric Club Hostels for Limbless Sailors and Soldiers; flag days (e.g. for prisoners of war); French refugees; Imperial Club for Nurses; King's Royal Naval Fund;

"IT'S 'OUR DAY.' WHAT MAY I PUT YOU DOWN FOR?"
Part of the caption reads: 'The British Red Cross Society is spending £60,000 a week on our sick and wounded and £40,000 a week on our prisoners. Mr. Punch earnestly appeals to his generous friends to help him to send a really useful contribution to the fund of "Our Day".' (Punch, 23 October 1918)

Our Day (Red Cross Society and the Order of St John); POWs' Flag Day; Primrose League; Prince of Wales's National Relief Fund; Queen's Nurses; Red Cross (France's Day); RFA Cadets; the wounded (especially at Christmas); troops (especially at Christmas); Waifs and Strays Society War Emergency Fund; War Work Depot; and the YMCA.

A splendid instance of corporate giving was the gift made in October 1918 to St Dunstan's Homes for Blinded Soldiers, Sailors and Airmen by the Grocers' Federation of Great Britain with the cooperation of the local branch. The extraordinary donation was the deeds to a large property – West House in Portland Place, Kemp Town – for use as a hostel and permanent training home for blinded soldiers. At a special luncheon held in the Old Ship Hotel on 16 October 1918 to mark the occasion, Sir Arthur Pearson, the founder of the charity, responded suitably and remarked that the 600 men at St Dunstan's, far from being sad and unhappy creatures, were 'bright and cheery mortals'.

West House (12-14 Portland Place) was built in 1847 and originally comprised three houses. It was renamed Pearson House in 1957. Its use by St Dunstan's ended in 1995. (Author)

In the afternoon, most of the luncheon guests went over to the building in Kemp Town, where the deeds were handed over to Sir Arthur. The grocery trade pledged to continue its help during the coming year by collecting money for the appropriate furnishing of the house. After the formalities, the visitors were shown over the splendid property and entertained to tea and a musical programme.

By contrast with the good work performed by the grocers, there were, regrettably, instances during the year of unionised labour taking militant action by protests and strikes. In January, when the food situation was a matter of grave concern, demonstrations were held in protest against the handling of food distribution in the town.

The first took place on Saturday the 12th, when some 600-700 railway workers of all ages left the railway workshops in New England Road in their working clothes and were formed into a procession by members of the Workers' Committee. About fifty children and women were at their head, one of whom carried a board which read, 'The wives and children of our fighters shall not want for food.' Other boards were held aloft in other parts of the procession, one of them worded, 'We are after food, come to your Food Control Committee.' Moving off just after noon, the procession made its way down New England Road, along London Road, where there were food queues outside some of the shops, and Grand Parade to the Old Steine, attracting a lot of public attention en route. When they reached the Food Control Office in the Steine, the marchers surged through the gateways and formed a dense crowd in front of the steps. Then Mr A.F. Gasston, of the Brighton and District Trades and Labour Council, mounted the steps and in a forceful address said the workers were there to demand a fair share of food from the Food Control Committee and that the worker should be supplied before the man who 'neither toils nor spins'. Any food coming into the town should be sent to the working class districts. The hotels had ample food.

George Rayner (Secretary of the BDTL Council) said the workers were very dissatisfied with the way the Food Committee in Brighton was distributing food. Many of those present were doing heavy manual work at the railway on dogfish at a shilling a pound, while people who had never done a stroke of work in their lives were still living on the best. If the Food Committee could not do their job, the workers could, and if they did not arrange for sufficient food and for its proper and fair distribution the workers would 'come down and kick them out of office'. He moved an urgent resolution calling upon the Mayor, as Chairman of the Local Food Control Committee, to at once inform

Lord Rhondda of the plight of Brighton's workers and their families. If they were to continue to work, they demanded that he take immediate action to increase the supplies to the town and that the Local Food Committee immediately allocate that food to working class areas.

The protest had admittedly been orderly throughout but attracted little sympathy in most quarters. The *Gazette* deemed the action 'all rather hasty and premature', the worst feature being the 'insinuation that the working classes are the only people suffering from food scarcity.' Many of the workers were actually far better off than some of the professional classes. The point was also made that 'If these men and women, instead of dragging themselves about the town in a dreary procession, had been bustling along from shop to shop, they would have procured all that reasonable men and women could desire in times like these.' In a letter published on 18 January, 'Spectator' agreed, adding 'what a splendid bag the recruiting officer could have made of the eligible young men in the procession.' Mayor Carden's view was that the Food Control Committee, if left to get on with its work undisturbed, could deal with the matter without demonstrations.

One week after the first rally came the second, trade union leaders having originally planned to stop all business in the town. However, the event, scheduled for the working day of Thursday, 17 January, had to be postponed until Saturday the 19th due to rain. Councillor T. Ernest Marsh, Secretary of the Labour Institute, a member of the Brighton Food Control Committee and a future Mayor of Brighton, repeated the workers' grievances to a press representative and expressed support for a rationing scheme. 'We claim that there should be equality of sacrifice all round.'

The *Gazette* described the event:

'A large crowd assembled outside the north end of The Level to witness the marshalling of the procession by Mr. G. Rayner (Secretary of the Council), Mr. Frank Ingham and other members, and when it moved off there were about 1,000 people in it, and probably three times as many followers, to say nothing of a very large number of children, who were running around in obvious glee and apparently regarding the whole proceedings as an entertainment.

'Several hundred railway workers were in the procession, and

there was also a strong contingent of the Women's Trade Federation, with their banner, munition workers of both sexes, and a few tram girls. The flaming red banner of the Workers' Union was carried, as were numbers of boards, on which were such inscriptions as "Protesting against queues, food for soldiers' wives and children"; "We are after food, come to your Food Control Committee"; "More food for workers, less for hotels"; and "Wives and children of our fighters shall not want for food". Several young fellows had bugles, and their favourite selection on the march appeared to be Come to the cook-house door. The route taken was Viaduct-road and Preston-road to Preston Park, where the processionists and escorting crowd formed up in a dense mass in front of one of the seats under the trees at the north end of the park to hear addresses by the leaders.'

H.B. Elliott, President of the Trades and Labour Council and a member of the Joint Committee, declared he would do all he could to see that the poorer districts got their fair share of the meat coming into the town. Lord Rhondda should be told that the time had come for a compulsory rationing scheme. Mr Rayner read a letter from the Mayor reporting that the Food Controller fully appreciated the position and was doing his best to ration food supplies fairly, taking particular steps to see the working classes got their fair share.

This demonstration also attracted censure. On 23 January, the *Gazette* claimed that processions were calculated to do more harm than good. Everyone was in the same boat in this emergency and class distinctions did not apply. The promoters had only themselves to blame for raising a feeling of widespread resentment in Brighton and Hove, especially on account of their allegations that visitors were sheltering from air raids and indulging in excesses, or that the better class residents were getting preferential treatment over the working population. The borough was not prepared to destroy the good reputation it had built up for itself during the war at the dictates of a few irresponsible malcontents. In February, the paper deplored the efforts by the 'so-called champions of the workers', who treated residents and visitors with utter disdain, to dominate the Food Control Committee from within, having failed to make an impression by outdoor demonstrations.

Mayor Carden took direct and memorable action to deal, in some measure, with the meat shortage problem. On Thursday 10 January, he and F.A. Besant Rice, Brighton's Food Control officer, bought ninety sheep which had been sold at Haywards Heath market to a butcher, Charles Kingston, the owner of a dozen shops in south-west London. Arriving late that evening at a Volunteers' recruiting rally at the Drill Hall in Church Street, Carden explained that he had been engaged all day in connection with the food supply of the town. 'During the last ten minutes,' he added, 'I have bought ninety sheep which were in a truck at the railway station on their way to London.' He had stopped the truck, he said, paid for the sheep, and hoped they would be in Brighton's shops the next day.

The general impression in London following this transaction was that the animals had been commandeered. The Mayor admitted as much, having stated on a receipt to Kingston: 'I hereby acknowledge that I have with your consent, commandeered the truck of 90 sheep at Brighton Station, and am paying you cheque for £299 2s, the cost of the said sheep to you, and I will pay all charges since.' The butcher claimed he had felt pressured to sell, stating in one of the points he made in a letter of complaint sent to Carden on the following day that he had parted with his sheep on representations to him by Brighton's Executive Food Officer that the situation locally was so bad that unless supplies were forthcoming for Saturday there would be serious trouble from railwaymen and other workers.

Brighton's whole batch was carefully distributed among seventeen retail butchers' shops deliberately chosen because they were all situated in densely-populated working-class districts in the town; a list of the shops was supplied to the Brighton Trades and Labour Council. None of this sat well with the people in the area Kingston supplied or in London generally. On the Saturday, the following notice was posted in the windows of his shops in Tooting:

'Why We Are Short of Meat

Ninety sheep bought by Mr. Charles Kingston at Haywards Heath Market for the people of Tooting have been commandeered by the Sussex officials for the people of Brighton.'

To this a London evening paper added the comment:

'Naturally the Tooting people are asking why meat intended for those who are remaining at their posts and homes, facing the dangers of air raids, should be taken to supply wealthy people who have cleared out of London to this south coast resort in order to be out of all danger.'

In an editorial, the same paper added:

'The munition workers who remain to live and work in South London will be interested to learn to-day that the rich people who had run away to Brighton to escape air raids will have 90 sheep which were purchased by London butchers to supply their customers. The Mayor of Brighton, it seems, learning that 90 sheep which had been bought at Haywards Heath were in Brighton en route for London, proceeded to commandeer them for the benefit of the population of Brighton, including the timid and idle rich.'

This, countered the *Gazette*, was blatantly untrue. There was a distinct shortage of meat in Brighton and in the poorer districts this was particularly acute. Not a scrap from the ninety sheep went to the so-called 'idle rich'.

Kingston made other points in his letter criticising the administration of food control in Brighton but glossed over the fact that he profited from his purchases in Sussex due to the price difference for fatstock between that county and London:

Carden's purchase of the sheep won him admiration in the town, with the *Gazette* remarking: 'It was a bold stroke, and those who know Alderman Carden can realize the spirit in which he clung tenaciously to his capture. The incident establishes a new war time Mayoral precedent.'

The hotels, for their part, put up a stout defence against the accusations levelled at them by malcontents. At a meeting held on 15 January, the Brighton Hotels Association passed a resolution protesting vigorously against the inaccurate statements made by various persons in the town, which had the effect of stirring up class hatred and causing detriment to their business in Brighton. During the past twelve months, many food items, notably meat, had been rationed per head to all hotel guests and staff in Brighton, while, except in the case of sugar the public had not been so dealt with. Meanwhile, they would be very glad to meet the Food Committee again and stated they wished to work in unison with it in every way. In addition, all members were being instructed to adopt the Mayor's suggestion that there should be a meatless day every Wednesday.

Such a restriction had already been in the government's sights at the beginning of the month. On the 26th, *The Spectator* reported:

> *'Lord Rhondda has made a drastic new Order, severely restricting the consumption of meat, sugar, bread, and butter or margarine in all hotels and boarding-houses, restaurants and clubs, throughout the kingdom. There are to be two meatless days each week – Tuesday and Friday in London, and Wednesday and Friday elsewhere. No meat is to be served at breakfast. ... The daily meat ration for four public meals is reduced from twelve ounces to six ounces; the daily bread ration is increased from eight to nine and a half ounces.'*

In his *Hove and the Great War* (The Cliftonville Press, 1920), H.M. Walbrook looked back at the meat distribution problem which had, of course, affected both towns:

> *'... the system of meat distribution ... has been such a boon to the general public of Brighton and Hove during the past two years. In the early days of 1918, a Brighton and Hove Meat Advisory Committee was formed ... This committee purchased each week the whole of the meat required for the two towns, and sold to each butcher the exact quantity required for his registered customers with absolute fairness as to quality. It was the only scheme of its kind in the country organised exactly on these lines, and worked most smoothly, saving the retailers a great deal of trouble, and securing the maximum of public convenience possible in those difficult times.'*

The first meeting of the Committee for Brighton and Hove was held in mid-January 1918 in readiness for the launch of the new scheme on the 29th.

January and February were the worst months for queues for margarine and meat in the town. On 4 January in Brighton, margarine was generally available in many shops while

The meat card allowed the use of four fivepenny coupons per week, all to be used or else forfeited. (Punch, 27 February 1918)

shopping for meat was largely futile. The weekend of 19-20 January was one of the busiest ever as far as shopping in person was concerned – yet butter, margarine, cheese, and bacon were almost unprocurable. 'Never', reported the *Gazette*,

> *'have the streets of the town presented such remarkable scenes. From early morning until dark ladies were rushing from shop to shop in search of the needful provisions. ... It was an unpleasant business to tramp about with a basket or a bag for articles that were formerly brought to the door or achieved on order.'*

On the 25th there were margarine queues of amazing length, especially in London Road. 'This horrible business is the most disgraceful thing that has ever happened in Brighton', declared Chairman E.G. Waters, to vociferous support, at a well-attended meeting of the Brighton, Hove and District Trade Protection Society at the Old Steine offices on the evening of 4 February. It was 'a most pitiful thing to see people standing outside shops at six o'clock in the morning, with frost on the ground, insufficiently clad and without proper boots on their feet.' The *Gazette* sympathised. It also praised the police for preserving order and fairness.

EVERYONE A FOOD-CONTROLLER. First Lady (in tram car after two hours in the queue). "Did you see that food-'og in the check coat and skirt wiv a 'alf-pound of margarine in each pocket?" Second Lady. "Why, yes—I pinched one." First Lady. "So did I!" (Punch, 27 February 1918)

On 25 February, the queuing ended. On that date, the scheme for rationing meat, butter and margarine, affecting 14 million people, came into operation in London and the Home Counties. Everyone was to receive a meat and food card from the local food committee and register it with his butcher and grocer. The arrangements came into force nationally on 7 April, with registration necessary as from 5 May to obtain bacon. After registration, each individual's ration of 16oz of meat, 5oz of bacon and 4oz (5oz from June 1918) of butter and margarine every week was guaranteed. There was plenty of margarine in the town by early March and towards the end of the month, rationing was reported to be going surprisingly well. In early July, butchers' shops were at last well stocked with prime English beef and choice Southdown mutton. Tea, too, had resumed its place in shop windows in the town.

The first food item to be rationed, at 8oz per person until September 1919, had been sugar as from 31 December 1917. Meat, including bacon, fats, sugar, and lard, with jam included for the first time in early November 1918, were the only articles of food which were rationed nationally. Cheese was rationed by a number of committees across the country but in Brighton, people found the arrangements difficult to understand. When government cheese was introduced it was thought the stocks would be regularly maintained, like tea and rice, but by the end of March 1918 cheese of all sorts had been unprocurable in Brighton for nearly three weeks. As late as the end of August, Mr H.L. Treherne of 6, York Grove sent a complaint to the Ministry of Food concerning a shortage of cheese and syrup in Brighton. The reply he received stated that retailers should now be receiving a supply of cheese under the Distribution Scheme fixed according to their 1916 supplies.

Potatoes remained the mainstay of the nation. Lloyd George wrote in March 1918 that there was no crop under existing war conditions which could compare with it in importance as a food for either man or beast, and it would be quite impossible to plant too many potatoes that spring. In the previous year he had appealed to the farmer to grow more potatoes and the farmer had responded by beating all records. The premier was appealing again in 1918, and with even greater earnestness, because the need was twice as great. Brighton and Hove were certainly doing their bit; a local reporter, walking around the outskirts of the twin towns, remarked that one would not imagine there was much more room for potato patches. They seemed to meet the eye in all directions.

The arrangements for the production and distribution of food were the responsibility of the Food Control Office located initially in the Old Steine then, from mid-March 1918, at 1, Richmond Terrace. This hive of industry, together with the Food Control Committee, made the year 1918 memorable for triumphs in food organization. For their part, the local authorities ensured the numerous regulations governing trading and consumption were complied with. In June 1918, Brighton Police Court came down heavily on William Robinson, of Denbigh House, 70-73, Grand Parade, for a string of offences (some withdrawn in the proceedings), the heaviest penalty – £65 – being imposed for 'failing to secure that the total quantity of meat consumed in the establishment did not exceed the amount of meat represented by the coupons, declarations, and emergency cards, and other like authorities, on 20th April.'

One of the success stories in easing the food supply situation of individual households was the introduction of communal catering. The first National Kitchen (Lord Rhondda's preferred term) was opened on 21 May 1917 in London by Queen Mary at 104, Westminster Bridge Road – with Her Majesty staying on to serve some of the meals herself. By August 1918, there were 600 National Kitchens across the country. Locally, Hove led the way, with its establishment in Livingstone Road opened in September 1917.

Brighton's Kitchen, at 40, St James's Street, near High Street, was officially opened on 30 May 1918 by Alderman Spencer, Director of National Kitchens, who stressed that the facility was for all classes and remarked that in London it was in fact middle-class people who patronised the kitchens most. By noon, a long queue had already formed; an hour later the meals were entirely sold out and a great many people had to be turned away. Opening hours were from 12 to 2 (except

on Sundays) and there was capacity to serve about 1,000 portions daily to begin with. The paid staff, under Miss Morton, provided patrons every day with soup, a meatless dish, fish,

National Kitchens provided nutritious and inexpensive meals for the local population. (IWM Q54564)

vegetables and at least two kinds of puddings, one of which was a milk pudding. To cope with demand, equipment was installed enabling an additional 400 portions to be cooked daily. By the summer, the facility had fully proved its worth and was financially sound. The Kitchen Sub-Committee of the Council's General Purposes Committee accordingly opened a second Kitchen. The premises selected were part of the police station at Preston Circus, given up temporarily on certain conditions.

At £1,370, the total outlay was within the £1,450 budget. The rent was £55 a year, with an undertaking given as to maintenance. The planned distribution was 2,000 portions of food per day. By mid-November 1918 the adaptation and equipment of the premises were nearing completion but no report of the opening appears to have been published in the *Gazette*. We do know, however, that both establishments continued to provide their welcome services until their closure in November 1923.

Their success was due to the efficiency and indefatigable efforts of a band of committed and patriotic women. 'Nothing', commented the *Gazette* in mid-April, 'has more clearly demonstrated the value of women's help in municipal affairs.' Women kept the town running in so many ways. It was, therefore, a bitter disappointment to townspeople and visitors when, in August the tramway girls suddenly went on strike.

They had already taken action on 26 June 1917 in protest against certain arrangements made for extra conductresses on the cars being paid at the same rate as the regulars, the loss of Saturday or Sunday as an off-duty day and eligibility for war bonuses. Some sixty strikers had attended a private meeting in the Queen's Hall, Queen's Place, London Road, and afterwards had held an open meeting on the Level to air their grievances. Here they had been joined by hundreds of people. Despite

Brighton's trams to the racecourse were well patronised before the war. The wartime ban on meetings was lifted briefly in October 1917. (Pamlin Prints)

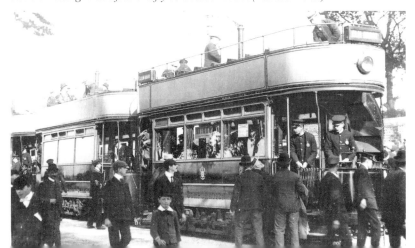

only one conductress in ten venturing out on their cars, the authorities had managed to maintain the service and the dispute, dismissed as 'all small beer' by the *Gazette*, had been amicably settled after the third day.

On the afternoon of Monday 19 August 1918, without warning, their second strike began. Both the Corporation tramway service in Brighton and Tilling's bus services for Brighton, Hove, Portslade, Patcham and Rottingdean were abruptly discontinued. The *Gazette* reported:

'So far as could be ascertained neither tramway nor 'bus employees had any grievance. The wages and war bonuses of staffs of both services have been adjusted from time to time with sympathy and liberality, but on receipt of telegraphic communication from the London Vehicle Workers' Union, the tram cars were driven to the depot in Lewes-road, and the 'buses to their garages, and, in spite of remonstrance from the management, no further 'bus service was run for the rest of the day and only a few trams could be got out. ... Munition workers and the limbless soldiers at the diamond factory in Lewes-road were especially badly inconvenienced, many of the disabled men being quite unable to travel without the aid of the cars or some other vehicle.'

Also affected were hundreds of soldiers from Shoreham and district accustomed to using the Portslade service, while wounded and sick soldiers wanting to return to distant hospitals – Dyke Road, Elm Grove and Portland Road – were also stranded. The paper recorded that:

'Mr. Marsh, the Tramways Manager, thanks to the loyalty of motor men and a few of the conductresses, was able to run seven cars and to alleviate to some extent the inconvenience to the public; but considerable obstruction was met with from disorderly strikers in New England-road, and after reducing the service to five cars between 7 p.m. and 9 p.m. the trams were returned to the depot for the night.'

Marsh was especially grateful to the 'silver badge' ex-servicemen who came to his aid. Cars were run early in the morning for the benefit of the Allen West munition workers, although one of the seven conductresses who stuck to her work was pelted with fish offal and bad tomatoes, which soiled both her uniform and the seating. The rowdy element, reinforced by some London strikers, held up trams near the Level in the late afternoon by deliberately disconnecting the trolley arms from the wires and removing the reversing arms from the motormen's platforms. It was largely owing to the pluck of some of the 'silver badge' men that the service was continued at all. No bus services were available in Brighton, Hove and district on the following day,

The Corporation's Tramways Committee met to consider the situation and shortly thereafter the Town Clerk, Hugo Talbot, issued an official statement. Two of the points made were that the strike was called by the executive of the Employees' Union in London by telegram and that it was a sympathy strike in support of the London Women Tramway and Omnibus Employees against the decision of the Committee on Production, the Tribunal set up by the government for the decision of such disputes, in an arbitration case; this centred on a national war bonus matter decided in the previous month after the formal hearing of both sides.

More violent action took place on the morning of Wednesday the 21st, when the cars were again attacked and, most alarming of all, the points at the North Road and Waterloo Place junctions were found to have been interfered with. Police officers had to be drafted to the locations. Elsewhere, in the early afternoon,

> '... the strikers were reinforced by a contingent of 'bus drivers from London, who made strenuous efforts to bring the tramway service to a complete standstill. Threats were hurled at the drivers and the conductresses who had remained on duty from shortly after 5 a.m., and by three o'clock the strain they had endured decided them upon their course. The cars were returned to the depot, and the faithful few sought a few hours' rest, but there still remained other motormen willing and anxious to undertake duty should it be deemed prudent to resume the service of cars.' (Gazette, 24 August 1918).

Pending arbitration in London, the strikers returned to work on Thursday the 22nd. The cost to the company in Brighton was a reduction of £451 in receipts and a drop of 97,544 in the number of passengers carried compared with the corresponding period in 1917.

To this had to be added whatever sum the motor bus services lost. Other towns had also been affected, including Bath, Bournemouth, Bristol, Folkestone, Hastings and Weston-Super-Mare. Over 15,000 bus and tram workers were involved overall. Yet the action was successful in gaining a full backdated increase for the women of the 5 shillings war bonus paid to men for which they had come out.

For Brighton women in general, 1918 was something of a landmark year. By the end of it, they had voted for the first time (Britain's first woman MP was also elected), the first female councillor had taken up office and a trio of women police was employed in the regular force.

The town had been slow to accept 'real' policewomen, despite the strong backing for the idea voiced in late 1917 and its constant support by Chief Constable Sir William Gentle. Support also came from Dorothy Peto, Director of the National Union of Women Workers' patrol training school in Bristol in a letter to the *Gazette* dated 25 March 1918, seeking 'an unlimited number of gentlewomen from 27 to 45 years, height above 5ft 4in with good physique, initiative, and knowledge of the world', who would receive training and a starting salary of £2 a week plus uniform; the work could be taken 'either temporarily, or as a permanent profession'. On 6 February 1918, a conference of representatives of fifteen women's societies was held in the Oddfellows Hall, Queen's Road, to consider the matter. In their resolution, they affirmed their support 'in favour of the immediate appointment of Women Police in Brighton.' Other boroughs had them,

Formidable members of the Women Police Service (WPS), strict guardians of morals in wartime urban society. Before 1915 they had been named Women Police Volunteers (WPVs). (Hulton Archive/Getty)

namely Bath, Bexhill, Birkenhead, Birmingham, Carlisle, Folkestone, Grantham, Glasgow, Huddersfield, Hull, Oxford, Reading and Southampton.

Meanwhile, Brighton had between forty and fifty ladies who, almost since the outbreak of the war, had done – and were still doing – excellent voluntary work as women patrols, nightly patrolling the town and rendering invaluable service. Sir Edward Henry, who retired that year as head of the Metropolitan Police, wrote a letter warmly extolling their work in Brighton. Letters full of praise were also received, in June, from the Mayors of Brighton and Hove and Brighton's Chief Constable, the latter stating: 'I am happy to say ever since the patrols were formed the streets of Brighton have been supervised with a thoroughness that would have been quite impossible without them. The excellent work of the patrols and their leader, Mrs. Lay, has earned for them lasting gratitude.' This lady referred in late April to the beneficial results achieved by her force in a letter, written jointly with the Chief Patrol for Hove, Mrs Annie Sargeant, to the *Brighton and Hove Society* magazine seeking new recruits. It reminded readers of the duties entailed:

> *'The work of the Women Patrols is to guide and befriend young girls who, in the strain and excitement of these days, are apt to lose their sense of responsibility. The qualifications desirable in a Woman Patrol are tact, sympathy and leisure to give not less than two hours at a time once or twice a week. Patrols work in couples, and each Patrol, after a short training by the Chief Patrol, will be furnished with an armlet and card signed by the Chief Constable.'*

At the business meeting in November – after the Armistice – it was stated that more patrols were urgently wanted in both Brighton and Hove.

In July, Sir William reported to the Watch Committee that he had engaged two policewomen who had been trained under the Chief Constable of Carlisle. By late August, the women had, the *Brighton and Hove Society* magazine tells us, been officially incorporated into Brighton's police force. What was more, Sergeant Blanche Irwin and Constable Glover, had only the previous week used their power of arrest on a drunken soldier, Henry Brown, who had been molesting women on the beach and had conveyed him to the Town Hall where, next day, he was fined 20 shillings or 11 days in default.

Both those officers, and a third (Constable West), were welcomed and received a warm tribute of appreciation for their supportive cooperation from Mrs Lay at a business meeting convened by the Brighton Women Patrols Committee at the Sussex Pioneer Club, New Road, on Saturday 16 November.

The contribution of women to the war effort, nationally and locally, uniformed and not, was immeasurably valuable. Premier Lloyd George recognised the importance of their work on the land in an urgent appeal on 26 June 1918 for help with the forthcoming critical harvest. 'I have,' he wrote, 'watched with deep interest and admiration the splendid work

Their punctuation's not great but they certainly did their bit for Britain! Women workers at the Allen West factory, where the munitions made included the 106 Fuse, the Mills bomb, a spring-loaded bomb thrower (supplies of which were stored temporarily under the grandstand of Brighton Racecourse), aeroplane parts, and the famous Stokes mortar. (Chris Horlock collection)

already done. Never have British women and girls shown more capacity or more pluck.'

Some time earlier, the vital services women were rendering for their country had been highlighted by a recruiting campaign on behalf of the WAAC, the Women's Royal Naval Service, the Women's Land Army and the Women's Forage Department. An exhibition was held at the Ministry of Labour Recruiting Office at 130a, Western Road, where a large number of people attended the formal opening on 6 March. Miss Annie Gardner OBE, Divisional Officer for the Ministry of Labour, presided and was supported by civic officials and dignitaries. The Mayor of Brighton expressed the hope that the exhibition would generate a great deal of interest and induce a large number of women to join one of the sections. He believed there were many girls in Brighton who might volunteer their services and do a bit more than they were. Thousands more women were wanted for service in France and on the land. Those who joined were certain to be well fed, better than civilians in the foreseeable future.

The Countess of Chichester made an eloquent appeal for recruits for the Women's Land Army. Miss Fairbairn (Recruiting Controller, WAAC) said how glad they were to 'have in their ranks the fine type of girl Brighton sent them'. Although she went to many parts of the country she had 'never seen a better set than those from Brighton'.

Members of the Women's Army Auxiliary Corps tending graves in France. The Corps supplied women cooks, domestic workers of all kinds, clerks, motor drivers and driver mechanics, and women for many other classes of work thus releasing men for the Army. (Brighton and Hove Society, *20 December 1917)*

Miss Gardner mentioned that the approximate number of Sussex women already enrolled in the WAAC was over 600.

The meeting was preceded by a parade of about a hundred girls, including representatives of the Forage Department, wearing buff-coloured smocks and green hats, the WAAC, in khaki and the Land Army, dressed in white smocks and carrying milking stools, rakes or forks. Two farm wagons were in the procession which, to the sound of the bugle band of the Sussex Yeomanry Cadets, marched along the sea front and along a number of other main roads in Brighton and Hove. They were afterwards drawn up in line in Montpelier Road and inspected by the Mayors of Brighton and Hove, who warmly

WAACs march past the Royal Sussex Regiment memorial in Regency Square on Victory Day, 19 July 1919. (Robert Jeeves/Step Back in Time)

congratulated them on the way in which they were doing their bit for their country.

The year's harvest proved to be a splendid one in practically every part of the country – the best for grain yield per acre for fifty years, according to Sir Charles Fielding, the Director of Food Production.

The last of the series of public meetings in connection with the

Women of the Land Army in procession on an unrecorded date (but very probably 6 March 1918) pass the Royal Albion Hotel on King's Road as part of a recruitment event. (IWM Q054600)

Women's War Services exhibition in Brighton was held on Saturday 16 March 1918 at the Western Road offices. Major R.L. Thornton DL JP, who presided, emphasised the very great importance and extreme urgency of women's war services. Thousands had thrown themselves into munition-making in order to sustain the men at the Front, while others worked long hours in offices or shops, on railways and in various other ways, such as on the land, in hospitals or performing clerical

Munition workers at 67, Eastern Road Kemp Town, September 1917. Here valuable work was done on the premises of an upholstery business. (Peter Booth collection)

duties in the army. Brief speeches by ladies in support of the recruiting campaign followed.

Two women who had played a key role in assisting our troops abroad were Mrs Anna Volk, wife of Magnus, the noted engineer and inventor, and former Mayoress Audrey Otter, by now Lady Otter.

By the end of 1917, Mrs Volks' 'Comforts for Soldiers' War Work Depot, the first to have started – on 8 August 1914 – had already raised a total of over £2,000. It was registered in October 1916 under the War Charities Act and the report and statement of accounts up to 31 December of that year showed that £1,313 17s 11d had already been disbursed on 'extras', usually garments, for our fighting men, with food, tobacco and other necessities also sent to prisoners of war. At the depot's annual tea held on 19 December 1917, the President was able to show that her depot had sent out over 25,000 articles. Initially based at 38a, Dyke Road, it moved next door in 1918 to No 39, where rooms

The Volks' home at 38 Dyke Road (today's No 128), where much good work was done producing comforts and necessities for the sick and wounded. (Peter Booth collection)

and a large hall were loaned to the cause. By the summer of 1918, the number of workers at the depot exceeded 150.

On 15 August, a matinee concert was given on the Palace Pier by the RAF (Roehampton) Concert Party to raise funds for the charity. The party included G.H. Elliott, the 'Chocolate-Coloured Coon', who would one day make his home near Brighton.

The depot held its final sale on 11 and 12 December 1918 and here Mayoress Carden expressed admiration and congratulation for the achievement of Mrs Volk and her working party, whose fundraising figure had now reached £3,000. The large hall was attractively adorned, with patriotic decorations and stalls laden with goods of practical value.

In 1918, four of the original ladies involved with Lady Otter's Fund – Mrs Charles N.T. Jeffreys, Mrs E. Leslie Beves, Mrs C.Y. Hudson and Mrs Milner Black – were still on the staff and all now held important positions. On 15 November, ex-Mayoress Otter wrote to the *Gazette* thanking all concerned and declaring:

> '*The work of the Brighton War Work Depot, begun on 12th August, 1914, is finished. The last parcels to our prisoners of war were sent from it last Wednesday to Holland to greet them on their arrival there, and the Depot will be closed except for the completion of the contract which I have with the Army Clothing Department for shirts, which I hope may continue until the new year.*
>
> '*I beg you also, Sir, to accept my thanks for your kindness in publishing each week contributions to the funds and the names of the prisoners of war to whom parcels had been sent and their acknowledgments of the same. The relatives of the prisoners have appreciated highly this service. Yours, &c.'*

A War Work Depot buttonhole flag showing the North Street address. (Author)

The story was not quite finished, however, for on Saturday 14 December a grand fundraising pageant, starring Clara Butt representing Britannia, was held at the Hippodrome on behalf of the Depot and the Hove War Hospital Supply Depot jointly. Sir John Otter and the Mayor of Hove both attended and each made an inspiring speech.

POWs also benefited from a flag day held on their behalf on 3 August. This raised over £600 from various sources, including collections at places of entertainment (£5 was raised at the Palladium from the sale of a letter from Lloyd George).

Conditions for British captives in Germany were grim. Many Brighton men were held at a major camp at Limburg an der Lahn, in the State of Hesse. Others were recorded elsewhere, such as at Thuringia, Cassel, Mecklenburg and Dülman. In various other cases, the place of detention was not specified.

A public insight into life in the camps was afforded in Brighton by Ernest Lionel Pyke, who was confined in Ruhleben civilian prison camp, a converted racecourse near Berlin, for three and a half years. He was released on 6 March under the agreement relating to the repatriation of prisoners over 45 years of age. He had a thrilling story

British civilian prisoners and their quarters at Ruhleben POW camp.

to relate and a striking set of photographic slides, smuggled out of Germany, to illustrate his recollections. He wrote *Desperate Germany*, published in 1918, which revealed the current appalling conditions in that country. He gave his talk several times at the Hippodrome between Monday 8 and Saturday 13 May inclusive. In the crowded stalls were numbers of officers and men in khaki, wounded men in blue and many well-known people, some visiting and some resident.

The first six months spent in the camp were positive hell but things improved. Parcels of food from home kept them alive. He had had many opportunities to observe the wretched conditions in Germany generally and – as the camp's kitchen inspector – in Berlin in particular. The starving city was lacking in almost everything.

A fellow-sufferer at Ruhleben, Rupert Burden, then resident at 129, King's Road, had been in business in Germany's capital for twenty-four years prior to the outbreak of the war. His comment on Pyke's lecture was that it 'did not deal with half the enormities practised there.' He was, of course, able to corroborate in every detail the story told by the lecturer of the 'Hunnish abominations and the fiendish cruelties of the enemy in their treatment of prisoners.'

On 3 December 1918, Private Leonard Brown told Sussex VADs at a meeting in St John's Hall, Carlton Hill, that of his ten months in Germany, four were spent working in a coal mine. Although rough in their manner, the Germans did not knock him about in any way. There he suffered semi-starvation; at one time he was kept so short of food that he had to eat what he could from a swill tub. Things improved after July when in hospital due to his general weakness. There he remained until a fortnight before the armistice. The best thing was when he received parcels from the British Red Cross.

Hubert James Baird RAMC (1896-1961) spent some unpleasant time in Germany as a POW. (Graeme Davis)

'I only had eight months in the hands of the Germans, but that was quite enough', Private Hubert James Baird RAMC of 8, Elm Grove told a local reporter. Repatriated on 7 December 1918, the 23-year-old soldier was delighted to be back in Brighton. Educated at Ditchling Road School, he was an old RAMC Territorial. He had gone to France in November 1917 and was in an advanced dressing post near St. Quentin when he was captured on 21 March 1918. He and several others were moved to the rear of the German lines and were made to do dressings and ambulance work for the enemy. With several other RAMC men, he was then moved to Bachant, a major centre for wounded men and prisoners some fifteen kilometres from Mons, and remained there for some weeks until they were sent to Germany. Every day, parties of prisoners returned from work behind the German lines. They were mere bags of bones and all of them were ill. In Germany he was held in Dülman Camp, near the Westphalia Mines. There he was treated well, due to the presence of the British Help Committee Representatives of the British Red Cross. At Dülman there were about 2,000 prisoners captured on all fronts, and they included British, French, Italians, Russians and Portuguese. On 22 November Baird and his fellow-prisoners were released from the camp. He returned to England via Holland, then Hull, where the YMCA gave him and his fellow-POWs as much food as they could carry and showered them with cigarettes and tobacco. He was later the recipient, with other returning POWs, of a letter from Buckingham Palace in which King

George, joined by Queen Mary, welcomed him on his release from the miseries and hardships he had endured with much patience and courage over many months.

It was, surprisingly, only some way into 1918 that a formal heading 'Casualties' (non-RSR), with names within sub-categories below it, would make its appearance in the *Gazette*. The wounded brought to Brighton, fresh from the battlefields, could recuperate in the town and enjoy the specialist care for which it was famed. The convoys arrived relentlessly at the station throughout the year until the end of November. Ironically, the last batches included men who had been wounded in the capture of Mons – a name with a strong local resonance, for in 1914 it was from the battle there, fought on 23 August, that numbers of 'Old Contemptibles' were brought in the first Red Cross train to arrive in Brighton. Now our warriors had their perfect revenge by capturing the Belgian town on the very day of the enemy's surrender. Decked with flowers by the delivered townsfolk, our conquering troops paraded through garlanded villages.

During the year, the average number of wounded arriving at the station each month, as listed in official returns in *In The Service Of Mankind,* was 11,496, although there were wide variations. In February, for example, just three convoys, consisting of 391 men, were

Members of the 13th Sussex VAD in 1918. Standing second from right is Charles James Mercer, a wheelwright by trade, who sadly died that year. He is the grandfather of local historian and author, Peter Mercer, of Seaford. (Peter Mercer)

recorded. The figure in the worst month of April, with 2,188 wounded, was nearly six times as bad. Other months with over 2,000 casualties were August (2,164 men) and October (2,181).

Describing the conveyance of our courageous heroes to the various hospitals, the *Gazette* noted:

'A large fleet of ambulances in attendance included two of the new ones provided by means of the fund set on foot by Lady George Nevill, one being the gift of members of the Jewish community. The new cars have a very wide body and the bunks are slung from the roof, there being no uprights fixed in the floor, an arrangement that permits the lower as well as the upper bunks to be used for cases with extended arms, &c.'

(2 November)

'They [sixteen lady drivers of ambulances] were to be seen this morning handling the wounded men like experts who had nothing to learn. They met 92 Red Cross trains last year, and already this year they have attended at 75. It is a record to be proud of.'

(18 November)

'The officers being taken to the Clarendon-terrace Hospital [not referred to in the paper before 1918], and the whole of the men going to the Kitchener Hospital, special tramcars being utilized for the "sitting" cases.'

(20 November)

On occasion, the wounded were transported *from* Brighton to other destinations:

'Later in the afternoon, the same train was utilized for the transfer of 153 wounded American soldiers from Brighton to Portsmouth.'

(27 November)

On their recovery, men could be found employment locally at, for example, the Lord Roberts Memorial Workshop in St James's Street and, in particular, the diamond-cutting works in Lewes Road/Coombe Road, opened on 17 May 1918. This was an enterprise by Bernard Oppenheimer, a South African/British diamond merchant and philanthropist. The first building accommodated some 300 workers. A major new extension, built across the road on the south side of Coombe Road soon housed some 2,000 workers and was opened by the Prince of Wales on 1 February 1921 – the same day as he unveiled the Chattri

The extension of the diamond cutting factory on the south side of Coombe Road in December 2012. Lewes Road is out of sight on the right.

Indian memorial on the Downs at Patcham (see Appendix 1) and visited the Lord Roberts Memorial Workshop. Oppenheimer died in that year and three years later his enterprise went into receivership. The buildings still exist, however, the smaller premises as stylish residences and the larger as a self-storage facility.

In late April 1918, at the second Brighton and Hove Home Life Exhibition at the Aquarium, representatives of the Ministries of Labour and Pensions showed how discharged soldiers and sailors could find employment. Also to assist returning servicemen, the YMCA opened, on 21 October at 28, St James's Street, Brighton, an employment office known as 'The Red Triangle Employment Bureau', at which no fees were charged.

In August, Brighton and Britain marked the fourth anniversary of the war. Strangely to our ears, the day was referred to then as Remembrance Day. A united war memorial and intercession service, conducted entirely by laymen, was held on Sunday 4 August on the Level, where an address was given by a prominent legal figure, Arthur O. Jennings JP, Registrar of the Brighton County Court and District Registry and Superintendent of the Brighton Force of Special Constables. The event was huge:

> *'People were streaming on to the Level nearly an hour before the service began. There is no computing the thousands who ultimately stood in huge masses all round the platform. ... The band of the 1st Sussex Volunteers, seated in front of the platform, played the accompaniments to the hymns. As the band were marching to the Level they could be heard in the distance playing in spirited style Sussex by the Sea. When Sir John Otter [deputising for the Mayor] stood up he faced thousands, and more thousands were behind him, gathered under the trees, clusters of people all down the railings almost as far as the eye could see.'*

> *(Gazette, 7 August)*

In his statesmanlike address, Jennings said this war was the nation's war, and that meant that the whole of the nation was in it. Never before in the whole history of wars had there been anything like this volume of bloodshed and pain, misery and death. Various aspects of our struggle were positively considered and at the end of his address he moved the following resolution:

> *'That the inhabitants of Brighton here assembled on Remembrance Day, 4th August 1918, silently paying tribute to the Empire's sons who have fallen in the fight for freedom on the scattered battlefields of the world-war, whether on sea or shore, and mindful of the loyalty and courage of our sailors, soldiers, airmen and men everywhere, and those who are working on the munitions of war and helping in other ways for the preservation of civilization, unanimously resolve to do all that*

David Lloyd George (1863-1945), prime minister 1916-22, inspired the nation to 'hold fast' in August 1918.

in their power lies to achieve the ideals on behalf of which so great a sacrifice has already been made.'

A show of hands was called for and a sea of them went up.

Churches across the town held services to observe the anniversary and on the following day, in all places of entertainment, a message from Prime Minister Lloyd George was read out. The key words in it were 'hold fast' – words which instantly resonated with the masses:

'The message which I send to the people of the British Empire on the fourth anniversary of their entry into the war is "Hold Fast." We are in this war for no selfish ends. We are in it to recover freedom for the nations which have been brutally attacked and despoiled, and to prove that no people, however powerful, can surrender itself to the lawless ambitions of militarism without meeting retribution, swift, certain and disastrous, at the hands of the free nations of the world. To stop short of Victory for this cause would be to compromise the future of mankind. ... But the battle is not yet won. ... Having set our hands to the task, we must see it through till a just and lasting settlement is achieved. In no other way can we ensure a world set free from war.

HOLD FAST!'

At the Theatre Royal, packed for *The Gondoliers*, this text was read in an interval between two acts. As the curtain rose, disclosing the entire D'Oyly Carte company and their manager, Lawson Lambert, the audience fell silent. Mr Lambert then broke open an envelope with a big red seal and read the contents, after which the rapt listeners broke into a prolonged outburst of cheering. *God Save the King* was then resoundingly sung by both the cast and the audience in what was one of the most thrilling patriotic demonstrations ever witnessed in Brighton. Similar scenes were enacted at all the other entertainment venues. Over at the Hippodrome, following the entertainment, the speech was read out in stirring fashion during two intervals by Alderman A.R. Sargeant JP, Mayor of Hove, in the absence of the Mayor of Brighton. He called for three cheers, which were heartily given and followed by the national anthem.

This outburst of patriotism melded with the holiday mood permeating the town. On Friday the 2nd, the Queen, Princess Mary and

The gateway to and from Brighton. Note the long line of waiting horse cabs on the far right. (Author)

Prince George had visited. Londoners and others were desperate to reach the coast for the weekend. At the station, the crowded midnight train from London had even brought in over 200 determined passengers who had nowhere to stay. The railway authorities allowed them to remain in the station for the rest of the night, some being accommodated in the waiting rooms.

The resort was packed, especially during the week 12 to 18 August. Despite the absence of the well-appointed fleet of pleasure steamers and a reduction in the number of pleasure sailing-boats available, other delights were to be had. Hundreds enjoyed boating and bathing; even at six in the morning the beach was swarming with bathers. Air displays were a source of general interest. Both the piers were besieged throughout the day for the entertainment they offered, while their facilities for angling were greatly enjoyed. Taking August as a whole, all wartime records for the numbers of pier visitors were beaten. The scenes on the beach equalled those witnessed on many Bank Holidays in pre-war times, even the memorable August of 1911. Tram and bus services were overwhelmed and every kind of refreshment place was crowded out at mealtimes. At the end of the month, the *Gazette* remarked:

> '*It will be something for the generation to tell their children and grand children that Brighton really felt the pinch of war more in the August of 1914 when hostilities were commenced than in this fifth August of Armageddon.*'

Fierce action during the Second Battle of the Marne (15 July – 6 August 1918), the last major German Spring Offensive on the Western Front. The artist's name is unclear.

Mingling with the crowds were servicemen of various nationalities, reminders of the war. The tide had begun turning against the enemy at the end of July/early August. At the end of the latter month, morale at home was further boosted by the exceptionally exhilarating tone of the message from Sir Douglas Haig describing the brilliant military operations of the armies under his command.

By September there was elation over what the Allies were achieving. On the 7th, the *Gazette* noted:

> '*War news has monopolized attention in Brighton this week. It is all so wonderful that people are almost bewildered by the succession*

of brilliant achievements, and optimism has been raised to a pitch rarely experienced in this vital struggle. ...The most profitable thing to do is to make the most of the stimulating influence of these glorious deeds upon our own attitude towards the war. Now is the time for everyone at home to back up the splendid men at the front. We ought to be intensely proud of them all. What a joy it is to read of the rivalry in patriotism between the Londoners and the boys of the home battalions, the clever tactics of the Australians, the invincible dash of the Canadians, the dogged determination of the Highlanders, and the brilliant élan of the French poilus. Every element seems harmonized.'

Within a few weeks, the Allies were sweeping all before them along the whole Western front from the Scheldt in the north to Sedan at the southern end, after a simultaneous attack by over 200 divisions. Supported by British, American and French troops, King Albert's twenty-eight Belgian divisions delivered crushing blows in Flanders where the war had begun. All along the line, the Germans avoided battle wherever possible, making a stand only in order to cover their retreat. Bulgaria surrendered after Allied troops, advancing from northern Greece, took less than a fortnight to smash its army even with its stiffening of German troops. A month later, Turkey surrendered and the Dardanelles were reopened to Allied shipping. And on 3 November, Austria signed an armistice with the Allies, its Emperor Karl abdicating on the 11th. On that day, in a guarded railway carriage in the forest of Compiègne, some thirty-seven miles north of Paris, Germany admitted defeat and signed an armistice. After four and a quarter years of war, the guns fell silent on the battlefields of Europe.

At Roedean School, the co-principal, Penelope Lawrence, noted:

'One of our parents has heard from her brother at the War Office that the following telegram [a wireless signal sent by 2nd Australian Division] has been received:

'Text reads: "Message from General Foch to Commander in Chief BEF reads Hostilities will cease on the whole front on the 11th November French Time 11 o'clock. The Allied troops will not cross until further orders the line reached on that date at that time. Signed Foch 6.35 am."'

'So this', she wrote, 'means an end of the killing. I have just read it to the School. We are not having a holiday.'

Directly the official news of the Armistice reached Col. Maurice, the CO at the Pavilion Hospital, the men were ordered to assemble in the Recreation Room. A roar of applause greeted his appearance on the stage. He then relayed the glad tidings to 'the Boys'. The privilege was enthusiastically received. At York Place he performed a similar pleasant duty.

On the 13th , the *Gazette* described the deep contentment prevailing in Brighton:

'Armageddon is over. The signing of the Armistice produced a feeling of intense relief. There was no disposition to indulge in wild demonstrations of joy. The memories of the past four years had chastened public sentiment. ... But beneath the surface there was a feeling of profound thanksgiving and a reverent realisation of the work of Divine Providence. In the twinkling of an eye there burst forth in every district of both towns a galaxy of flags, the simple symbol of a pleased people.'

A poem, *The Happy Warriors*, skilfully penned by a local contributor signing himself/herself simply as 'M.M.R.', was published in the same issue. The following is an extract:

Oh Happy Warriors! You have fought the fight –
And know the joy of battle bravely won,
Bathed in the glow of Victory's golden light,
Yours is the commendatory 'Well done'!
And in our joy to-day we feel you near,
Glorying in the triumph you hold dear.

The paper has left us a vivid overview of the townspeople responding to the splendid news of the newly-won peace in Brighton and Hove:

'Holiday, holiday, holiday! That was the popular mood in Brighton and Hove on Monday, and, after the long agony, nothing could have been more natural. All of us have borne quite enough, many have suffered very terribly, and the blessed word peace (even when it is called armistice) had come to have a sweet and welcome sound. No one who went about the two towns during the afternoon will need to

be told that the rejoicings of the crowds were admirably restrained. Of course the younger generation couldn't help letting themselves go, but a prolonged walk through many streets in the most frequented parts shewed no sort of conduct that could be described as disorderly. ... Of the tens of thousands of people who had come out to share in the celebration of Armistice Day thousands were in mourning. ... Every thoughtful person must in his heart have remembered the great multitude of the valiant dead, and paid silent homage to their dear and heroic memory ... So Brighton and Hove rejoiced temperately but very sincerely.

'A few minutes after the Morning Argus sent the glad tidings throughout the towns, people began to hang out trophies of victory, and from hour to hour the vari-coloured magnificence grew, till many streets "beat all records" in this kind of display. ... The Brighton Town Hall was hardly recognizable under its many gigantic flags. ... All round these flags, simply deluging enormous upper spaces of the Town Hall, were the emblems of all the triumphant Allies – a sight to remember, such as has never before been seen there, crowds gathering in Bartholomews and East-street to gaze

Reveller: "Say, mate, yer hat's on straight!" Victory celebrations as seen by Punch, *20 November 1918.*

and perhaps to ponder the world-wide significance of the hanging of the banners of the nations upon the walls of the great English town. ... It is not possible to tell of all the remarkable displays. ... Right up to the fall of twilight they were still being put out at public buildings, places of business, and private homes. If you hadn't a flag and couldn't get one for love or money you did the next best you could with a piece of coloured cloth. ... East-street presented a richly diversified appearance, particularly that part of it towards the sea, which had a charmingly artistic aspect, thanks to the effective use of streamers across the street.'

(Issue of 13 November 1918)

The Pavilion was bedecked, in record time, with flags and bunting galore.

A colourful postcard celebrating the end of hostilities and hoping 'for happy times to be'. (Author)

'In the town, the spontaneity of the displays was something of a mystery. ... when the news reached Brighton, nearly everybody managed to produce some sort of symbol or decoration. After dark, the streets were made more inviting by the removal from shop

interiors of the shading which had been imposed for so long, and although shop windows were still in the shade, ... people could at least see where they were. The perfect autumn day on Wednesday the 13th concluded with one of the most gorgeous sunsets of the season.'

(Gazette, 16 November)

Two wounded soldiers in overcoats, one with four gold stripes on his sleeve and the other with three, were wearing caps so thickly covered with little flags that their faces could hardly be seen. A high-spirited small group of their fellows came marching along Western Road arm in arm, singing some weird medley of popular songs, almost holding up the traffic with their antics. They survived the conflict. Many did not. Our nameless local poet reminds us:

> *And they who miss you, in the years to come,*
> *Shall know your sacrifice was not in vain.*
> *History shall bear you whilst the ages run,*
> *Telling the story of your deathless fame;*
> *You, who in England's greatness played a part,*
> *Shall ever live enshrined within her heart.*

Appendices

Appendix 1   Timeline of Selected Events (from the Armistice to the end of December 1918)

Appendix 2   GALLERY – Post-War Remembrance and Recognition, 1919-22

Appendix 3   Theodore Wright VC and Edward 'Mick' Mannock VC

Appendix 4   Poem *9 November* by Irene Snatt

Appendix 5   The Plaque in Holy Trinity Church

Timeline of Selected Events
(from the Armistice to the end of December 1918)

11 November	The Local Government Board and the Ministry of National Service announce that **all recruiting under the Military Service Act is to be suspended**. All outstanding calling-up notices, whether for medical examination or service, are cancelled. **All cases pending before Tribunals to be suspended**.
	(Brighton's Tribunal had had 308 sittings and had dealt with over 12,000 cases).
16 November	The musical revue, *The Passing Show*, plays to a packed Hippodrome.
	Business meeting called by the Brighton Women Patrols Committee at which the **first three Brighton women police** (Sergeant Irwin, Constable West and Constable Glover) were welcomed.
	Large tea party and entertainment given by a Mrs A.E. Minett at the Hotel Metropole to 150 wounded men from the Kitchener Hospital.
17 November	**Victory Sunday**.

20 November	Letter from the Mayors of Brighton and Hove published in the *Gazette* appealing for clothes and bedding for the dispossessed in devastated areas of France and Belgium.
23 November	Report of new regulations imposed by the Local Government Board and applying to all places of public entertainment to help control the spread of **influenza**.
	War Office announces the suspension of recruitment to the **Volunteer forces**.
	Grand boxing tourney attended by at least 2,000, held at the Drill Hall, Church Street, in aid of the 1st Volunteer Battalion, Royal Sussex Regiment.
25 November	Bruce Bairnsfather's *The Better 'Ole* plays for a week from today at the Hippodrome.
	An Order in Council repeals a number of Defence of the Realm (**DORA**) regulations, a large group of which controlled recruitment and exemption from military service.
30 November	The *Gazette* reports the issue by the Admiralty, War Office and Air Ministry of announcements reminding the public that **general demobilisation** had not yet begun.
11 December	Gathering to mark the closure of Mrs Magnus Volk's **War Work Depot**, which had produced comforts for the troops since 12 August 1914.
14 December	**General Election**, with the announcement of results postponed until 28 December. Major George Clement Tryon, MP, Unionist Member for Brighton elected in 1910, and Charles Thomas-Stanford (Mayor of Brighton, 1910-13, and likewise, since 1914, Unionist Member for Brighton) retain their seats.

This was the first election in which women, and all men over the age of 21, could vote and also the first at which organised Labour made a separate stand.

Pageant of Freedom starring Clara Butt as Britannia at the Hippodrome in aid of Brighton's War Work Depot and Hove War Hospital Supply Depot (the *Pageant* had previously been performed in London, at Queen's Hall, Langham Place, on 7-13 May).

17 December
The members of 'D' Company, 1st V.B. Royal Sussex Regiment, celebrated the Allies' victory by holding a social gathering at St. Augustine's Hall, Stanford Avenue.

18 December
Postponed **opening of new YMCA lecture and concert hall** by Mrs Walter Long at the Kitchener Hospital, where a Canadian unit had been in charge for nearly two years; in the last 20 months about 20,000 wounded had passed through its hands.

19 December
The Council's **Lighting** Committee reports that the lighting of the Front from the Aquarium to the western boundary was being done as fast as possible. The reason for the delay was the awful condition of the lamps. Councillor Weller put in a strong plea for attention to the lighting of the eastern end of the Front.

20 December
Brighton's **Allied Victory Dance** at Hove Town Hall in aid of the Jubilee Fund of the Queen Alexandra Hospital for Sick Children, Brighton. At one point nearly 400 people were dancing and some 240 were viewing the event from the balcony. Among the fancy dress personages represented was DORA, hampered in the dance by sundry coils of government red tape.

21 December	**Italian War Photograph exhibition** at Brighton Art Galleries opened by Colonel Sir Filippo de Filippi, who stated that of the five million Italians called to the colours, as many as 1.3 million had been killed or permanently disabled.
23 December	***Romance***, a play by Edward Sheldon (claimed to be 'the most beautiful love story ever written'), performed at the Theatre Royal and repeated during the week.
	The Lighting, Heating and Power Order, 1918, is revoked by the Board of Trade.
25 December	**Victory Christmas** celebrated by the wounded at Brighton Pavilion Hospital, where the Banqueting Room was now one of the largest wards. The recent appeal in the local press meeting for 'extras' for the men met with a response of over £70.
	'It was in fact, as in name, a Peace Christmas. ... In hundreds of homes at Brighton this Christmas the fire seemed to burn brighter because of the presence of one who had been absent for two or three years. In many more, the knowledge that the prisoners of war in German hands were being restored to friends contributed to a freer celebration of the day. It was like a new experience after the gloom and anxieties of the past, and it explained the demeanour of reverence and spiritual thanksgiving observed in the church services and social gatherings.' (Gazette).
26-28 December	Afternoon and evening **dances at the Grand Hotel**

Gallery
Post-War Remembrance and Recognition

Victory Day, 19 July 1919

What we know as Peace Day was celebrated as Victory Day in 1919. The highlight was the Victory March, in which the local discharged soldiers, the Royal Garrison Artillery and the patients from both the Kitchener and Pavilion Hospital participated. The legless cases, conveyed in a fleet of charabancs and motor buses, led the march, closely followed by the arm cases. Soldiers and ex-soldiers paraded in full force. A splendid meal, provided by the people of Brighton, was served on the roof of the Aquarium. The final event of the day was a firework display on the Palace Pier.

H.R.H. THE PRINCE OF WALES DEDICATING THE CHATTRI, PATCHAM.
FEB.1. 1921.
WILES HOVE 13

Dedication of the Chattri, 1 February 1921

Lieutenant Das Gupta of the Indian Medical Service approached Mayor Otter in August 1915 for permission to erect a memorial on the site where the cremations of the Hindus and Sikhs who died in hospital in Brighton took place. The memorial on the Downs at Patcham now known as the Chattri (which means 'umbrella' in Hindi, Punjabi and Urdu) was built to the design of E.C. Henriques from Mumbai. The dome and eight pillars of white Sicilian marble symbolise the protection offered to the memory of the dead.

Presentation of tank, 10 January 1920

A First World War tank was a feature of Preston Park for over twenty years. On January 10 1920, the Mayoress of Brighton, Miss E.R. Palfrey, smashed a bottle of champagne over the tank and 'christened' it *Brighton*. The tank was a gift to the town in recognition of Brighton's contribution to the war savings campaign.

UNVEILING OF BRIGHTON WAR MEMORIAL BY EARL BEATTY - OCT-7-1922.

Unveiling of the War Memorial in the Old Steine, 7 October 1922

The memorial, whose pylons bore the names of 2,597 men and three women of the town who fell in the war, was unveiled by Earl Beatty, who was presented with the freedom of the borough at a special town council meeting. At the unveiling, guards of honour were provided by the Sussex Division of the RNVR, the Home Counties Brigade RFA and the Home Counties Divisional Royal Engineers. Ex-servicemen assembled for inspection by the earl. The memorial was designed in the form of a Roman water garden by Brightonian Sir John Simpson. The statue of George IV which had originally stood on the site was removed to the North Gate of the Royal Pavilion.

Dedication of the Pavilion South Gate, 26 October 1921

The new southern gateway to the Royal Pavilion grounds, a gift from the people and princes of India commemorating Indian soldiers nursed in Brighton's military hospitals, was dedicated by Bhupinder Singh, Maharaja of Patiala. The structure is of Bath stone and its design is said to derive from 16th century buildings in Ahmadabad, the principal city of Gujarat. One of the two inscriptions on the gate reads: 'THIS GATEWAY IS THE GIFT OF INDIA IN COMMEMORATION OF HER SONS WHO STRICKEN IN THE GREAT WAR WERE TENDED IN THE PAVILION IN 1914 AND 1915.'

During the ceremonials, the Mayor presented the Maharaja – who in his speech humorously coined the term 'Doctor Brighton' – with a gold key as a gift which was a copy of the original key to the Royal Pavilion.

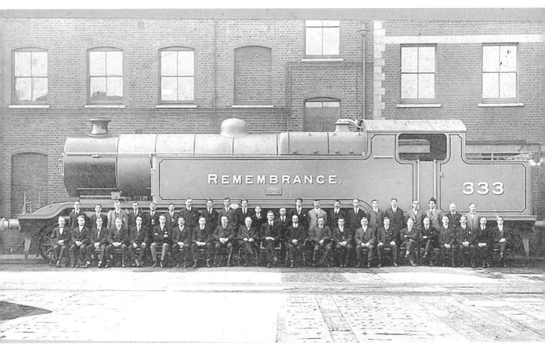

LBSCR Locomotive Remembrance

No. 333 *Remembrance* was the last new locomotive built (in May 1922) by the London, Brighton and South Coast Railway before it became a part of the Southern Railway on 1 January 1923. The commemorative plaque below the name reads: *In grateful remembrance of the 532 men of the L. B. & S. C. Rly. who gave their lives for their country, 1914-19*. It is on display at the National Railway Museum, York, together with the nameplate which the locomotive carried in later years. (*June Churchill*)

Theodore Wright VC and Edward 'Mick' Mannock VC

As part of a national scheme whereby every VC recipient of the War is commemorated with a paving stone and a plaque, three 'Brighton VCs' were selected to be so honoured, namely Theodore Wright, Ernest Beal and Edward Mannock, one hundred years after their deaths.

Captain Theodore Wright was killed in 1914. He was born in 1883 and educated at Clifton College, Bristol, before going to the Royal Military Academy in Woolwich. He joined the Royal Engineers in 1902 and served around the world before being sent to France with the BEF when the war broke out. During the Battle of Mons, he was ordered to blow up eight bridges over the Mons-Condé canal. Despite being injured he continued to set charges under the bridges and managed to blow up a key crossing. For his bravery during this operation he was awarded the VC. He was killed in the following month at Vailly while helping wounded men to shelter. His cross has been left to the Royal Engineers Museum in Gillingham, Kent.

Brighton and Hove City Council's information plate states that Captain Wright was born in Brighton. He was not. His birth certificate states that he was born on 15 May 1883 at 119, Lansdowne Place, Hove. On that basis, his name and achievements have had to be recorded in this separate section rather than in the body of this volume. Brighton and Hove Bus and Coach Company's Bus No 480 on Route 5 has carried his name since 3 September 2014.

The two other VCs, to be honoured in 2018, are Ernest Beal (see Chapter 5) and Edward 'Mick' Mannock. The latter's name – as Mick Mannock – was carried on Bus No 912 from September 2006 to March 2008, when it was replaced by that of Anita Roddick. The bus company affirms in the notes to its listing that he was born in Ballincollig, County Cork, Ireland. By way of a Brighton link, it states that 'the Air Cadet building in Preston Barracks is named in his honour.' This ties in with some sources claiming that the fighter ace was actually born in the Barracks.

A number of Mannock's biographers admit, however, to the total confusion surrounding the pilot's place of birth, which has been mooted as Brighton, Aldershot, Cork, Canterbury and even India. Mannock himself clouded the issue by recording both Brighton and Cork on documents. Biographer James Dudgeon was told by family members that Cork was correct. As in the case of Theodore Wright, no local references during the years 1914-18 have been found by this author.

The VC recipient acknowledged by Brighton itself in 1918 as the town's only other holder of the medal apart from Ernest Beal was Captain John James Crowe, concerning whom full details are provided in Chapter 5. Crowe deserves to be commemorated at the Old Steine. Perhaps one day he will be.

Mention may be made by way of a postscript of Air Commodore Ferdinand ('Freddie') West, the last surviving British VC of the 1914-18 war at the time of his death on 8 July 1998 at the age of 102. Some sources (e.g. *The Daily Telegraph Book of Airmen's Obituaries* compiled by Edward Bishop, reprinted 2008) refer to him receiving part of his education at the Xaverian College, Brighton. Having been born in 1896 and with the College opening in 1909, he could only have attended from the age of thirteen. The time spent there is not recorded. Most of his education was actually received in Italy, where, Bishop states, he attended the Lycée Berchet in Milan and Genoa University, where he read international law.

9 November

In Preston Park there is a tank.
Relic of the Battle of Cambrai.
Its rusty treads loom over,
Threatening.

I play with Army buttons,
Unwind some tattered puttees.

On corners of the shopping streets
The blind and maimed
Are selling matches.

Some veterans march.
A brass band plays
Sussex by the sea,
And Mother sighs and says
Before the Marne,
Before the Somme,
She watched the boys in khaki
March away.

By Irene Snatt (1920-) from *Childhood at Brighton* and *Wartime Verses,* published May 1996.

The Plaque in Holy Trinity Church

This plaque was uncovered in the church of the Holy Trinity, Ship Street, Brighton, exactly 100 years after the outbreak of the First World War. It bears the names of seventeen soldiers who lost their lives in the conflict (thirteen of them in France) and of seventy-eight men, many of them evidently brothers, who served during the war but survived.

The Grade-II listed Anglican church of the Holy Trinity in Brighton's Ship Street closed in 1984. Subsequent plans to convert it to a museum of Brighton did not materialise, although in 1996 the premises were converted to an art gallery, its current use.

By an extraordinary coincidence, the plaque pictured was uncovered on 4 August 2014, the centenary of the First World War to the very day, after being covered up for three decades. The current leaseholders of the church, the Fabrica Gallery, Brighton's centre for contemporary art and a non-profit arts charity have, in partnership with Strike a Light (a non-profit community arts and heritage organisation) and Brighton & Hove Library Services, received £9,300 through the Heritage Lottery Fund's First World War: then and now programme to conduct research into the names commemorated, under a project running from 2015-2017 entitled The Boys on the Plaque.

Fabrica and Strike a Light hosted a free event, Centennial, on 11 September 2014, which profiled and examined aspects of experiences of the war through the use of diaries, moving image, songs, creative workshops and talks, exploring shared and personal memories and stories relating to the war.

Archivists, artists, historians and the local community are, at the time of writing, working together through research, creative activities and heritage events to discover the hidden histories of the ninety-five names listed. A number of well-researched and detailed results have already been achieved. The findings will be digitally recorded and an online, open access, archive of 'The Boys' will be created as a focus for discussion, the sharing of views and the pooling of contributions.

The year 2017 will mark the bicentenary of the church itself and will be an additional occasion for commemoration and reflection.

SOURCES AND FURTHER READING

A: NEWSPAPERS, PERIODICALS & MISCELLANEOUS PAPERS

Brighton and Hove Society and Hove Gazette

Brighton Gazette, Hove Post, Sussex and Surrey Telegraph

Brighton Graphic and South Coast Illustrated News

Brighton Herald and Hove Chronicle

The Brighton Season - A Record of the Season's Social Happenings (1914-15 to 1918/19 inclusive, 1919)

The Sunday Times

The Times

THE ROYAL PAVILION as an INDIAN MILITARY HOSPITAL 1914-1916, folder published by The Royal Pavilion, 2014 (Bacon, Kevin & Beevers, David, Eds.)

B: BOOKS

Adland D., *Brighton's Music Halls*, Baron Birch for Quotes Ltd, Whittlebury,1994

Arscott D., *A Century of Brighton & Hove - Events, People and Places over the 20th Century*, Alan Sutton, Gloucester, 2000

Beavis J., *The Brighton Races*, Jim Beavis, [Brighton?], 2003

Bilton D., *The Home Front in the Great War - Aspects of the Conflict*, Leo Cooper, Barnsley, 2003

Brown V., *Women's Hospitals in Brighton & Hove*, Hastings Press, Hastings, 2006

Bullock A. & Medcalf P., *Palace Pier, Brighton,* Sutton, Stroud, 1999

Carden D. & Carden A., *Carden of Brighton*, David & Arthur Carden, Brighton, 2008

Carder T. & Harris R., *Seagulls!: The story of Brighton & Hove Albion F.C.*, Goldstone, Hove, 1993

Carder, T., *The Encyclopedia of Brighton*, East Sussex County
    Libraries, Lewes, 1990.
Collins J., *Dr Brighton's Indian Patients - December 1914 –
    January 1916*, Brighton Books, Brighton, 1997
Corum M. *et al.,* Blighty Brighton, QueenSpark, Brighton, 1991,
Fraser H., *Women And War Work*, G. Arnold Shaw, New York, 1918
Gaston H., *Brighton's County Hospital, 1828-2007*, Southern
    Editorial Services, Newhaven, 2008
Gooch L., *A History of Brighton General Hospital,* Phillimore,
    Chichester, 1980
Gregory A., *The Last Great War – British Society and the First
    World War*, Cambridge University Press, Cambridge, 2008
Grieves, Keith *Sussex in the First World War*, Sussex Record Society,
    Lewes, 2004
Harkin, T., *Brighton and the Great War*, War Memorial Park
    Publications, Coventry, 2014
Harrison R. S., *Brighton Quakers 1655-2005*, Brighton Preparative
    Meeting (Society of Friends), Brighton, 2005
Hill D., *The Great War – A Pictorial History*, Atlantic Publishing,
    Herts., 2013
Horlock C., *Brighton: The Century in Photographs, Volume I*, S. B.
    Publications, Seaford, 2000
Horlock C., *Brighton: The Century in Photographs, Volume II*, S. B.
    Publications, Seaford, 2001
Jones M. D. W., *Brighton College, 1845-1995*, Phillimore & Co.
    Ltd., Chichester, 1995
Manning Foster, A. E., *The National Guard in the Great War*, Cope
    & Fenwick, London 1920
Mayhew E., *Wounded – From Battlefield to Blighty 1914-1918*,
    Bodley Head, London, 2013
Meades E. E., *A Brief History of St. Mary's Hall, Brighton 1836-
    1956*, published by the School, Brighton 1956
Mercer D. (Ed.), *Chronicle of the 20th Century*, Longman, London,
    1988
Middleton J., *Hove and Portslade in the Great War*, Pen & Sword,
    Barnsley, 2014
Moore J. (Ed.), *Memories of Roedean - The First 100 Years*, S. B.
    Publications, Seaford 2008

Parker G., *The Tale of a Boy Soldier,* QueenSpark Books, Brighton, ca. 2001,

Paul A., *Poverty, Hardship but Happiness - THOSE WERE THE DAYS 1903-1917*, QueenSpark Books, Brighton, 1971

Roberts H. D. (Ed.), *A Short History in English, Gurmukhi and Urdu of the Royal Pavilion, Brighton, and a Description of it as a Hospital for Indian Soldiers* Brighton Corporation, Brighton, 1915

Roberts J., *British Bus and Trolley Systems: No. 4. Brighton & Hove,* Transport Publishing Co., Glossop, Derbyshire, 1984

Shelton, David *For the Service of Mankind*, CreateSpace Independent Publishing Platform, 2014

Snatt, I. *Childhood at Brighton and Wartime Verses*, Book Guild Publishing Ltd, Lewes 1996

Various, *Who was Harry Cowley?*, QueenSpark Books, Brighton, 2003

Walbrook H. M., *Hove and the Great War*, Hove, The Cliftonville Press, 1920

West A., *The Allen West Story,* Allen West & Co Ltd, Brighton, 1960

C: INTERNET

Below are listed just some of the numerous websites accessed for this history:

Locally relevant:

Brighton's Roll of Honour website (compiled by Christopher Comber) :
http://www.roll-of-honour.com/Sussex/Brighton.html

My Brighton and Hove:
http://www.mybrightonandhove.org.uk/index.aspx

Brighton & Hove Libraries Online Catalogue:
http://www.brighton-hove.gov.uk/content/leisure-and-libraries/libraries

The Keep:
http://www.thekeep.info/

First World War Centenary Site for Brighton & Hove:
http://www.visitbrighton.com/first-world-war

Nationally/internationally relevant:

***The Times* Digital Archive, 1785-2006 and *The Sunday Times* Digital Archive, 1822-2006**:
(both available online via public libraries)

Findmypast:
http://www.findmypast.co.uk/

Commonwealth War Graves Commission:
http://www.cwgc.org/

CWG casualty records:
https://search.livesofthefirstworldwar.org/search/world-records/commonwealth-war-graves-commission-cwgc-casualty-records

Hansard 1803–2005:
http://hansard.millbanksystems.com/

The Gazette (Official Public Record)
https://www.thegazette.co.uk/

The National Archives:
http://www.nationalarchives.gov.uk/
http://discovery.nationalarchives.gov.uk/

Wikipedia [numerous accesses/retrievals]:
https://en.wikipedia.org/wiki/Main_Page

Index

Accommodation, 26, 31–2, 40–1, 43, 65
see also Hotels
Admiralty, 80, 123, 145, 246
Agriculture, 149, 187, 188, 223–6
Albion, PSS, 13
Alcohol, 138, 193
see also Public houses and inns
Alexandria, 78, 101
Alien(s), 23–4, 50, 110–11
Allen West, 219, 223
Allies, 25, 76, 109, 153–5, 158, 207, 238, 240, 247
Allotment(s), 159, 184, 186–91
Ambulance(s), 33–4, 46, 56–7, 77–8, 80–1, 131, 168–9, 181–2, 230, 232
American(s), 21, 109, 152, 159, 176, 238
see also Fund(s)
Aquarium, 42, 70–1, 74, 88, 94, 97, 108–10, 150, 166, 174, 191–2, 233, 247, 249
Argus, *The*, 14, 174, 240
Armistice, 204, 222, 230, 238–9, 243, 245
Army:
Bulgarian, 238
British, 53, 59, 88–9, 91, 93, 101, 104, 108, 118, 120, 123, 125, 171, 177–9, 184, 224, 226, 228, 256

Indian, 47, 64, 127
Territorial Force, (Territorials), 15, 18, 103
Australia(n)(s), 62, 68, 132, 156, 237–8
Austria(n), 23–4, 50, 238

Bairnsfather, Bruce, 165, 246
Baron, Bernhard, 114, 131, 167
Battles:
Aisne, 38–9, 99–100
Arras, 168, 173
Cambrai, 38, 168, 257
Loos, 100, 131
Marne, 38–9, 99, 237, 257
Mons, 29–30, 37–8, 99, 170, 230–1
Somme, 17, 132, 255, 257
Ypres, 17, 59, 99–100, 132, 135, 172
Beal:
2/Lt Ernest Frederick VC, 202, 255–6
John W., 202
Messrs John & Son, 102
Belgian(s), 14, 24–8, 37, 59, 68, 80, 158, 165, 183, 231, 238
Belgium, 25, 29, 37–8, 60, 80, 99, 179, 201, 207, 246
see also Battles; Louvain
Blackout, 57, 181
see also Lighting

Blaker, Sir John, 17, 87–8, 90, 93, 119, 123, 125, 179
Boarding houses, 82, 84, 113, 160
Boulogne, 13, 56, 97
Brewery, 17, 90
Brighton:
　Art Galleries, 248
　Battalion Boys' Brigade, 203
　Board of Guardians, 64
　　see also Workhouse
　Brighton Queen, PSS, 12–14
　Corporation, 17, 44
　　see also Brighton Town Council
　County Court, 233
　Food Control Committee, 209–10
　Gazette, 19, 24, 39, 46, 117, 119, 124, 129, 132, 135, 143, 146–9, 157, 162, 172, 176–7, 187, 189, 191–2, 195–8, 200, 203–204, 210–11, 213, 215, 218–20, 227, 231, 234, 236–7, 241, 246, 248
　Graphic (and South Coast Illustrated News), 28, 58, 76, 80–1, 84–6, 103–104, 110, 145, 148, 158
　Home for the Queen's Nurses, 181
　Hotels Association, 191, 213
　Nursing Division (of St John Ambulance Brigade, qv.), 168
　Poor Law Institution, 32
　　see also Workhouse
　Relief Committee, 147
　　see also Employment
　Season, The, 137, 139, 147–8, 150, 164
　Station, 19, 34–5, 55–7, 66, 98, 113, 131–2, 147, 153, 155, 168, 172, 212, 231, 235
　Town Council, 43, 96, 172
　Town Hall, 24, 40
　Trades and Labour Council, 212
　War Work Depot, 171, 208, 227–8, 246–7
　　see also Brighton and Hove
Brighton and District Trades and Labour Council, 209

Brighton and Hove:
　Albion, 173
　Bus and Coach Company, 255–6
　Butchers' and Pork Butchers' Association, 23
　City Council, 255
　Gas Company Limited, 17, 179
　Grocers' Association (BHGA), 89, 192
　Ladies' Golf Club, 69
　Meat Advisory Committee, 214
　Society, 18, 23, 32, 36, 42, 44, 50–2, 54, 85–6, 88, 107, 111, 127, 139, 142, 152, 160, 165, 177, 196, 199–200, 222, 224
　Trade Protection Society (BHTPS), 89, 215
Brighton, Hove and Sussex Horticultural Society, 191
Britain, 11, 14, 127, 142–3, 150, 159–60, 167, 187, 194, 208, 221, 233
Canada/Canadian(s), 23, 27, 50, 117, 132, 152–5, 158, 207, 238, 247
Carden, Alderman/Mayor Herbert John, 156, 176, 187–8, 193, 195, 205–206, 210–13
　Mayoress, 227
Charity/ies, 52, 129, 146, 207
　see also Funds
Chattri, 234, 250
Chichester, 15, 57, 97–8, 149, 175, 183–4, 224
Christmas, 47, 51–3, 78, 109, 112–15, 156–8, 165, 195–7, 199–200, 208, 248
Church(es):
　Holland Road Baptist, 94
　Lewes Road Congregational, 68, 189, 195, 201–203
　Norfolk Road Wesley Methodist, 169, 199
　Preston Parish, 109, 174
　St Anne's, Kemp Town, 27, 55, 175
　St Margaret's, 105
　St Mark's, Kemp Town, 10, 175

St Martin's, 176
St Peter's, 75, 174, 201
Union, 68
United Methodist, 68
Conscientious objectors, 120–1,
    179–80, 199
    see also Pacifists; Pelham Committee
Conscription, 76, 93–4, 96, 118
Convalescent homes, *see* Hospitals
Corn Exchange (before use as hospital),
    12, 18
    see also Hospitals

Dome (before use as hospital), 14, 20,
    25, 40, 42–5, 48, 128
    see also Hospitals
Dover, 55–6, 131, 168

Eastbourne, 13, 56, 93
Employment, 26, 28, 49, 76, 87, 122–3,
    142–3, 147, 149, 232–3
    see also Labour
Enlistment, 16–17, 20, 37, 60, 76, 88,
    90–1, 93, 97–9, 101, 103–104, 119,
    148, 178, 184
Entertainment(s), 14, 47, 51, 68–9, 76,
    113–15, 135, 156–7, 163–6, 168,
    172, 210, 228, 234–6, 245–6
Exhibition:
    Brighton and Hove Home Life, 233
    Flying, 91
    Horticultural, 191
    Italian War Photograph, 248
    Patriotic Housekeeping, 134
    Women's War Services, 223–5

Fish/fishing, 122, 124–5, 127, 160,
    190–1, 217, 219
Fishermen/fishmongers, 123–6
Flanders, 56, 131, 238
Folkestone, 14, 221–2
Food:
    bread, 22, 122, 141, 156, 190–1, 193,
        214
    butter, 23, 156, 214–16
    Control Committee, *see* Brighton
    Controller, 190, 193, 211, 215

margarine, 195, 214, 215–16
meat, 22, 43, 112, 122, 190–1, 193,
    211–17
    Advisory Committee, *see* Brighton
        and Hove
    bacon, 22, 27, 215–16
    meatless days, 191, 214, 217
    potatoes, 27, 184, 189, 191, 193,
        216–17
    rationing, 157, 210–11, 213–16
    rhubarb, 192
    sugar, 23, 27, 190–2, 213–14, 216
France, 25, 28, 39, 53, 55, 60, 77–8, 80,
    101, 127, 131, 153, 165–7, 169–70,
    184–5, 204, 207–208, 224, 230, 246,
    255, 259
    see also Boulogne
French, 24–5, 78, 162, 182
    Convalescent Home, Kemp Town, 9,
        78
    FM/Vis, Sir John, 16, 135
    Fraser, Maj Campbell, 104, 107–108
    Prisoners of war, 230
    Red Cross, 183
    Refugees, 207
    Soldiers, 238
    see also Hospitals
Fund(s), 155-6, 169, 232
    Belgian Relief, 24, 183
    British Empire Union, 170
    Children's Welfare, 207
    King's Royal Naval, 207
    Lady Otter's, 227
    Prince of Wales's National Relief, 38,
        78, 208
    Prisoners of War, 170, 172, 228–9
    Queen Alexandra Hospital for Sick
        Children, 247
    Queen Mary's, 49
    RAF (Roehampton), 227
    Red Cross, 153, 207
    Tobacco, 80
    VTC, 80, 105
    Waifs and Strays Society War
        Emergency, 208
    Water Ambulance, 181

Gallipoli, 97, 102–103
German(s), 23–4, 28–9, 37–8, 47, 50,
    81, 87–8, 92, 99, 107–108, 111, 121,
    165, 170, 230, 237–8, 248
Germany, 14, 20, 23–4, 111, 157–9,
    170–1, 199, 228–30, 238
Grantham, Maj William W., 93–4
Grocer(s), 89, 121, 123, 192, 208–209,
    216
Gurkhas, 44, 57–9, 61, 70

Hanningtons, 13, 90, 160
Hassocks, 65, 70–1
Hastings, 13, 56, 93, 154, 165, 221
Holland, 228, 230
Hollingbury, 137, 187
Hoskyns, Archdeacon B., Vicar of
    Brighton, 174
Hospital(s), 60, 68, 70, 101, 113–14,
    123, 126–7, 132, 145, 155, 166, 169,
    171, 181–2, 226, 230–1, 250
    2nd Eastern General, Dyke Road –
        SEGH, (ex-Brighton, Hove and
        Sussex Grammar School), 32, 34,
        36, 38–9, 47, 56, 59, 69, 131–2,
        148, 156, 167, 182, 186, 219
        Lewes Crescent, 62–4
        Stanford Road, 33, 68–70, 115,
    British Water Ambulance Hospital,
        Cherbourg, 181
    Chichester Hospital for Women, 183
    Clarendon Terrace, 232
    Corn Exchange, post occupation by
        Indian wounded, 135
    Crescent House Convalescent Home,
        26
    Dome, post occupation by Indian
        wounded, 135, 137
        see also Indian General
    Eastern Terrace, 62
    French Convalescent Home, Kemp
        Town, 9, 78
    Fulham Military, 167,
    Hove Military, 64, 131, 228, 247
    John Howard Convalescent Home,
        30–1

Indian General, 66
    Corn Exchange, 45, 61, 127
    Dome, 44–5, 58–61
    Kitchener Indian (formerly Poor
        Law Institution, now Brighton
        General), 32, 57, 59–60, 64,
        66–7, 129
    Pavilion, 42–8, 57–60, 64, 66–7,
        80, 127–9, 134, 249, 252-3
    York Place (and Pelham Street),
        57, 59–60, 129
    Kitchener (post occupation by Indian
        wounded), 129–32, 134, 155–6,
        167, 219, 232, 245, 247, 249
    Lady George Nevill Hospital, Hove,
        182
    Military Hospital, Skopje
        (Macedonia), 170
    Pavilion Military Hospital for
        Limbless Soldiers, 129, 134–7,
        155, 238, 248–9
    Queen Mary Convalescent Auxiliary
        Hospital, 136
    Portland Road, Hove, 219
    Red Cross, Hove, 56
    Royal Alexandra Hospital for Sick
        Children, 52, 196, 247
    Royal Crescent, 64
    Royal Sussex County Hospital
        (RSCH), 52, 57, 68, 131–2, 196
    Sanatorium (later Bevendean
        Hospital), 189
    Sussex Eye Hospital, 56, 68, 131
    Third Avenue Red Cross Auxiliary
        Hospital, Hove, 131
    Women's Hospital, West Street, 33
    York Place (post occupation by
        Indian wounded) 129
Hotel(s), 11, 24, 50, 73, 113, 154,
    159–60, 178, 191, 196, 209, 211,
    213–14
    Bedford, 154
    Cricketers Arms, 159
    Grand, 49, 74, 81, 113–16, 158, 163,
        248

Metropole, 21–2, 50, 52–3, 74, 88,
113, 116, 150, 154, 163, 165, 245
Prince's, 128
Queen's, 109
Royal Albion 74, 170, 226
Royal York, 52, 113, 146, 196
Ship:
New Ship, 99
Old Ship, 115, 208
Unicorn, 104
Victoria, 118
see also Brighton Hotels Association;
Orchestras
Hove, 9–12, 15–18, 23, 25–8, 32–3,
35–8, 41–4, 46, 48, 50–2, 54, 56,
63–4, 69, 71, 76, 77–81, 85–91,
93–4, 96, 107–108, 111, 127,
129–33, 136–7, 139–40, 142, 148,
152–7, 160–1, 165, 167, 169–70,
173, 177, 179, 181–3, 189, 191–2,
196, 199–207, 211, 214–17, 219–20,
222, 224–5, 228, 233, 235, 239–40,
246–7, 255
Howard, Sir John, 30–1, 59, 151

Indian(s), 40–1, 43, 45, 47, 55, 57,
59–60, 64–6, 67, 70–1, 117, 127–9,
134, 232, 250, 253
Influenza, 246
Italy, 176, 256

Kaiser Wilhelm, 54, 88, 134
Kemp Town, 9–10, 26–7, 30, 45, 55,
59, 62, 64–5, 68, 78, 148, 171, 175,
181, 208, 226
Kitchener, Lord Horatio H., 17, 20, 31,
41, 60, 64, 67, 88, 90, 93–4
see also Hospitals
Kitchens, National, 43, 129, 193, 217

Labour, 76, 89, 125, 142, 147, 178,
209, 247
Female, 147, 150
Institute, 210
Labour Exchange, 17, 147
Labour Gazette, 149
Labour Party, 20, 134

Ministry of, 223–4, 233
see also Employment
Lancing, 28
London, 9, 19, 21–2, 25, 49, 62, 71, 73,
77, 81, 85, 87, 89, 105, 108–109,
134, 136, 141–6, 149, 152, 160–2,
166, 195, 203–204, 209, 212–20,
235, 247
London Brighton and South Coast
Railway, *see* Transport
Louvain, 28
Lyell-Tayler, Henry, 150, 164, 166

Mackintosh, E.A., 175, 184-5
Macleod, Lt Col J.N., 127–8
Mannock, Edward VC, 243, 255–6
Marlborough, HMS, 11–12
Munition(s), 91, 125, 143–4, 146, 178,
211, 213, 219, 223, 226, 234

Navy, Royal, 11, 18, 118, 121, 125, 171
see also Royal Naval Volunteer
Reserve
Newhaven, 18, 123
Nurses, 32-3, 45, 81, 123, 137, 181,
207–208
see also Brighton

Orchestras:
Brighton Municipal, 25, 42, 150,
164, 166, 178
Grand Hotel, 81, 115
Hippodrome, 164
Metropole, 113
Royal York, 52, 113
Otter, Mayor John, 16, 20, 41, 48–9,
58, 77, 81, 86–7, 89, 92, 94, 96, 104,
123, 127, 130, 170, 172, 227–8, 234,
250

Pacifist(s), 40, 120–1
see also Conscientious objectors
Palfrey, Mayoress E.R., 207, 251
Palladium Opera House (Cinema), 80,
88, 105
Pankhurst, Emmeline, 48, 143
Pelham Committee, 18, 66, 179–80
see also Conscientious objectors

Peto, Dorothy, 221
  see also Police
Pier(s):
  Palace, 11, 13, 51, 70, 73, 108, 150,
    152–4, 158, 163, 165–6, 227, 249
    see also Theatres
  West, 11, 13–14, 52, 73, 88, 97,
    150–2, 163–5
Police, 16, 23–4, 34, 52, 81–2, 84–6,
  87, 94, 145, 153, 215, 220, 222
  Commissioner, London, 145
  Constable(s):
    Special Constables, 82–4
  Court, Brighton Police, 111, 217
  Policewomen (in regular force),
    221–2, 245
  Station, 111, 218
  Surgeon, 141
  Women Police:
    Patrols, 85–6, 222
    Patrols Committee, 145
    Police Service (WPS), 221
    Police Volunteers (WPVs), 85–7
Pollak, Mrs Frances, 46, 68–9, 131,
  133, 154, 156
Portslade, 25–6, 37, 88, 142, 194, 196,
  219
Postmen/-women, 112, 143, 147
Potatoes, see Food
Preston, see also Church(es), 142, 175
  Barracks, 16, 29, 256
  Harry, 113, 130, 146, 196
  Park, 70, 80, 104–105, 154–5, 188,
    190, 206–207, 211, 257
Prince:
  of Wales, 232, 235
    see also Fund(s)
Princess:
  Helena Victoria, 167
  Henry of Battenberg, 60
  Louise, (Duchess of Argyll), 60, 134
  Mary 59, 183
Prisoners of War, 7, 30, 108, 149,
  169–72, 181, 207, 227–30, 248
  see also Fund(s); Ruhleben

Public houses and inns, 13, 86, 111,
  138
Punch, 23, 76, 79, 83, 122, 161, 190–1,
  194, 207, 214–15, 240

Queen Mary, 58–9, 61, 75, 77, 217
Queen Mary's Workshops, 137, 217,
  230
  see also Fund(s)

Race Hill, 66, 91, 131, 188
Races/racecourse, 17, 218, 223, 228
Railways/trains see Transport; Brighton
  - Station
Railwaymen, 179, 209–10, 212
Rally, 92–3, 210, 212
Rationing, see Food
Royal Army Medical Corps (RAMC),
  33, 46, 55, 58, 230
Red Cross, see Hospitals and Societies;
  Fund(s)
Recruitment, 16–17, 19–20, 33, 76,
  86–8, 91–4, 97–8, 223–4, 226, 246
Recruits, 15–17, 20, 87–9, 93–4, 96–8,
  105, 222, 224
Regiments, 126, 131–2, 158, 172
  English:
    East Surrey, 103
    East Yorkshire, 29
    Hampshire, 169
    Middlesex, 173
    Royal Dragoon Guards, 30
    Royal Engineers, 253, 256
    Royal Field Artillery, 16, 18, 92,
      98, 102, 104, 183, 208, 253
    Royal Garrison Artillery, 51, 152,
      249
    Royal Horse Artillery, 29
    Royal Sussex, 15, 37, 88, 97,
      99–101, 172, 175, 225, 246–7
    Sussex Yeomanry, 18, 101, 123,
      225
    Warwickshire, 169
    Worcestershire, 203
      see also Volunteers
  Indian, 66

Irish, 29, 34
Scottish, 34, 37, 68, 99, 184
Rhondda, Lord, 190, 195, 210–11, 214, 217
Roehampton, 136, 227
Rottingdean, 78, 108–109, 146, 219
Royal Flying Corps (RFC), 28–9, 148
Royal Naval Volunteer Reserve (RNVR), 92, 252
Royal Pavilion (before use as hospital), 10, 12, 254
see also Hospitals
Ruhleben POW camp, 228–9
see also Prisoners of war
Russia(n), 23, 25, 76, 162, 170, 176, 230

St John Ambulance Association/Brigade, 46, 80,168–9
see also Brighton
Saltdean, 108–109
School(s) and colleges, 24, 34, 173, 187
Belvedere, 103
Brighton and Hove High, 183
Brighton College, 79, 103, 184–5
Brighton Hove and Sussex Grammar (now BHASVIC), 9, 32–3, 39–40, 79, 186, 202
see also Hospitals
Brighton Secondary and Technical, 175
Christ Church, 145
Ditchling Road, 230
Lewes Road Boys', 103, 173
Municipal Technical College, 134, 146
Pelham Street, 18
see also Hospitals
Roedean, 9, 55, 180–3, 238,
St Mark's, 55–6
see also Hospitals
St Mary's, Portslade, 25
St Mary's Hall, 9, 180–1
Stanford Road Council, 33–4, 55, 68–70, 115
see also Hospitals

Windlesham House, 65
Xaverian College, 185–6, 256
York Place Municipal Secondary, 18, 58, 129, 187
see also Hospitals
Shoreham, 17, 32, 38, 87, 97, 166, 219
Shrine(s), 173, 175–6
Sikh(s), 43, 58, 250
Societies:
British Red Cross, 62, 77, 80–1, 181–2, 207–208
see also Hospitals
Society of Friends, 121
Sussex Record, 107
see also Brighton and Hove; Fund(s)
Southampton, 17, 40, 44, 57, 222
Station, Brighton Railway, see Brighton
Sugar, see Food
Sussex, 10, 15, 20, 32–3, 40, 46, 57, 75, 78, 89, 152, 212–13, 224

Tank(s), 205–207, 251, 257
Theatres, 51, 69, 178
Court, 79
Grand, North Road, 47–8, 51, 69, 113
Hippodrome, Brighton, 13–14, 47, 51–2, 68, 89, 134, 163–7, 205, 228, 235, 245–7
Palace Pier, 70, 158
Theatre Royal, 51, 69, 113, 158, 165, 235, 248
West Pier, 151
Thomas-Stanford, Charles, 90, 94, 246
Thomas-Stanford, (Mrs), 130
Transport, 57, 111, 123–4, 147
Bus(es), 74, 141–2, 148, 195, 219–21, 236, 249, 255–6
Conductors/ Conductress(es), 142, 147, 218–20
Tilling,
Charabanc, 47
Messrs, 142
Thomas Tilling Ltd, 141–2
see also Brighton and Hove Bus and Coach Company

Railways/trains, 11, 15, 19, 34, 46, 49, 55–8, 66, 98, 113, 117, 131, 133, 149, 151, 155, 162, 168, 197, 206, 226, 231–2, 235, 238
Brighton Works, 49, 90–1, 103, 209
London Brighton and South Coast Railway (LBSCR), 15, 19, 71, 90, 149, 180, 254
Southern, 254
Volk's, 73
Trams/tramcars, 17, 142, 147, 174, 195, 211, 215, 218–21, 232, 236
Tramway(s), 17, 74, 103, 117, 179, 218–20
Trench(es), 17–18, 35, 46–7, 53, 57, 101, 103, 110, 119, 131, 165, 169, 173, 184, 203
Tribunal(s), Military Service, 96, 118–22, 125–6, 176–80, 245

Victoria Cross, 5, 59, 202–204, 243, 255–6
Visitors, 11, 46, 50–2, 60, 69, 73, 76, 109, 117–18, 127, 129, 131, 146, 150–1, 153–4, 159–60, 163–4, 196–8, 205, 207, 211, 218, 236
Volk, Mrs Anna, 48, 227, 246
Magnus & Mrs Anna, 227
Voluntary Aid Detachments (VADs), 46, 132, 168, 229, 231
Volunteer(s), (for the armed services and home defence), 17, 76, 93, 98, 104, 134, 177, 212, 246
Central Association of Volunteer Training Corps, 105, 107
City of London National Guard, 108–109
Home Protection Brigade, 107
National Association of Volunteer Training Corps, 105
Sussex Home Defence Volunteer Corps, 91
Sussex Home Protection Volunteer Brigade, 107
Sussex Volunteer Regiment, 170
1st Battalion, 108, 234, 246
Volunteer Training Corps (VTC), 73, 79, 93, 107–108, 121, 125, 178
1st (Brighton) Battalion, 79-80
see also Recruits

Whiting, Robert W. ('Bob'), 173
Women's Army Auxiliary Corps (WAAC), 223–5
Women's Auxiliary Force (WAF), 145–6
Women's Land Army, 223–6
Workhouse, 17, 32, 168, 178
see also Brighton
Worthing, 15, 76, 89, 93, 108
Wounded, 7, 30–40, 46–8, 56–9, 62, 67–70, 78, 81, 94, 99, 101, 114–15, 121, 130–5, 146, 148–9, 154–6, 167–9, 172, 181–3, 201, 203, 207–208, 219, 227, 229–30, 232
Indians, 43–5, 55, 58–60, 64, 66, 70, 127–9, 241, 245, 247–8, 253
Wright, Theodore VC, 5, 255–6

Young Men's Christian Association (YMCA), 101, 156, 166–7, 208, 230, 233, 247